INDIA'S FILM
SOCIETY MOVEMENT

INDIA'S FILM SOCIETY MOVEMENT

The Journey and Its Impact

VK CHERIAN

Los Angeles | London | New Delhi
Singapore | Washington DC | Melbourne

First published in 2017 by

 SAGE Publications India Pvt Ltd
B1/I-1 Mohan Cooperative Industrial Area
Mathura Road, New Delhi 110 044, India
www.sagepub.in

SAGE Publications Inc
2455 Teller Road
Thousand Oaks, California 91320, USA

SAGE Publications Ltd
1 Oliver's Yard, 55 City Road
London EC1Y 1SP, United Kingdom

SAGE Publications Asia-Pacific Pte Ltd
3 Church Street
#10-04 Samsung Hub
Singapore 049483

Published by Vivek Mehra for SAGE Publications India Pvt Ltd, typeset in 10.5/12.5 pt Minion Pro by Fidus Design Pvt. Ltd., Chandigarh 31D and printed at Chaman Enterprises, New Delhi.

Library of Congress Cataloging-in-Publication Data Available

ISBN: 978-93-859-8563-8 (HB)

SAGE Team: Shambhu Sahu, Neha Sharma and Ritu Chopra

The book is dedicated to the 60 glorious years of *Pather Panchali*, the first and historic filmy contribution of the Film Society Movement to world of films from India.

and

To my late parents—Thankamma (Mary) Kurian and Philipose Kurian—who inspired me to look at the world differently!

Bulk Sales

SAGE India offers special discounts
for purchase of books in bulk.
We also make available special imprints
and excerpts from our books on demand.

For orders and enquiries, write to us at

Marketing Department
SAGE Publications India Pvt Ltd
B1/I-1, Mohan Cooperative Industrial Area
Mathura Road, Post Bag 7
New Delhi 110044, India

E-mail us at **marketing@sagepub.in**

Get to know more about SAGE

Be invited to SAGE events, get on our mailing list.
Write today to **marketing@sagepub.in**

This book is also available as an e-book.

Contents

CHAPTERS

List of Images

Chapter 1

Chapter 2

Chapter 3

Chapter 8

Chapter 9

List of Abbreviations

ACJ	Asian College of Jouralism
BARC	Bhabha Atomic Research Centre
BDA	Bangalore Development Authority
BFS	Bombay Film Society
BRPSE	Board for Reconstruction of Public Sector Enterprises
C&S	Cable & Satellite
CBFC	Central Board of Film Certification
CDS	Centre for Development Studies
CENDIT	Centre for Development of Instructional Technology
CET	Centre for Educational Technology
CFS	Calcutta Film Society
CPI(M)	Communist Party of India (Marxist)
CPI	Communist Party of India
CPSE	Central Public Sector Enterprises
CSDS	Centre for Study of Developing Societies.
DD	Doordarshan
DFS	Delhi Film Society
DPI	Director of Public Instruction
DTH	Direct To Home
DVDs	Digital Versatile Discs
FACT	The Fertilisers and Chemicals Travancore Limited
FFC	Film Finance Corporation
FFSI	Federation of Film Societies of India
FICC	Fédération Internationale des Ciné-Clubs.
FICCI	Federation of Indian Chamber of Commerce and Industry
FSM	Film Society Movement
FTII	Film and Television Institute of India
I&B	Information and Broadcasting

ICAF	International Cine Appreciation Foundation
ICEC	Indian Cinematograph Enquiry Committee
ICS	Indian Civil Service
IFFI	International Film Festival of India
IFFK	International Film Festival of Kerala
IFFS	International Federation of Film Societies
IFSON	Indian Film Society News
IIFS	International Federation of Film Societies
IIM	Indian Institute of Management
IIMC	Indian Institute of Mass Communications
IIT	Indian Institute of Technology
IMPEC	Indian Motion Picture Export Corporation
IPTA	Indian People's Theatre Association
IPTV	Internet Protocol Television
ISRO	Indian Space Research Organisation
IT	Information Technology
JNU	Jawaharlal Nehru University
KPAC	Kerala Peoples Arts Club
KSFDC	Kerala State Film Development Corporation Ltd
LCD	Liquid–Crystal Display
MD	Maryland
MFS	Madras Film Society
MOA	Memorandum of Association
MPEG	The Moving Picture Experts Group
MSO	Multi System Operators
NASSCOM	National Association of Software and Services Companies
NCERT	National Council of Educational Research and Training
NFAI	National Film Archive of India
NFDC	National Film Development Corporation
NFHM	National Film Heritage Mission
NGO	Non-governmental Organisation
NIAVE	National Institute of Audio Visual Education
NMIC	National Museum of Indian Cinema
NRI	Non-resident Indian
OHSL	Open Health Systems Laboratory
OUP	Oxford University Press
PCM	Prabhat Chitra Mandal
PIL	Public Interest Litigation

RBI	Reserve Bank of India
RTI	Right to Information
SAHAMAT	Safdar Hashmi Memorial Trust
SITE	Satellite Instructional and Television Experiment
SRFTII	Satyajit Ray Film and Television Institute of India
TIFF	Trivandrum International Film Festival
TV	Television
UFC	University Film Council
UGC	University Grants Commission
UK	United Kingdom
UNESCO	United Nations Educational, Scientific and Cultural Organization
UNICEF	United Nations Children's Fund
USIS	United States Information Service
VCD	Video CD
VC	Vice Chancellor

Foreword

VK Cherian's treatise on the Film Society Movement—a predominantly post-independence voluntary initiative in our country—charts the sporadic beginnings, its enthusiastic course of growth and the excitements and travails of sustenance over a period of nearly seven decades.

Adoor Gopalakrishnan
Courtesy: Author.

At a time when the cinemas of Europe and the East were inaccessible to the *cinephiles* of our subcontinent, film societies provided us with the special privilege of watching, relishing, debating and writing about the very best of world cinema. We became enriched in the process with the aesthetic experience of the most nascent of all art forms.

At the dawn of independence, our national leaders had the vision and commitment to build up a nation of enlightened citizens capable of accessing and appreciating what was new in world culture, thereby enabling and encouraging them to contribute their might to the world in return.

Realising cinema's intrinsic capability to duplicate and distribute widely, the United States was quick to market it worldwide as an article of immense commercial potential. In the Soviet Union, where the early American productions (DW Griffith's *The Birth of a Nation* and so on) were studied and analysed by stalwarts like Pudovkin and Eisenstein in their 'Labs', it was eventually developed into an effective tool for propagating and consolidating the gains of the Bolshevik revolution ('For us, Cinema is the most of all arts,' proclaimed VI Lenin in 1917). No wonder, in India, cinema was brought under the Ministry of Information and Broadcasting (I&B). The Nazi Germany used cinema (Leni Riefenstahl's *Triumph of the Will* and so on) as a means of unmitigated propaganda.

It was in the Soviet Union and Europe that cinema was treated as an art form in the league of painting, theatre and litera-ture. Many well-known artists of the period saw it as an extension of painting. All the early 20th-century movements and trends in painting (expressionism, impressionism and so on) were applied to cinema with fantastic results.

The European masters put cinema on such a high pedestal that it gained a unique status to be seen, appreciated and studied seriously. So were born film clubs, mainly patronized by artists and intellectuals in Paris, London and elsewhere, who would debate and analyse films for their content and form, technique and aesthetics.

In India, we followed the British and film societies were set up first in Bombay (1942) and then in Calcutta (1947) by small groups of film enthusiasts and intellectuals. Significantly, in Calcutta, it was led by Satyajit Ray and Chidanand Dasgupta.

It was a great start and the movement gave the right fillip and inspiration to many artists and professionals to look up to cinema as a new realm of artistic pursuit.

VK Cherian faithfully follows the progress of the movement with utmost care and, in the meantime, uncovers the saga of passion and commitment as evidenced in the work of some of the pioneers.

It is, of course, not an easy task to register every little develop-ment that took place in each corner of this subcontinent. However, the author seems to have achieved the impossible.

Until the middle of the 1960s, West Bengal had held the enviable position of having the largest number of film societies in the country. The situation was soon to change. By the 1970s, Kerala overtook West Bengal and claimed the first position in the number of film societies functioning in a state.

In the last three decades, the situation slowly and steadily started to change. With the introduction of the VHS tape, many films, otherwise inaccessible, came to be circulated in the new mode. Soon the technology was to be replaced by the compact discs and then digital video discs and lately by the blu-ray discs, each an improvement on the previous in terms of quality of image and sound reproduction. The most dreamed of situation was finally on hand. All the classics of world cinema had become available to the genuine film enthusiast. Film societies lost the unique position of being the one and only window to world cinema.

Fortunately, the advantage of community viewing and sharing the uncanny pleasure of watching a film with like-minded people and the discussion and debate following a screening, all still hold its charm to this day. In addition, film societies continue to be relevant even with a smaller number of patrons than before.

The author's extensive research and study of the Film Society Movement has resulted in a comprehensive and impressive volume, a significant reference for those who wish to trace the roots of the offbeat cinema in our country.

I take great pleasure in introducing this book to film lovers, students and scholars.

Adoor Gopalakrishnan

A Note by Shyam Benegal

Shyam Benegal, film-maker
and a former FFSI President.
Courtesy: His Unit.

I cannot recollect at what stage of my life I got addicted to the Cinema. Perhaps, it all started when I saw films for the first time projected on a silent 16 mm projector, a prized possession of my father that he set up ceremoniously to show the films he kept making of his ten children—each of the ten children had a film made on them, from the time they were born until the next child came along. These were films all of us loved to see and comment on. However, he tended to reserve such shows only for occasions when he had special guests over for a dinner. Having a regular cinema, at a stone's throw from our home also helped greatly. Indian, American and British films were shown at that cinema which was built for the army garrisoned in the cantonment where we lived. Incidentally, the cinema was also called Garrison. By the time I was in college, going for a film had become not only my main recreation but also a chronic addiction. The twin cities of Hyderabad and Secunderabad, where I grew up, were sadly lacking in any film clubs or societies that could screen classics of world cinema like the film societies in Bombay and Calcutta did.

It was the desire to see film classics from countries other than India, UK and the USA, that motivated me and some of my friends to start a film club. We called this film club rather grandly, "The Cultural Group". This was sometime in 1955/56. Having heard of *Pather Panchali* I wrote to Satyajit Ray to ask him if we could get his film to screen at our film society. He graciously sent an introductory letter to his producers, who in turn sent us a print quite unhesitatingly for a screening. It was with this film that the Cultural Group was inaugurated at a cinema in Secunderabad on a Sunday morning. After this we managed quite successfully to arrange film screenings, every Sunday morning with a film that we managed to obtain from different foreign embassies in Delhi or through their consulates in Bombay. Over the next two years, the Cultural Group screenings became exceedingly popular and the membership soared. The screenings were usually prefaced with an introduction to the film, its director and a short background to the film industry of the country of its origin and so on. This helped to prepare the audience for the cultural character, form and content of the film. At the end of each screening there was a certain amount of time allowed for discussion on the film that had been screened.

Apart from embassies and consulates of countries; we acquired films from film distributors and sometimes even exhibitors who had prints of some great classics they had simply forgotten about in their godowns. The easiest films to get at the time were Soviet classics such as the ones made by Pudovkin and Eisenstein, and Mark Donskoi's *Gorky Trilogy* and even some classics of the silent era. Satyajit Ray films made until that time were special favourites and also Hindi films such as *Dharti Ke Lal* by Khwaja Ahmed Abbas and *Neecha Nagar* by Chetan Anand. All the 1930s Prabhat film company classics were part of the Cultural Group's repertoire.

The Cultural Group came to an abrupt end when I left Hyderabad to seek a livelihood in Bombay. There was a functioning film society in the city at the time called the Bombay Film Society which had started in 1942 and had its screenings at the Eros mini theatre from time to time. As it faded away, a new and dynamic film society was started by Mr Gopal Dutia called Anandam in 1959. Five years later, yet another film society called Film Forum initiated by the film-maker Basu Chatterji became active both in the city as well as the suburbs of the city.

In the late 1960s Sudhir Nandgaonkar and some of his colleagues started the Prabhat Chitra Mandal which has not only survived to this day but has grown in size and has extended its activities through campus film societies in practically all the Universities of Maharashtra. This is probably was among the most active film societies of the country today.

I am not sure to what extent the Film Society Movement has helped in adding to the ranks of film literates and cineastes in the country. However, one thing is certain. It has contributed to inspiring a significant number of young film enthusiasts to become filmmakers. These are among the filmmakers who have contributed to the development of the alternate or parallel cinema of the country. A substantial number of highly respected Indian filmmakers such as Satyajit Ray, Mrinal Sen, Adoor Gopalakrishnan, Aravindan, Gautam Ghose, Buddhadev Dasgupta, Girish Karnad, Girish Kasaravalli, Jabbar Patel and scores of others are among those who benefited from the Film Society Movement.

The book on India's *Film Society Movement: The Journey and Its Impact* by VK Cherian has captured the history of the Film Society Movement in India from the advent of the Calcutta film society and the formation of Federation of Film Societies by some of the most prominent Indian filmmakers of the time, who were the pioneering spirits driving the movement. He also deals with intervention and support that the government of the time gave to films that did not follow the conventional form of Indian Cinema, which in turn, helped evolve what is termed as Alternate or New Wave Cinema in our country. Mr Cherian's book is a valuable addition to the somewhat spare shelf of serious books on the Indian Cinema and certainly among the very rare ones written about the Film Society Movement.

Shyam Benegal

From the Desk of FFSI President—Gautam Kaul

Gautam Kaul – FFSI
President 2015.
Courtesy: Author.

One baneful effect of the First World War that engulfed much of the developed nations was the destruction of stable civilisations, developing within the nations of both the European and the American continents.

In Asia, the First World War destabilized the Far East. In particular, it opened Japan to the winds from across the Pacific and the first entry of US interests into the island kingdom. The map of the Middle East was drastically redrawn. The African continent was only marginally touched and in South Asia, India was missed in all destructive action.

The imperial government on the subcontinent still used the resources of its colonialism to underwrite the burden of financing the Big War and enforced punitive measures that exercised more control on both speech and media to put down the sentiments which would fuel the ongoing struggle for independence against the British administration.

A stray action that was enforced was to ban the import of films by some film studios from the United States and fill this scarcity with the fare what we called then 'dominion cinema'.

The end of the Big War also saw the film industry of England almost dead, and threatened by a new invasion from the studios of the United States. The British government provided subsidies to its indigenous industry to make films and forced the theatres to show only local products to boost up viewership, setting aside other products desperate for screen time by independent film-makers. This dilemma was resolved by the creation of an alternate system of film circuits for such films, and this laid the foundation of the Film Society Movement in England.

Nothing happened here in India. Cinema was silent, and the films that were fed into theatres in the urban pockets were either made in the country by local merchants or imported from England. However, low-quality films from the United States still managed to be imported, which did not figure the works of the banned film directors like Charles Chaplin. These American films were 'girlie' types and roused the anger of Indians who wanted them to be banned. In 1927, this outcry led to the Dewan Sir Rangachariar report on the cinema industry, which sought many reforms. The report also recommended the creation of a film school to train Indian film-makers. However, sound emerged by 1929, and made many of the recommendations a bit outdated.

In 1937, a ship from England docked in the Bombay harbour bringing a British film enthusiast who wanted to introduce the system of alternate film circuit in India. He received little interest for his suggestion in the commercial world, but found still some film critics with interest to receive other world cinemas, and agreed to create a platform for such cinema. BD Garga and Khwaja Ahmad Abbas were among this group and they created the Amateur Film Club, which can arguably be called as the founding of the Film Society Movement in India.

In 1939, England again entered into the Second World War, and the Indian film industry was roped into the 'war effort', rendering the idea of 'an alternate cinema' a dead letter for the time being. The rest of the details of the effort and how this effort progressed over the years form part of the narrative of the book.

The Film Society Movement in India was never crafted to be a mass movement. It was elitist from the very beginning. It was introduced to educate a class of Indians who would lead the country into the modern age; it was nurtured to open new windows for the young film-makers to see what was happening elsewhere and not get swamped with the new emerging technologies. It was supposed to arouse curiosity, and not create a habit. To that extent, it has served its purpose.

It would be wrong to surmise that this movement has outlived its time and utility. Cinema is undergoing vast changes, and the movement managers have accepted the challenges of the impending changes. An effort is now underway to hand over this movement to a new generation of film-makers, students and audiences. We expect the course of alternate cinema to also exist as we have allowed other forms of cinema to stay with us in the past century and more.

Gautam Kaul
(President FFSI, 2014–16)

Preface

After 30 years of a life full of hustle and bustle in New Delhi as a communications professional, I had begun to frequent Thiruvananthapuram, the capital city of Kerala, from 2010. The city was the cradle of the Film Society Movement that sprouted in the state 50 years ago and I was a part of it as a student. My frequent visits to the city (thanks to my flat there) led to the revival of old friendships from the film societies, the media and films. I was curious to find out whether the Film Society Movement was still active or not and found that it existed in a new format and had different patrons. I also noted that veterans like Adoor Gopalakrishnan, MF Thomas, Kulathoor Bhaskaran Nair and Vijayakrishnan were not active with the movement in Kerala and a new leadership had taken over. I met Adoor, whom I knew from my *Chitralekha* days in the 1970s. He talked about the plight of the Film Society Movement in India and Marie Seton, arousing my inherent journalistic curiosity and that led me to plan the book with a pan-India embrace. Until then, I never thought I would end up writing a book on the history and travails of the movement across India.

I travelled to all the major film centres, starting with Kolkata, Pune, Bangalore, Chennai and Hyderabad, meeting film society activists, both former and current ones. Thanks to U Radhakrishnan, the former secretary of the Federation of Film Societies of India (FFSI) in the northern region, I could track almost all old and new players across India. Soon, I caught up with my old friends from the film societies in Delhi and Kolkata and had discussions. At Pune, I went through documents in the National Film Archive of India (NFAI). Here, I met PK Nair and had a discussion with him on the state of film societies. PK Nair has always been a surprise for me with his deep commitment to good films. Nair *saab* (sir) is a unique person who has never made a film, but knows everything about films and has inspired three generations towards 'good film' culture. Till his death in 2016, he stayed around NFAI, which he created from scratch, like a guardian angel.

I have been meeting Gautam Kaul, who was a police officer, in International Film Festival of India (IFFI) at Delhi, even when he was heading the special protection force during the regime of Prime Minister Rajiv Gandhi. Kaul led me to his friend and colleague in the Film Society Movement, Anil Srivastava, whom I had seen as Delhi's first video technology evangelist in the mid-1980s. He had emigrated to the United States with his wife, Shampa (daughter of Karuna Banerjee, the lead actress in Ray's first movie *Pather Panchali*). I met the couple when they were visiting India.

I was surprised to know that in Kolkata, my Indian Institute of Mass Communications (IIMC) colleague, engineer-turned-professor Asoke Bhattacharya, who was the director of Department of Adult, Continuing Education and Extension, Centre of Jadavpur University and a former Director of Roop Kala Kendro, film and social communication institute of the Government of West Bengal, (a brain child of Satyait Ray—the name was given by him and Buddhadev Bhattacharya, the former Chief Minister of West Bengal), was also the treasurer of the historic Calcutta Film Society.

That meant an easy gateway to the history of the city's Film Society Movement. A visit to the maestro Satyajit Ray's home to meet his son was like taking a pilgrimage. I saw the empty, big chair where Ray used to sit, surrounded by books. At that moment, I regretted never having met the great man, despite Safdar Hashmi, my friend, pushing me to do so in the 1980s. A visit to the CFS office at Bharat Bhavan, meeting Mrinal Sen, Sajjal Dutta of Cine Central at the Ganashakthi office and dinner with the old film buff and writer Abhijit Ghosh Dastidar at Calcutta Club, were all a part of the perks of enquiry into the Film Society Movement. Meeting *Akka*, Vijaya Mulay, was an eye opener into the enormous political patronage which the movement enjoyed. *Akka* was a good friend of Marie Seton, the evangelist who drummed up the movement, and of Indira Gandhi who extended patronage to the movement and pushed it to what it is today. At 94, *Akka* continues to be as energetic as ever with her sharp memory.

I had been occasionally meeting Bikram Singh, an ex-Indian Railway Service officer-turned film-maker, before his demise in

2013. Singh was associated with the Film Forum, Delhi Film Society (DFS), Film Censor Board and the 1980 Film Enquiry Committee. He enlightened me on the enormous effort undertaken by the government until 1984, to create the new Indian Cinema. He shared with me the Dr Shivaram Karanth film enquiry committee report of 1981 and asked me to look up the 1955 Film Seminar documents. Thanks to Malayalam film artist Sajitha Madathil, who joined Sangeet Natak Akademi by then, I obtained the entire edited volume, which further confirmed the Nehru–Gandhi agenda on films.

However, my first visit to NFAI, Pune, and its library was a huge disappointment, as a library official even denied of having books of Marie Seton there. Despite spending three days, I was unable to get what I wanted. It was only during my second visit that I obtained all that I wanted and much more. Thanks to Nair *saab* and Arti Karkanis, I found the old documents and press clippings, which were a treasure house of information and spoke volumes of the rise, decline and state of the Film Society Movement. I could validate many anecdotes, which I had heard from various players during the past five years that I had invested in my research for this book.

For those of us who were born in free India, and have only heard about Freedom Movement or remember the 'Make in India' effort of Chacha Nehru, connecting the dots of the 1950s and 1960s was like revisiting history. I have heard and met most stalwarts who played an instrumental role in the Film Society Movement from 1975 onwards, but never sat down to talk about their work and the movement itself. Chelavoor Venu, whom I helped to procure Hungarian films in the early 1980s, recognised me on a phone call after almost 25 years, when a common friend, film-maker TV Chandran, connected us. One person I missed in the search in Kerala was Chinta Ravi, film-maker and writer, who grew up with Venu and his Aswani Film Society in Kozhikode. In memoriam, I must mention that Ravi was an inspiration for a lot of us in our quest for a better worldview.

My search for the last book written by Chidu *da* was quite a handful as it was out of print and even the second hands were highly priced on various shopping websites. Thanks to Geedha, a research scholar from Jawaharlal Nehru University (JNU), who helped me procure the book by Chidu *da* as well as the thesis on the Film Society Movement by Abhija Ghosh.

When I finished the book, I realised that what I had done was an enquiry into the deep passion and worldview that I carried all my life, on good films and appreciation of art in general. The book, indeed, is a look at the social, political, systemic and personal influences and a movement that forced me into such a passion.

In the process, if I can get to the origin, progress, decline, trials and tribulations of the Film Society Movement, with its players and their success, failures and survival tactics, I have achieved my goal.

I remain thankful to film-maker and *Karnavar* (head man) of the fraternity Adoor Gopalakrishnan, who read the first draft and made immensely valuable suggestions and wrote an introduction. Shyam Benegal, the eminent film-maker, also spared his valuable time to look at the contents and write a small note for the book. Thanks to my senior friends, Vijaya Mulay (*Akka*), Anil Srivastava and Gautam Kaul for writing short notes for the book. For want of space I could use only Mr Kaul's note fully, but have extensively quoted *Akka* and Anil, and profiled them in the book. A special thanks to the late PK Nair and Bikram Singh, MF Thomas, Asoke Bhattacharya and U Radhakrishnan for their friends' valuable suggestions and encouragement in every phase of writing this book. My search for old images of the history of the Film Society Movement was equally laborious. But for the 84 year old *young* enthusiast, Mr Pradipta Sankar Sen, the Executive President of CFS, who went through the CFS photo-archive, this book would not have the touch of that Golden period. So was Ram Rahman of SAHMAT, who helped me with reaching out to Jean Bhownagary's family ensuring a profile of the man and rare pictures of him. Thanks to Meera Sahib, Adoor's first assistant director for years, I could get a rare picture of the studio complex of *Chitralekha* Film Cooperative. I must also thank FFSI-Keralam's Sasi Kumar for ensuring the copy righted pictures of many film makers, as my efforts to get them from NFAI failed miserably. Professor Satish Bahadur's son, Apporva Bhadur and his sister, Anil and Shampa Srivastava and Gautam Kaul, the Current FFSI president and Nara Hari Rao (former FFSI President) were all every ready to help with details of their historical associations with the Film Society Movement and rare images adding to rare collection of pictures. I have to also thank my former Editor, YC Halan (Financial Express), Arti Karkanis of NFAI and Mahesh Rangarajan (former director Teen Murti) for their valuable help in accessing historical documents.

I am also thankful to the following eminent personalities for their interviews/discussions, valuable inputs and suggestions: Mrinal Sen, Adoor Gopalakrishnan, Shyam Benegal, Girish Kasaravalli, Kumar Shahni, TV Chandran, Vijaya Mulay, K Bikram Singh, Khalid Mohammed, Shoojit Sircar, PK Nair, Sashidharan & Arti Karkanis (NFAI), Samik Bandopadhyay (Art and film writer), Anil Srivastava & Shampa Banerjee (USA), Peter Sutoris (UK), Sudhir Nandgoakar (PCM-Mumbai), Pradipta Sanker Sen and Asoke Bhattacharya (CFS), Sajal Datta, (Cine Central), Mihir Bhattacharya, formerly Jadavpur Univesity, (Kolkata), Kulathoor Bhaskaran Nair, MF Thomas, Meera Sahib (*Chitralekha*) George Mathew (Chalachitra), Dr Rajakrishnan, Sunny Jospeh, KR Manoj, V Sasikumar, CS Venkiteswaran (Thiruvananthapuram), Venu Chelavoor (*Aswini*-Kozhikode), Nara Hari Rao (Former FFSI President) and Prakash Belavadi (*Suchitra*-Bangalore), YC Halan (DFS), Gautam Kaul (DFS - FFSI), U Radhakrishnan (DMFS-Delhi), Partha Chatterjee, Deepak Roy, Abhijit Gosh Dastidar, Vijayakrishnan, KN Shaji (film writers) Ms Shyamala Vanarse and Apurva Bahadur, (Pune) Govindaraj, Madras Film Society, Madhukar Upadhyaya, Sheetal Singh, Jan Morcha, Faizabad, NK Sharma and Ram Rehman (Sahamat), Janine Bharucha (Paris), S Jayachandran Nair (Ex-Editor Malayalam Varika), VK Joseph, Mohan Kumar, FFSI, Keralam and Satish Sehegal, artist, Delhi.

This note would simply remain incomplete, if I do not express my deep gratitude to Sunmita Shinde, who took the painstaking effort, despite her busy schedule, to go through each page, checking the flow of the chapters and initial editing of the manuscript. Karuna John, a family friend, further chiselled my copy and a big hug to her too.

A big thanks to the team at SAGE for the professional handling of the publishing of the book.

I am delighted that the book is being published coinciding with the 60th anniversary of the release of *Pather Panchali*. The book is also my humble tribute to the great maestro of Indian films, Satyajit Ray.

To all my readers, I sincerely hope that you would enjoy reading the book as much as I have enjoyed researching and penning it for you.

VK Cherian

CHAPTER 1

A Nation Awaits a
Pather Panchali

Pather Panchali *introduced Indian cinema to the West as cataclysmically as Kurosawa's Rashomon had done for Japanese films. A human document of timeless simplicity and exquisite beauty.*

—Ephraim Katz, T, *The Macmillan International Film Encyclopedia*, 1998

INTRODUCTION

In 2012, the British Film Institute and its legendary film journal *Sight and Sound* asked its panel of 846 critics, programmers, academia and distributors to vote for the best film ever. The voting saw the end of a 50-year reign of the *Citizen Kane* by Orson Welles. The panel, instead chose *Vertigo* by Alfred Hitchcock as the best film ever.[1]

But for Indians, the list becomes important as there is one film that still remains among the top 50 of all-time greats: Satyajit Ray's timeless classic *Pather Panchali*. This film of 1955 still adorns the celebrated annals of world's top 50 films ever made, with its unparalleled human document, touching the hearts of millions of people across the continents over generations.

Reams of analysis have been carried out on the film. Critics have looked at the film from all perspectives and adjudged it as one of the best, from India. Some have ridiculed it as a depiction of India's poverty and misery portrayed in front of the entire world. Ray's contemporary, Mrinal Sen, recalled, "certain Friday in 1955, came as surprise, the biggest of all big surprises—a *coup d'état,* so to speak, conceived and staged almost conspiratorially. Yet, *Pather Panchali* was not an accident, it was overdue," he wrote in the official brochure of the CFS founded by Satyajit Ray one and a half months after India attained its much sought-after political freedom. Sen, indeed, was voicing the words of his fellow contemporary Indians about the advent of the *Pather Panchali* era in Indian films.[2]

Image 1.1 Apu—Screen grab from Pather Panchali.
Note: The film gave the biggest boost to the Film Society Movement in the 1950s and 1960s.
Courtesy: The producers: Government of West Bengal.

For the Indian film industry, the advent of *Pather Panchali* was a watershed, which divided the history of the Indian film industry as the period before and after *Pather Panchali*, a film that is still rated as one of the best among the top 50 after having bagged the national and international awards in a row and breaking all box office records, as far as earnings were concerned. The film, which was made with ₹1.50 lakh, earned over $50,000 from the United States alone. Unquestionably, Ray's film was the first to put India on the world map. Although films were being shown and even produced in India since colonial times and after the Lumiere Brothers had made cinematic experience possible through their invention, yet no other film has got into the history of the global film-making the way Ray's film has. "The international interest in Indian cinema which

Pather Panchali had created *continues* to grow. Indian films are now eagerly invited by major international film festivals," observed the Report of the Working Group on National Film Policy, headed by Dr Shivarama Karanth in 1980, firmly affixing the official stamp of approval for "…as watershed among Indian films."[3]

HISTORY OF THE FILM AS A MEDIUM: STUDIES AND APPRECIATION

Alongside the development of the Indian film industry, there was a parallel development of films as a medium and its study and even appreciation as an art form. These flourished in the film centres, especially in Bombay (now Mumbai) and Calcutta (now Kolkata). According to Vijaya Mulay, the founder of the Patna Film Society and also the first joint secretary of the Federation of Film Society of India (FFSI), "it first happened (the first film society) in The Amateur Cine Society of India started by Ference Borka, a cameraman of Hungarian origin serving in the British Army unit. For creating healthy and good cinema, it was necessary to create *rasiks* from the populace."[4]

PK Nair, the first director of the NFAI, recounted about the origin of film societies in India[5]:

> The first official film society in India, the Bombay Film Society was started in 1940 with the blessing and support of the colonial rulers, but obviously with different intentions. Namely, to expose budding Indian documentary film makers to the best of world documentary especially the works of Grierson, Wright, Jennings and others so that they could be engaged to make effective war effort films for the Raj.

Ference Borka registered his film society in 1943, under the Societies Registration Act of Bombay. The society started with nine members and conducted one film show a month. The half-yearly membership fee was ₹12. Gradually, the strength increased to 60 members by 1961. The best attractions in this film society were the discussions where Borka used to keep the members enthralled by his active participation. "The Bombay Film Society (of Borka) did signal service to all true lovers of cinema in Bombay by holding shows of films with outstanding, technical, historical, artistic merit, initiating discussions about films and promoting the Film Society Movement," wrote Shanti P Chowdhury from the CFS.[6]

What is a film society all about? "The Film Society, so to say, is an international, intellectual, non-political and cultural movement dedicated to the study of cinema as a serious art form," the first conference of the FFSI held in 1967, defined the Film Society Movement.

"By screening, discussing, reading and writing about good cinema all over the world, they created a higher level of artistic taste and this builds up to a better and bigger audience for good films within the country," commented Chidananda Das Gupta, one of the founders of CFS along with the celebrated film director Satyajit Ray.[7]

The document of NFAI, "How to form a film society" defined:

> A film society can be defined as a non-profit cultural organisation formed to encourage the appreciation of cinema both as an art and as a medium of information and education, by means of showing films, discussing them and supplying its members with information about cinema.

The term 'film club' appeared for the first time in April 1907, with the creation of Edmond Benoit-Lévy's *Film Club*. Located at the 5 Boulevard Montmartre in Paris, France, the 'Film Club' was to preserve and place at the disposal of its members all the existing cinematographic documents and productions. It was also equipped with a projection room. The website of the International Federation of Film Societies (IFFS) described its version of the origin of the film society.

The Film Society Movement originated in France during the time period between the two world wars, just as the films originated there. Soon after the Second World War, an international association was set up in 1947 in Cannes (France), among the groups of film societies in countries throughout the world, and this association was called Fédération Internationale des Ciné-Clubs (FICC). It has now taken the shape of an international body for film societies, namely, the IFFS, an organisation supported by the United Nations Educational, Scientific and Cultural Organization (UNESCO).

The Italian film theoretician Ricciotto Canudo, who had been living in Paris since 1921, founded one of the first film societies, sparking the academic study of the film as a medium and as an art.

After the First World War, film director and film critic Louis Delluc founded one of the first film societies with an important film magazine *Cinéa*.

In 1930, Jean Vigo founded the first film club in Nice, Les Amis du Cinéma. In 1935, Henri Langlois and Georges Franju founded the film society, Cercle du Cinema, which became the *Cinémathèque Française* in 1936 to show and to preserve old films.

After the Second World War, the movement of cine clubs boomed. In 1945, the Film Society of Annecy was founded, from which originated the Annecy International Animated Film Festival. In 1948, André Bazin, together with Jean-Charles Tacchella, Doniol-Valcroze, Astruc, Claude Mauriac, René Clément and Pierre Kast, founded the avant-garde film society, *Objectif 49*. Jean Cocteau became its president. This film society became the cradle of the *Nouvelle Vague*. *Objectif 49* organised the Festival du Film Maudit, which took place in Biarritz in 1949.[8]

The first film society of the United Kingdom was established in London in 1925 by a group of Left-wing intellectuals interested in films from Europe which could not be shown in public cinemas for political reasons. It was called the Film Society, but is often referred to as the London Film Society, as it was followed by many others in the next 15 years. These included the Edinburgh Film Guild (1929, still in existence), the Salford Workers' Film Society (1930; this became the Manchester and Salford Film Society, still in existence) and many others.[9]

Film societies have been extremely influential in fostering film cultures in a number of different countries, celebrating non-commercial cinema and film as art, and promoting film appreciation and cine literacy. This activity has been instrumental in encouraging varied forms of film practice (the British Documentary Movement, the *Nouvelle Vague*, New American Cinema, New Indian Cinema and so on) and in the development of film studies as a discipline, says a definition of a film society.[10]

CFS AND THE SEARCH FOR NEW IDIOM IN FILMS

Independent India saw the film society bug affecting the Indians with artistic lineages. The CFS was founded on 5 October 1947 and the 19 founding members met in a garret in South Calcutta. Prominent among the founders were Satyajit Ray, Chidananda Das Gupta, Hari S Das Gupta, Hiran Sanyal and Radha Mohan Bhattacharya. The founding fathers of the film society wanted to create an ambience for 'intelligent film-making'. Their activities included screening of outstanding feature films and documentaries, which are generally outside the commercial circuits. They also held discussions on such films and planned to bring out a journal on them. They even wanted to make 16-mm documentaries. "It was a period of discovery. Suddenly we saw what cinema could mean and how different it could be from what it went under its name," stated Chidananda Das Gupta, in whose garret the first meeting of CFS happened.[11]

Satyajit Ray—a commercial artist with a British advertising firm then—bitten by the film bug was experimenting with his scripts and conventional producers, in Tollywood, of Calcutta.

Marie Seton noted in her official biography of the film-maker[12]:

> Following the cancellation of the contract for the script of *Home and the World*, Ray's interest in cinema increased rather than diminished. It was stimulated by the return of Hari Das Gupta from Hollywood, who was to become known as a maker of documentary films and for the formation of the Calcutta Film Society.

Nation building in all spheres, including culture, was weighing heavily on the film industry, and a quest for an Indian idiom in films began earnestly after the country attained its freedom from the British Raj in 1947. Prime Minister Jawaharlal Nehru, an Oxford scholar, freedom fighter and writer of many insightful books on India and its history, had already initiated many steps to build institutions in various cultural fields, including films. The government had constituted an expert committee on films with SK Patil as the chairman, ably assisted by the likes of V Shantaram and BN Sircar. As against the earlier Rangachariar committee, during the British Raj, which deliberated only on film censorship, this committee under Patil had the mandate of exploring the development of the film industry as a whole.

In its recommendation, the Patil committee observed:

> In our view remedy lies neither in *Laissez-faire*, nor in regimentation, but curing all the various elements of their defects and deficiencies and ensuring, that they combine and cooperate in a joint endeavor to make this valuable medium a useful and healthy instrument of both entertainment and education, as well as a means of upliftment and progress, rather than degeneration and decay.[13]

The year was 1951 and the Indian film industry owes it all to Patil's insightful and wise recommendations for its further development in the new republic. Until the Patil committee report, the Government of India had never considered films as a medium that needed detailed attention of the State apparatus. The reason was that, even with all its mass appeal, the medium was not perceived an art form worth consideration or given status equivalent to other art forms. The entire production, funding and structure of the film industry was considered almost 'barbaric', by the State, as the funding was considered to be from black money and people associated were not from related cultural fields. Hence, the sanctioning of films for exhibition, that is, censorship, is under the Union list (seventh schedule of the Indian Constitution) and its actual exhibition and taxes were on the State list, ensuring a double control on the production and exhibition of films.[14]

Needless to say, the then government accepted the recommendations of the Patil committee and went about implementing its suggestions.

The first act was to flag off the Indian international film festivals, in 1952 itself. A French Indian was appointed at the Indian information ministry as an advisor, to plan the Indian international film festivals and laid down the foundations of the first institutions that were meant for the development of Indian films. The government had identified the country's film industry, which had by then emerged as the world's third largest film-making centre, as one of its cultural priority.

As Ray was running around to complete the making of *Pather Panchali*, the French Indian, Jean S Bhownagary, was making his plans to make India the first Asian country to have its own international film festival.

Bhownagary has also been credited for the actual implementation of SK Patil's committee report on promotion of films and film-based institutions such as the Film and Television Institute of India (FTII), NFAI, Film Finance Corporation (FFC) and International Film Festival of India (IFFI), which have contributed to a sea change in the approach towards Indian cinema over 60 years. "He (Bhownagary) asked me to wait and apply for the Archives job in the soon to be established Film Institute at Pune," recollected PK Nair, who built up NFAI from scratch, recalling his first meeting with Bhownagary in New Delhi in the 1950s. Nair, who was an apprentice with many studios and eminent directors of Bombay during the period, had gone to meet Bhownagary to seek a role in the exciting new plans of this French Indian for Indian films.[15]

"Everyone was excited about building a new nation from scratch. We never knew what we were doing will be a success, but we did an honest effort," noted Vijaya Mulay, who later held many positions related to films with the Government of India for promotion, as well as for policy making.[16]

Bhownagary and his team did flag off the IFFI, which is an annual event, in Goa, now.

Prime Minister Jawaharlal Nehru said in his message to the first IFFI held in Bombay from 14 January to 1 February 1952[17]:

> I hope that films which are just sensational or melodramatic or as such make capital out of crime will not be encouraged. If our film industry keeps this ideal before it, it will encourage good taste and help pave its own way, in the building of new India.

The festival moved to Madras, New Delhi and Calcutta during the same year, opening up a new window to the world of film-making, other than that of English-speaking countries to the Indian audience. Nehru was sure that the festival, which also had an exhibition on film equipment, will help Indian films, with regard to both content and technology. "The Festival and the Exhibition will bring new ideas from other countries. I hope that we shall profit by these ideas," Nehru hoped.[18]

CHALACHITRA AKADEMI: AN UNREALISED DREAM

Having defined his idea of culture, the scholar statesman Nehru went on to propose a Chalachitra Akademi to promote his ideas. Nehru had already defined his idea of a cultured mind in his 9 April 1950 speech at the inauguration of the Indian Council for Cultural Relations, New Delhi:

> Culture, if any value, must have a certain depth. It must also have a certain dynamic character. After all, culture depends on a vast number of factors. If we leave out what might be called the basic mould that was given to it in the early stages of nation's or people's growth, it is affected by geography, by climate and by all kinds of other factors.[19]

Prime Minister Nehru had already constituted academies for arts, literature, music, dance and fine arts at the central level. He, as a scholar and author of great repute, was also the president of the Sahitya Akademi. As the Sahitya (literature) Akademi president, he urged the Sangeet Natak Akademi (music and dance) to organise a seminar for laying down the foundations of the Chalachitra (Film) Akademi so that it could promote good films with the Indian cultural stamp on it.

The Chalachitra Akademi was still a pipe dream for the film fraternity, but Nehru made his intentions clear even before a film like *Pather Panchali* had hit the Indian film scene surprising everyone. "It is melodrama that interests large numbers of people, whether in India, England or America or elsewhere. Public taste, to some extent, moulds what is presented to it. At the same time, what is presented should mould public taste," Nehru told the film seminar, attended by who's who of the then film industry from all regions of India, as early as on 27 February 1955 at the Sangeet Natak Akademi in New Delhi. Devika Rani and Prithviraj Kapoor were the directors of the seminar and Indira Gandhi was the social secretary.[20]

The Sangeet Natak Akademi of India recognised the independent strength of films and organised the seminar accordingly. "Film was a distinct form with a separate artistic individuality," declared PV Rajamannar, the first chairman of the Akademi, at the seminar.[21]

The planning and conduct of the seminar were placed almost entirely in the hands of reputed artists and other professionals of the film fraternity. As joint and executive director of the seminar, actor Devika Rani Roerich played an instrumental role in organising the event, working in tandem with the joint director and actor Prithviraj Kapoor. One could see a young Raj Kapoor, Prithviraj Kapoor's son, as a silent participant in many of the seminar sessions, where personalities like Bimal Roy, KA Abbas, a Leftist and the script writer of many a Raj Kapoor film, actively participated in the seminar.

The seminar, which had participation from every sector of the film industry and all principal aspects of film-making from all zonal centres, was 'well structured' and ensured an extensive and detailed discussion on the state of contemporary cinema. The seminar saw Bimal Roy urging the government for entertainment tax exemptions for good films.

The Government can exempt the twelve best pictures of a year from entertainment tax, or the best picture of a year from entertainment tax, or the best picture of a year could be awarded a lump sum amount which may inspire the producer concerned to pursue his good services to the society.

The veteran film-maker's suggestion was implemented by the government, as the film policies unfolded later.[22]

In his inaugural address, Prime Minister Jawaharlal Nehru was at his visionary best as far as films were concerned:

I see a great future, a glorious future, for Indian films. Before long, I expect Indian films to be exhibited to crowded houses all over the world, and they will earn not only money for our country but also a reputation for beauty, goodness and truth. India must and will make its distinctive contribution to the film art of the world and I am confident it will.[23]

For Nehru, the scholar statesman, cinema was a medium of public influence and he wanted the budding republic to take serious note of it. He also declared that the government cannot be a mute witness to the trends in the film industry. The Prime Minister stated as follows at the seminar[24]:

You may consider it in terms of high art, well and good, but regardless of that, in terms of moulding … the people of the country, the new generation; it is of high importance…. It has to be treated realistically as something of the highest importance, a Government must be intimately concerned with it.

Years later, the Dr Shivarama Karanth committee on films instituted by the then Prime Minister Indira Gandhi recommended the formation of a Chalachitra (Film) Akademi to the government. Just as the unfulfilled dream of the first prime minister, his daughter's effort too did not meet with success, although many state governments were taking the route of Chalachitra Akademi to promote regional cinemas. Curiously enough, the only other political figure who addressed the seminar was the then Indian ambassador to the United Nations (1952–1962), VK Krishna Menon. He emphasised on the employment opportunities that films could create across India from production to screening, but he was keen to see the Indian films

reach the masses in the villages. "Until we can really take entertainment into the fields of rural India and be able to understand the
response of the villagers, there can be no universal development in
this direction," Menon reminded the film fraternity. The 10th session
of the seminar saw Krishna Menon asking the fraternity to have similar seminars in other metro cities, promoting the participation of local
talents and proposed an organisation for the assessment of public
opinion.

Krishna Menon told the participants of the seminar[25]:

> At the present moment, all your assessments of public response is
> merely guesswork. You must study how to condition that response,
> how to educate that response. You cannot do it all on a sudden. It
> is a gradual process of cultivating and educating public taste itself.

Krishna Menon stopped short of uttering the words 'film society'!

Nehru, who was also the president of the Sahitya Akademi in
those days, took his cultural role very seriously. He had earlier cabled
India's high commissioner and his friend VK Krishna Menon in
London to find an expert of British origin to evangelise on educational
quality of films. Menon, in turn, asked his (high commissioner's)
social secretary, Pamela Cullen, to search for the right candidate for
Nehru's assignment, even before arriving in India to take over as the
defence minister.

ARRIVAL OF THE EVANGELIST MARIE SETON

As Satyajit Ray, having flagged off the CFS with his friends, was busy
shooting and running around to complete his first film, *Pather
Panchali*, in 1955, Cullen was finalising an old Indian league associate
of Krishna Menon, Marie Seton, on Nehru's assignment on films. She
had just come back from the erstwhile Soviet Union, after a couple of
years of association with the legendary Soviet film-maker Sergei
Eisenstein and was invited for a lecture tour in India on film appreciation. The tour was to be conducted by the Ministry of Education, in
association with the British Film Institute. Marie, an activist of the
British Labour Party, had once 'barged' into Mahatma Gandhi for a
meeting. She was excited about going to India and being a part of the
young nation's efforts to build a new film culture. "I first met Marie
Seton in 1955 when the Indian ministry of education, in association
with the British Film Institute, commissioned her to lecture on film

appreciation at many of India's flourishing film societies," Pamela Cullen wrote later.[26]

Marie Seton and her friends from the British Film Institute later had a major role in promoting *Pather Panchali* in the Western world, not that Ray was a greenhorn to the London film scenario at that point of time. Marie had arrived in India soon after the seminar of 1955 to become the lifelong family friend of the Nehrus (both father and daughter). As history points out, with the International Film Festival in 1952, the seminar of 1955 and arrival of Marie Seton, Prime Minister Nehru earnestly took up the effort to give Indian cinema the right direction it needed.

Marie Seton remained an *Indophile* till the end of her life in 1985 and was single-handedly responsible for drumming up and giving the sporadic flicker of film societies, the shape of a national movement. Her multicity lectures and the excitement created by the success of *Pather Panchali* resulted in the formation of the FFSI in 1959. *Pather Panchali*, which got India a place on the world film map, just about the time when *Rashomon* of Akira Kurosawa (Japan) took the world of films by surprise.

Seton's first booklet remains as the first effort by the Indian government towards giving films an academic orientation.

Marie Seton wrote in the first chapter of her booklet[27]:

> The first subject of the seminars—Film Appreciation—introduced the audience to the history of cinematic development. It showed how the film medium had been freed from theatre traditions and had developed a technique of presentation which was suited to the artistic possibilities of the motion picture camera. It also presented cinema from an international perspective and showed that in general a film, like a novel or play, becomes universal in its appeal (a) when it presents an important social or political theme, and (b) when it is nationally true to the country where it is created.

Seton had written the booklet after a series of lectures across various cities in India. Her tour in India was not just for lectures, but also for screening 35 films and film extracts that she brought to be shown to the audience in India, in order to develop a taste for good films from the point of view of international cinema. Seton wrote two more booklets, which were published by the National Centre for Educational Research and Technology, titled *Film As an Art* and *The Art of Five Directors: Film Appreciation*.

Image 1.2 Marie Seton's book *Film as an Art and Film Appreciation.*
Note: The first book-let officially published by Ministry of Education, GOI.
Courtesy: Author.

Image 1.3 Indian Film Review—the first Indian film quarterly by CFS 1956.
Courtesy: CFS collection/Photo by the author.

There is no doubt that the terms 'Film Appreciation' and 'Film Society' were made popular in India by Marie Seton. She can be described as the first evangelist for *Film Appreciation* who gave a shape to the Film Society Movement, thereby spreading the excitement of a new art among the urbanites of India during the 1960s and 1970s.

What is the role and objective of the *Film Appreciation*, a concept that spread like wildfire in those days among the educated youth of India? Broadly, it was defined as the following, by an NFAI document on the subject years later. These include, "how to look at films differently than what you are accustomed to and to help one to find out the hidden layers of a well-made film and in the process lift your enjoyment to a higher plane."[28]

Based on these definitions, NFAI along with FTII, Pune, organises a film appreciation workshop for a month every year, as part of its effort to promote good film culture in India. NFAI also circulates a document—how to form a film society—to interested parties.

From 1956 to 1985, Marie visited India several times. In 1984, she was awarded Padma Bhushan, the third highest national honour by the Government of India, for her contributions to India and Indian films. "Indira Gandhi's sons, Rajiv and Sanjay, used to stay in her London house, when they were admitted for some short term educational courses in London," says Vijaya Mulay, who was a close friend of Marie.[29] The first professor of film appreciation of the FTII, Professor Satish Bhadur, who was the first academic initiator of film studies in India, was handpicked by Marie Seton, from Agra St. Johns College, during one of her lecture tours across Indian cities.

PATHER PANCHALI: A TOAST OF TIMES FOR THE COUNTRY, DEFINING INDIA'S IDIOM IN FILMS

In short, just as India awaited the film *Raja Harishchandra* to join the emerging medium of the industrial revolution during the British Raj, the new democratic republic was preparing itself for the arrival of a film like *Pather Panchali* in its cultural horizon and to have its own idiom in the world of films. The first show of Ray's film in New York organised by the Indian Embassy was after a sitar recital, sending out the message of the film as a true cultural product.

Though sceptics tried to deride the film as 'selling' Indian poverty abroad, Prime Minister Nehru himself defended *Pather Panchali*.

"What is wrong about showing India's poverty? Everyone knows that we are a poor country. The question is: Are we Indians sensitive to our poverty or insensitive to it? Ray has shown it with an extraordinary sense of beauty and sensitiveness," Nehru strongly defended the film.[30] Needless to say, the Prime Minister and his daughter Indira Gandhi became lifelong connoisseurs of such films and always promoted film-makers making similar films. Ray's first film won the best Human Document award at the Cannes Film Festival, along with several national and international awards, making the CFS founder a global celebrity in films.

The nation and the CFS celebrate *Pather Panchali* and the anniversary of its public screening every year. The film enthusiasts of the country realised that Ray's first film was not just a *Song of the Road*, but was indeed a song of the times. The film gave a new face to Indian cinema and sparked off a tremendous interest in not just *Pather Panchali*, but in a whole new genre of meaningful films. The entire Film Society Movement got a jump-start in many places with the screening of *Pather Panchali*, which was making waves nationally and internationally. The world acknowledges Ray's film as the advent of new Indian cinema. The film and the director of the film were historically identified as the pioneers of a meaningful cinema move-ment in India. Satyajit Ray, indeed, continued not just in being as the lifelong president of the FFSI, but still remains the sole stalwart of the new Indian films.

Marie Seton[31] wrote:

Where there is such a response to discussion of cinema and an interest in films which are not in accord with the conventional entertainment film, it is reasonable to suppose that there is growing public of a higher and more cultural character. The success of the Bengali film, *Pather Panchali*, is also indicative of this trend.

Malayalam film-maker Adoor Gopalakrishnan, who dedicated an entire chapter on *Pather Panchali* in his first collection of articles on films, stated:

No one ever thought, there will be a narrative on the folklore of life and a celebration of life itself, this way on the celluloid and that is why the *Pather Panchali* (Song of the Road) will be remembered as the harbinger of change in Indian cinema.[32]

Adoor, incidentally, was also a harbinger of the new film culture with his *Chitralekha* Film Society/Cooperative and is considered the leader of worthy successors of Ray and his genre of films.

The experience of Shyam Benegal, Adoor's contemporary, was no different. Benegal recalled his first experience of *Pather Panchali*: "The experience was indescribable. As the expression goes, 'it simply blew my mind.'"[33] Benegal had seen *Pather Panchali* in a Calcutta theatre on a visit to the city in 1955 and he saw it over and over after the first show by buying tickets continuously after each show. Such was his excitement!

Years later, Ray's own film society colleague, Das Gupta, explained the excitement that *Pather Panchali* created in India and abroad:

> Political independence and the beginnings of film appreciation are thus fused in my memory. Indeed there was more than a trace of messianic fervor in our attitude to film. A new cinema we thought would emerge as an art and social force. A country like India, with its honeycomb of identities defined by language, religion and a host of other criteria, would need social engineering of some scale to wield itself into a nation, and cinema would be an ideal force to supply the motivation.[34]

Looking back, Das Gupta, who was the prime mover behind the CFS and FFSI, remained prophetic even today. He walked his talk all his life, leading the Film Society Movement and the quest of India's idiom in films by the builders of modern India.

Anil Srivastava, another pioneer of the movement now settled in the United States, recollected the impact of the film on his life as such.[35]

> Earlier this year (2015), I was invited to watch the re-release of the digitally mastered *Pather Panchali* on the 60th anniversary of its world premiere at the Museum of Modern Art in New York. I sat in the darkness wiping my tears and reliving my viewing of the film in Bhopal. My involvement in the film society brought me to *Pather Panchali* and that was the beginning of a life long journey of learning to be a human being and not just another animal walking on two legs.

For the government, looking for moulding the taste of Indian films and film-goers, *Pather Panchali* was *manna* from heaven to showcase the new film to Indians and the world. The world began to see the new wave in Indian films, rather Indian films firmly perched itself to the global map with the Ray's first film. For Ray, but for the screenings of CFS, the visit of Jean Renoir, for the shooting of the film *River*, and films like *Battleship Potemkin*, by Russian legendary film-maker Sergei Eisenstein, and the Italian neorealist film, *Bicycle Thieves*, by Vittorio De Sica (1948), which he saw in post-Second World War, London, *Pather Panchali* should not have found its place in history.

The first film of the first film society organiser also became the first film to make into world film history for its new path-breaking approach to film-making. Hence, the film became the song and toast of the times, just as its title indicates 'Song of the Road'—*Pather Panchali.*

RAISING FILM AS A NEW ART AND DEFINING ITS AESTHETIC CONTOURS

Along with the Ray film, his colleagues from CFS began to educate the public on the need to look at films as any other art form, raising the status of the medium to a new level. But for the analysis of the Ray film by Das Gupta, Marie Seton and later Professor Satish Bahadur, the film, *Pather Panchali*, would not have perched itself at the highest status of the world film history for over six decades. Das Gupta was a star film critic of the prestigious daily, *The Statesman,* for years and wrote extensively on the evolution of Indian film as art in tune with the developing aesthetic tastes of the world. He inspired a generation of similar critics, who went on to write and analyse films using global aesthetic tools of the medium and contemporary arts, raising the medium to a higher art form, attracting the attention of the general cultural and intellectual arena to films. Till then, films as such did not arouse the curiosity of traditional cultural fields, as the medium was yet to evolve on its own, past the curiosity of the new medium.

The film societies not just sparked off a new creativity in films, but also gave rise to better film critics, film writers and historians, as the sole avenue for exposure to better films and film-makers of the world. The exposure to new trends in film-making and styles opened a new stream of film appreciation and studies. Along with the film screenings, the groups distributed pamphlets and other reading materials about the films and sometimes one of the members intro-ducing the film giving a background about the culture, film-maker and the film itself, placing the film in its cultural context. Many of the film societies brought out journals in their regions.

The first film quarterly, a serious academic journal on films, was also brought out by CFS, under the guidance of Marie Seton and Das Gupta, soon after the revival of CFS, after the roaring success of *Pather Panchali*. Years later, Calcutta's Jadavpur University became the first to offer a degree and postgraduate course in film studies, taking the film appreciation and studies to a different level. Now, over 200 universities in India offer various courses on film studies, and film institutes have sprung up across India to cater to the increasing fold of film-makers and technicians.

Pather Panchali and its makers put the country's films into a serious aesthetic and academic route, which years later Das Gupta analysed as two streams of the medium itself: the *Desi* and *Margi*. Desi indicating the popular mass culture and Margi indicating the classic culture. The film societies represented the Margi part of the film culture and, over a period of time, influenced the Desi culture, even raising the standard of Indian popular films equal to the best of the film industry, be it European or American, and strongly resisted a Hollywood takeover of Indian films. The ongoing interplay of Margi and Desi culture of Indian films overturned the viewing habits of Indians from 80 per cent foreign films in 1950 to 90 per cent Indian films by 2015, that too in all Indian languages, a dream that the founding fathers of the country were keen to achieve with their interventions in film field, during the first two decades of independent India.

(No history of Indian Film Society Movement is complete without the history and development of cinema as a medium in India and understanding the significance of *Pather Panchali* and its historic position: see Annexure 1.)

NOTES*

1. http://www.bfi.org.uk/news/50-greatest-films-all-time
2. CFS Silver jubilee brochure of *Pather Panchali*'s release. 1980.
3. Ministry of I&B, *Report of the Working Group on National Film Policy* (New Delhi: Ministry of I&B, GOI, May 1980), p. 9. Para 3.3.
4. HN Narahari Rao, ed., *The Film Society Movement in India* (Mumbai: Asian Film Foundation, 2009), p. vi.
5. *Reference: Article–collection of PK Nair from NFAI.* Retrieved from http://cherianwrites. blogspot.in/2016_02_01_archive.html
6. HN Narahari Rao, ed., *The Film Society Movement in India* (Mumbai: Asian Film Foundation, 2009), p. 25.
7. HN Narahari Rao, ed., *The Film Society Movement in India* (Mumbai: Asian Film Foundation, 2009), p. 19–20.
8. https://en.wikipedia.org/wiki/Film_society#France
9. https://en.wikipedia.org/wiki/British_Federation_of_Film_Societies

10. *Oxford Dictionary of Film Studies*, p. 174.
11. Chidananda Das Gupta, *Talking about Films* (New Delhi: Orient Longman, 1981), p. vii.
12. Marie Seton, *Portrait of a Director* (New Delhi: Penguin Books, 2003).
13. SK Patil Committee report, 1951, p. 185, para 523.
14. Rangachariar Committee 1913 and Patil Committee 1951 of Government of India.
15. Interview with PK Nair.
16. Interview with Vijaya Mulay.
17. *Selected Works of Jawaharlal Nehru* (New Delhi: Publications Division, I&B Ministry, GOI), p. 311.
18. Ibid., p. 311.
19. Ibid., p. 311.
20. RM Ray, *Indian Cinema in Retrospect: Speeches of the 1955 Seminar* (New Delhi: Sangeet Natak Academy, 1956 and 2009), p. 234.
21. Ibid., p. 234.
22. Ibid., p. 234.
23. Ibid., p. 234.
24. Ibid., p. 234.
25. Ibid., p. 234.
26. Marie Seton, *Preface of Portrait of a Director: Satyajit Ray* (New Delhi: Penguin Books, 2003).
27. Ministry of Education, *Film as an Educational Force in India* (New Delhi: Ministry of Education, 1956). Retrieved from http://cherianwrites.blogspot.in/2016/03/marie-setons-first-book-let-edited.html
28. http://cherianwrites.blogspot.in/2016/02/typical-film-appreciation-course-by.html
29. Interview with Vijaya Mulay.
30. Booklet CFS, *Pather Panchali*'s anniversary, 2012.
31. Ministry of Education, *Film as an Educational Force in India*, p. 27.
32. Adoor Gopalakrishnan, *World of Cinema* [in Malayalam] (Kerala: Kerala Bhasha Institute, 1983).
33. Sandeep Ray ed., *Deep Focus* (Delhi: HarperCollins, 2011), Foreword.
34. Chidananda Das Gupta, *Seeing Is Believing: Selected Writings on Cinema* (Delhi: Viking, 2008), Introduction.
35. http://cherianwrites.blogspot.in/2016/03/on-fsm-by-anilsrivastava-pioneer-and.html

* All websites accessed on 16 June 2016.

CHAPTER 2

The Growth Path: From Calcutta Film Society to the Federation of Film Societies of India

Building a new India was the buzzword of the countrymen in every sector, whether these were democratic institutions, economy, culture or new media such as films, in the years after its independence from colonial rule. "Tryst with Destiny" was a speech delivered by Jawaharlal Nehru, the first prime minister, to the Indian Constituent Assembly in the Parliament, on the eve of India's independence, on 15 August 1947 that reminded the people of India of bigger challenges of the future. "The achievement we celebrate today is but a step, an opening of opportunity, to the greater triumphs and achievements that await us. Are we brave enough and wise enough to grasp this opportunity and accept the challenge of the future?" Nehru wondered in his speech.[1] Citizens in each sphere, including films, were getting ready with their answers, inspired by the fresh atmosphere of optimism in the country.

Chidananda Das Gupta reflected on the advent of the first film society of the independent India[2]:

> India's Independence somehow launched me into an irrepressible enthusiasm for cinema. It was in October 1947 that some of us, including Satyajit Ray, got together and started the Calcutta Film Society (CFS) in an attic in Ballygunge, where I used to live. It was

a period of discovery. Suddenly, we saw what cinema could mean and how different it could be from what went under its name.

Das Gupta, along with his old time friend, Satyajit Ray, did not just stop short of organising a new forum called CFS, but went on to pave the way for a movement called the Film Society and New Indian Cinema in the following two decades. CFS, in its inception, was blessed with distinct academicians and cultural figures from the then Calcutta. The president of the CFS was an eminent economist, Professor PC Mahalanobis. The chairman of the executive committee was Hiran K Sanyal and the joint honorary secretaries were Satyajit Ray and Chidananda Das Gupta.

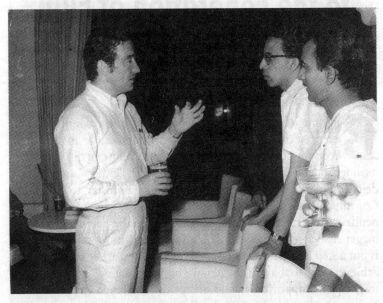

Image 2.1 French film-maker Louis Malle at CFS.
Courtesy: CFS Collection.

Decades later, Das Gupta, the trailblazer behind the Indian Film Society Movement, concluded that the quest of film enthusiasts was no different from that of the then leaders of the country. He pointed out in the report given by the Film Enquiry Committee of the Government of India in 1951, headed by SK Patil, which concluded that "the film industry was incapable of reforming itself" and proposed far-reaching changes through new institutions. "Nothing but a new cinema would suffice," he wrote.[3]

Ray's contemporary Mrinal Sen too noted the entry of CFS in the post-independence years.

Mrinal Sen, who turned 93 in May 2015, told the author, recalling his entry into films[4]:

> Since I have been reading lots of books on cinema, which were made available to me, mostly from the National Library; it used to be called the Imperial Library, during the British period. After independence it was re-named as the National Library. That is how I tried to understand films. After that when the film society started here (CFS); it was basically two persons, Satyajit Ray and Chidananda Das Gupta; there were others too. But they were the main force. I am no historian, but let me tell you that was the first film society born in India.

THE NASCENCE AND REVIVAL OF CFS

The CFS had an impressive kick-off with Jean Renoir's visit, and later a Russian maestro, Vsevold Pudovkin, also interacted with its members, making the society the leading cultural outfit in Calcutta. As Ray was engaged for three years in the making of *Pather Panchali*, the CFS had its first hiccup leading to a break in the first part of 1950s.

However, the success of *Pather Panchali* and the excitement and controversies that it created led to the revival of the society in 1956, that too with a journal, *Indian Film Quarterly*. Surely, the CFS founder's film pumped fresh adrenalin to the search for new Indian films and also for the budding Film Society Movement, which was eventually nurtured by the Central government and patronised by none other than Prime Minister Jawaharlal Nehru and his daughter Indira Gandhi, ensuring over four decades of continuous governmental and political patronage to the Film Society Movement.

"As the journal of the CFS, it represents and becomes the instrument of a new movement to promote the growth of better cinema and better audience," the editorial of the first issue of January–March 1957 had declared. Eighty-four-year-old Pradipta Sen, a media person, who was part of the revival of CFS, recalled the golden days of the society.[5]

Sen, who was the President of the CFS in 2012, recollected[6]:

> There were primarily three reasons for the re-starting of the CFS; impact and excitement about the success of *Pather Panchali*, frequent visits of Marie Seton, a British film expert and the growing number of film buffs in the city. From 250 members, the revived CFS grew to 2,500 members in five years and remained so till the 80s.

The CFS celebrates the August anniversary of its release of *Pather Panchali* almost every year. Indeed, the celebration had become a part of the cultural mosaic of Kolkata and of the city's proud Bengali cultural enthusiasts. "By 1956, with the success of *Pather Panchali*, first at home and then abroad, the film society scene opened out and took on an almost formidable aspect. Enthusiasm for cinema became respectable and wide range of people rushed into film societies," Das Gupta noted.[7] Obviously, cinema as it existed in India was till then looked down upon by other practitioners of other cultural forms, be it theatre or dance dramas or literature.

FILM SOCIETIES IN OTHER CITIES

Little did Das Gupta realise that there were small groups waiting to explore the new media, the cinema, in many other parts of the country following the excitement created by *Pather Panchali*. While Bombay already had its own film society to acquaint the film-makers with the theoretical and technical aspect of the emerging medium, through screening and discussing films of other countries, the other urban centres of the country were equally eager to join the bandwagon.

New Delhi, Patna, Lucknow, Roorkie, Bhopal and Chennai slowly got into the excitation mode with the film societies, exposing themselves to the experiments in this new medium happening outside India.

The Delhi Film Society

Muriel Wasi, one of the founders of DFS, in 1981, wrote[8]:

> It seems so long ago, but it was only about 25 years ago that the Delhi Film Society was founded by a small group of people—not more than 12–who were anxious to see outstanding films that were

not ordinarily screened at the commercial cinemas. These founding persons were professionals, journalists, businessmen, administrators, diplomats—but their common interest was the cinema and special thing that the cinema could do to criticize life.

DFS, founded in 1956, was one of the most privileged of the film societies in the country. The international embassies had their headquarters in the capital city of Delhi. The ministries and the government, prime ministers and other ministers promoting such films had their offices in Delhi. The last president of the now-defunct DFS was an Indian Police Service officer (retired) Gautam Kaul, who is also Indira Gandhi's cousin. The first screening of the DFS was a Hungarian film.

Marie Seton continued to be an inspirational presence for the film enthusiasts of the capital, as she was a guest of Ms Indira Gandhi at her home. Some of the early members of the DFS included dignitaries such as Indira Gandhi, Aruna Asaf Ali, IK Gujral (who went on to be a prime minister). By the early 1980s, the society that started with 15 members in 1956 had attracted over 2,000 film buffs of the capital into its fold. Nehru's close aide and Defense Minister Krishna Menon and a host of other VVIPs of the capital were regulars or guests at the DFS.

The DFS was at its peak during the 1980s, and the frequency of films shown was almost five to seven in a month. Slowly, a message went around that uncensored films were shown, and this led to the beginning of the decline of the DFS. Later in the 1990s, the Film Society Movement became dormant because of two reasons: the advent of TV and liberal import of films. The censoring policy also became liberal, observed YC Halan, who served as both the president and the secretary of DFS in 1970s and 1980s.[9] Memberships were not available to the then students, like this author in 1980, as DFS was full of "elite" members, and we were left to the mercy of various cultural centres of the diplomatic missions in the capital.

The strength of the DFS was its elitist membership as well as leadership, with the who's who in the government and power centres. It also attracted persons who were serious about pursuing a career in films. Many of them became film-makers, such as Pankaj Bhutalia, Gopi Gajwani and Bikram Singh. Many were politically and culturally powerful like Aruna Asaf Ali, Vijay Mulay, Usha Bhagat and Gautam Kaul. These people ensured that only serious members joined DFS. The DFS initially had limited its membership to 250 and then extended the limit to 500, and in 1980 it had grown over 2,500 members. There is an unconfirmed story that even Rajiv Gandhi, the son of the then prime minister, was denied a membership. Memberships were awarded after an interview in those days. The entry barriers helped to build up a quality membership. However, the waning of initial enthusiasm for uncensored films, and with the advent of the video and television, and lack of official patronage slowly put a curtain on DFS.

Bhopal's International Film Club

Anil Srivastava, who was also a founder of the Lucknow film society and a technocrat, recounted:

> My involvement with film society movement started with the International Film Club in high school (St. Josephs' Convent, Bhopal) in 1959. The father of two of my classmates, Saleem and Parvez Romani, had used a Bell & Howell 16 mm film projector. We used this to start showing films and started a film society on 4th August 1959. We began with 16mm film distributors like MGM, Columbia and NEIF Film Club. Tagore's birth centennial (1961) was coming up and from the newspapers we learnt about Satyajit Ray and his Teen Kanya based on Tagore stories, and Tagore documentary.

He went on to work with companies like Apple in the United States, after founding the first trust that promoted video and related technologies in a big way, and the Centre for Development of Instructional Technology (CENDIT), way back in the 1980s. CENDIT happened, even before India climbed on to the information technology (IT) bandwagon, and Anil, of course, was among the founding fathers of the National Association of Software and Services Companies (NASSCOM), the industry body of India's IT companies, before he immigrated to Mexico and then the United States.[10]

Anil Srivastva had the distinction of forming the first teenagers' film club way back in 1959 in Bhopal, where even Prime Minister Nehru was a VIP guest. Anil also became a disciple of Marie Seton, who had arrived to promote film societies in India. "I still have the long letters which Marie used to write," he said. A report in the *National Herald* in the year 1961 recorded all of it when the club made its first short film. "The teen-aged film unit of International Film Club of Bhopal has produced its first ever documentary to be made by the people entirely under seventeen years," the report said, featuring a photo of the production unit.[11] Taroon Kumar Bhaduri, the journalist father of actor Jaya Bhaduri Bachchan, was a patron to this film club and first of the films shown was *Pather Panchali*. Anil, whose life and work centred on films, later married Shampa, the daughter of Ray films' leading lady, Karuna Banerjee.

The Lucknow Film Society
Marie, who had not just inspired people in Delhi, but in distant Bhopal, had a young follower who went on to become one of the founders of the Lucknow Film Society.

Anil Srivastava recollected about the founding days of the Lucknow Film Society as follows[12]:

> I had finished my High School. My father's two-year posting in Bhopal was coming to an end. We were going back to Lucknow, I told Marie that I was very unhappy about having to leave Bhopal. She told me about Professor Kailashnath Kaul, director of the National Botanical Gardens (now National Botanical Research Institute) and suggested that I should meet him about starting a film society in Lucknow.

Professor Kaul's son Gautam Kaul, along with Anil, had become the beacons of the Film Society Movement in their adult days in Delhi and remained ardent film buffs. Gautam, who became an Indian Police Service officer, was also the office-bearer of the DFS, before the regular screenings stopped.

Anil recounted his nostalgic memories. Sheila Kaul later became a central minister:

> Marie had spoken to Professor Kaul in Delhi. I still remember vividly my meeting with Professor Kaul and his words how the botanical gardens are a place for nurturing the intellect and human culture. Walking through the botanical garden, he spoke of films and his stay at Kew Royal Botanic Gardens, in between, bending down pointing and describing the plants along our path. Films, he talked about, and plants he described seemed equally to preoccupy his thinking. He had a beautiful small film auditorium in the botanic garden which was the venue for most of the Lucknow Film Society's screenings. I don't know how the group came together. One person led to another and we all met at Professor Kaul's home. It was decided to start the Lucknow Film Society with Sheila Kaul as the

President; Wendy Vora, Devendra Mishra (father of film-maker, Sudhir Mishra); journalist CS Pandit; Harbans Mathur, KN Kacker and me as members. I was not even 18 but was treated as one. I was asked to be the joint secretary of the society.

The Madras Film Society

At almost the same time, post *Pather Panchali*, the Madras Film Society (MFS) was founded in October 1957, putting South India on the nation's film society map. Ammu Swaminadhan, a politician and mother of Mrinalini Sarabhai and Captain Laxmi Sehegal, was the founder-president of the MFS. Being the first film society in Southern India, it played a stellar role in inspiring other cities of the region to form their own film societies. KS Govindaraj, who was one of the founder members of the MFS, is presently the executive vice president. The MFS, which is nearing the 60th year of its existence, was started with a ₹12 annual subscription, and today the subscription is ₹700 per annum.

"Many film personalities have benefited by our screening of international films. The film-makers, K Balachander, Kamal Haasan, Singeetham Srinivasa Rao, Muktha Srinivasan, SP Muthuraman, Balu Mahendra, and popular actors Suhasini and Nazar were MFS's regular guests at the screenings," recalled Govindaraj.[13]

The Bombay Film Society

RE Hawkins, the former general manager of Oxford University Press (OUP), in 1981, reminiscences about the period in the FFSI's journal as follows:

> We normally had our screenings at 9.15 pm at Eros cinema. Ference Berko, our founder, was an enthusiast who at the end of the show would start a lively discussion in the miniature theatre where we met often, the one above the Eros Cinema–a discussion which would be continued in homes and cafes.

Hawkins, indeed, was the last chairman of the Bombay Film Society (BFS), which was founded by Berko in 1937. He was also the vice president of the newly formed FFSI in 1959. The last general body meeting of the BFS was held on 22 May 1962, which was attended by many people, including VM Vijakar and Jag Mohan (joint secretaries), VN Raji (treasurer), Tina Khote, ST Berkeley-Hill, KL Khandpur,

MV Krishnaswamy, Sudharshan Sharma and A. Bhaskara Rao. Jag Mohan, Khandapur and Krishnaswamy remained ardent film society activists till the end of their lives.

Jag Mohan, a leading light of the BFS, observed[14]:

> The BFS was an offshoot of the Second World War, when a group of serious-minded Britishers, mostly from the services stationed in Bombay, along with a few Indians, wanted some diversion. Typical of British and elitist approach to films prevalent at that point of time was that the members had drinks and dinner before seeing films.

The Patna Film Society

Just as in Calcutta and Bombay, in Patna, the UK-educated Vijaya Mulay and her friends, who were regulars at the morning shows of the English films in the city, decided to have their own club to view films of their choice. "In a way, these half empty morning shows proved a boon to the 15 or 20 of us, who founded Patna Film society in 1951," recalled Mulay, who went on to be one of the leading lights behind the FFSI from 1959 onwards. She still remains the best icon of the Film Society Movement even at the age of ninety-four. Mulay was bitten by the cinema bug while she was a student at Leeds University. She was a member of the University Film Society at Leeds, way back in 1947. On her return from the UK, she was posted with the government at Patna from 1949 to 1954, and her passion for cinema made her persuade her friends to form the Patna Film Society in 1952. The president of the film society was Prof Devi Chatterjee, and Mulay (fondly called *Akka*) was the secretary and Arun Roy Chaudhuri, the joint secretary. "Amongst the founder members were Akbar Imam, Kumar Durganand Sinha, Sita Sharan Srivastava, Gyan Chandra, NS Thapa (who later became the Chief Producer of Films Division)." Patna film society was also flagged off with the screening of *Battleship Potemkin*.

"We all knew each other very well and after the show there used to be passionate and almost endless discussions," Mulay recalled the good old days. After she moved to Delhi, the film society in Patna suffered many setbacks and was closed down in the 1960s. Later in 1974, the Cine Society of Patna was formed, and they continued to screen films, keeping Patna on the film society map of the country.[15]

The Roorkie Film Society

YC Halan, a Delhi University academic-turned editor, who was also secretary and president of the DFS, explained about how he got into the Film Society Movement:

> I was in Roorkie at the Central Building Research Institute in the early sixties. My uncle was the President of the Roorkie Film Society. I watched a Kurosawa film and realised how different it was. I was told that the best films, particularly non-commercial, from foreign countries were not shown in India. Also films from non-English-speaking countries were never shown in India. Those were the days when foreign films were not freely allowed. Such films were brought in by the embassies and were routed through film societies. Film society movement was at its peak as most persons like Usha Bhagat, Social Secretary to Indira Gandhi, and serious film buffs were interested in watching such films. Since these people were most influential in the society, the best films from the best directors were brought in by embassies and shown to society members.

The Roorkie Film Society, which was also among the first few to form the FFSI, was run by the academics at Roorkie, almost a campus film club of the Central Road Research Institute (CRRI) AK Rahman, who later became a scientist at Council for Scientific and Industrial Research (CSIR) in New Delhi, was running the Roorkie society.[16]

Agra and Faizabad Film Societies

Although Agra and Faizabad film societies came up soon after the formation of FFSI in 1959, it is also considered a milestone activity in the Northern Region.

Prof Satish Bahadur, who organised the Film Club, recalled in one of his notes:

> Based in the Institute of Social Sciences and the Institute of Linguistics and Hindi studies, the Agra University Film Club had about 150 post-graduate student-members. Almost all of them came from a middle-class urban or rural background, and almost none of them had any background of anything except the commercial Hindi cinema; a few of them, of the popular Hollywood films.

The society functioned from 1960 to 1963 and ceased to exist after the professor went to FTII as a staffer.

Going by the description of Professor Bahadur about the Agra Film Club, it was indeed a new experiment with film appreciation.[17]

The experiment, which was totally indigenous and voluntary by Professor Bahadur, impressed Marie Seton, the evangelist of the Film Society Movement those days, and she insisted on making Professor Bahadur, the first Indian professor of film appreciation at FTII. The professor took his post as lifelong mission and trained almost two generations of film-makers and film buffs through the FTII course, and an annual one-month residency run by him and PK Nair of the NFAI from 1967 onwards.

The Faizabad Film Society was established by a family that ran the newspaper *Hum Aap*, recalled senior journalist Madhukar Upadhaya, who belongs to the town. Despite repeated calls to the temple town of Ayodhya, details of this society were not forthcoming, although there is a non-affiliated Ayodhya Film Society functioning in the town.

Image 2.2 Marie Seton and Satyajit Ray.
Note: Marie Seton, the evangelist of film societies who also wrote a biography of Satyajit Ray, promoted him internationally.
Courtesy: FFSI/Asian Film Foundation, Mumbai.

THE POLITICAL AND GOVERNMENTAL PATRONAGE

No doubt both Prime Minister Nehru and his daughter Indira Gandhi, who was the I&B minister in Nehru's successor's ministry and later prime minister for over one and a half decade, remained patrons of new film culture and films, extending their total support to the Film Society Movement from 1950 onwards. Most of the initiatives of the government in films coincided with the advent and growth of the film societies in the urban centres of India. Nehru's trust with films was kicked off by the submission of the first Film Enquiry report led by SK Patil to the government in 1950. The committee had made wide-ranging recommendations with a view to effect far-reaching changes to films, which had emerged as the mass medium by then. The Indian film industry was only second to Hollywood, already by the 1950s, although none of traditional arts and its connoisseurs in India touched films by a barge pole. Films did not find a place in the list of coveted arts among Indians, just as music, theatre, or literature or arts.

The first in the government's agenda was to show case best of world films to Indians, so that it will attract the best of artistic minds. They had to depend on global Indians to undertake this, and hence a search was on right earnestly to get evangelists for the new Indian films. In 1951 itself, Nehru, on the advice of Indira Gandhi, brought in Jean Bhownagary, a French Indian, from UNESCO in Paris, as an advisor to ministry of I&B to flag off the IFFIs, which have become an annual feature now. The SK Patil committee in 1950 had made recommendations for many institutions to make Indian films world class. Bhownagary, who enjoyed the confidence of Nehru and Indira Gandhi, following the successful conduct of the Indian International Festival in 1952, was entrusted with the task of ensuring that the institutions that the Patil committee recommended were established. These institutions included the FTII, FFC and NFAI.

Nehru had also initiated the formation of a "Chalachitra Akademi" through a major seminar in Delhi in 1955, even before Marie Seton was brought in 1956 to popularise the new film culture. Marie could not have done what she did without the complete support from Prime Minister Nehru and his daughter.

Anil Srivastava, a veteran of the movement, recollected the involvement of Nehru as far back in 1959[18]:

Chacha Nehru was the universal uncle. We wrote to him about our film club in Bhopal. Our film projector was old and rickety. He was visiting Bhopal so it was natural to ask our beloved 'uncle' to gift us a new film projector. Lo and behold, he wrote back and promised to meet us. Marie Seton was a guest at Nehru's residence in Teen Murti Bhavan. On his return to Delhi he mentioned us to Marie and that brought me into the fold of the larger Indian Film Society Movement.

Both Marie and Indira Gandhi, who had developed a great personal friendship by then, had indeed initiated the formation of the FFSI in 1959, following Marie's successful all-India lecture tour on Film Appreciation. Marie stayed with the Nehrus at the prime minister's official residence Teen Murti Bhawan, and even penned a biography of Pandit Nehru.[19] Indira Gandhi remained on the post of vice president of FFSI, until she became the minister for I&B, under Prime Minister Lal Bahadur Shastri. Indira Gandhi was so much involved in the campaign for new film culture that she even asked Marie to show films to her sons and their friends at Teen Murti, so as to mould their film culture.

There were two major film enquiry committees under Prime Minister Nehru and the other under Indira Gandhi. "All film policies of Independent India began about that time (1947–61) so you can certainly imply that it was a Nehruvian policy initiative," Shyam Benegal, the veteran film-maker and director of TV series *Discovery of India* based on the writings of Jawaharlal Nehru, pointed out.[20]

KA Abbas, the veteran film-maker, in his autobiography describes an incident after the preview of the director's film, *Munna*, at the basement of the theatre in the Rashtrapati Bhavan, after being invited by Nehru for a breakfast chat along with a leading actor, a boy. Later, Abbas got a telegram from Nehru stating: "I liked the film and consider it good from many points of view. It was a simple story artistically told without too much embellishment or overstatement."[21] Abbas, who initiated neorealist films in India through his film *Darthi Ke Lal* in 1946, was another confidant of Nehru and Indira Gandhi in the film field. Abbas was also the successful screenplay writer for many of the popular films of Raj Kapoor.

Indira Gandhi remained an ardent supporter of the Film Society Movement and extended her political patronage in her official capacities, first as the I&B minister and later as the prime minister too. She also remained an ardent admirer of New Indian Cinema till her death, ensuring that FTII, FFC and NFAI had best of professionals manning them. The appointment of film-maker Ritwik Ghatak as the vice principal of FTII was at the instance of Indira Gandhi on the recommendation of Satyajit Ray. The FFC's golden era producing the landmarks New Wave films of Mani Kaul, Kumar Shashni, Adoor Gopalakrishnan and Mrinal Sen were all under her patronage. From playing an important role in the formation of FFSI in 1959 and to the formation of last of the Film Enquiry Committee headed by eminent cultural icon Dr Shivarama Karanth in 1980, she remained part of the new film culture of India. She brought in Jean Bhownagary from Paris in 1951 to mount the first India International Festival, which opened a new vista of diplomatic missions as a source for the best of films from across the world. The new avenue that opened up a non-commercial route for getting best of films of each country still remains as the biggest source of global films to film society network.

Indira Gandhi also ensured the French Indian remained as an advisor to ensure the institutions such as FTII and FFC were formed under the ministry of I&B. She also supported Bhownagary as the head of Films Division to mentor a new Indian documentary, with independent film-makers like Sukh Dev and MF Husain, who went on to make their mark globally.

Gandhi's special interest in the budding Film Society Movement was evident from the word "go." When she became a minister, and later prime minister of India, she deputed Usha Bhagat, her social secretary, as the joint secretary of FFSI, keeping a close eye on the activities of the movement. "As I remember, the Federation had at that time (1961) only nine film societies affiliated to it. The office work consisting of a dilapidated typewriter and a few files was carried on in a portion of the garage in my house," Bhagat recalled in 1981, in an article on *IFSON* (*Indian Film Society News*), the journal of DFS.[22]

From giving film import facilities to FFSI, ensuring entertainment tax waiver, censorship exemptions to the film society screenings and an annual grant, Nehru and Indira Gandhi patronised and promoted the Film Society Movement fully. The formation of the Federation of Film Societies on 13 December 1959 was ensured by Indira Gandhi with the active support of the government. An Indian Civil Service (ICS) officer drafted the memorandum of understanding of FFSI. Later in 1960, Nehru's confidant, a former finance secretary and the then chairman of the University Grants Commission (UGC),

CD Deshmukh was prompted to form a University Film Council (UFC) with a former I&B minister, RR Diwakar, as its chairman.

Apart from institutional support from the government, both Nehru and Indira Gandhi extended their personal support whenever the need arose for the new Indian film-makers. In 1956, *Pather Panchali*, which is the first product of the Indian film society culture, and also directed by the promoter of the first major film society of the independent India, ran into its own controversies, when some sections of the government raised a hue and cry about the portrayal of poverty in the film. However, the film received the whole-hearted endorsement of even the scholar-statesman prime minister of the country, who hailed its treatment of the subject of poverty with its aesthetic qualities. It appeared that Nehru, who pushed his agenda of a new Indian idiom in films, saw the success of *Pather Panchali* as an endorsement of his views on the new kind of films for the country. "What is wrong about showing India's poverty? Everyone knows that we are a poor country. The question is: are we Indians sensitive to our poverty or insensitive to it? Ray has shown it (poverty) with an extraordinary sense of beauty and sensitiveness," said Nehru about *Pather Panchali*.[23]

The personal support and involvement of Indira Gandhi to new the Indian film culture was total. So much so that MS Sathyu's *Garam Hawa* got clearance for public shows from none other than Indira Gandhi after a preview of the movie. The censors in those days had rejected the film, which remained a landmark in depicting the complex Indo-Pak divide and the question of the Hindu–Muslim relationship in independent India. David Lean's controversial film *Doctor Zhivago* was also cleared by Indira Gandhi with minimum cuts to "safeguard" India's relationship with the then Soviet Union, after a preview of the movie.

Combined with the liberal political thoughts of Nehru and the parallel efforts of the Leftist Indian People's Theatre Movement (IPTA), the movement towards new films and film appreciation got further push. The Communist Party of India (CPI) had identified films as an important medium of influencing peoples' thought towards their political and social ideologies. They identified KA Abbas, who had already written screenplays and a film critic of long-standing, to make a humane document on the Bengal famine in 1946, *Darthi Ke Lal*, which was in the neorealist tradition of the post-war world. With his involvement in two path-breaking films in Hindi, *Naya Sansar*

(1941) and *Neecha Nagar* (1946), as a screenplay writer, Abbas had made a name for himself. The trilingual (Hindi, Urdu and English) Abbas was also among the early film critics of India arguing for better films from 1935 through his newspaper *Bombay Chronicle*. Abbas remained in the Left camp all his life and is credited with forming the first trade union in the Bombay film industry and even promoting a film society, Film Forum, with the trade union.

John Wood, author of the book on the art film-makers of India, stated[24]:

> While IPTA transformed ideas of political and social reform into cultural substance, the film societies and the international film festivals allowed would-be film makers such as young Ritwik Ghatak and Satyajit Ray, for example, to learn from what they were able to see of masters such as Eisenstein as well as the best of con-temporary foreign directors, especially the Italian neo-realists, all of them heirs to a quite different tradition of cinema from that which had developed in India during the art's first half century.

There was confluence of thoughts of the liberals and Leftists, which gave a major fillip to the Film Society Movement. The liberals led by Prime Minister Nehru patronised the Film Society Movement by extending total government support as part of improving the aesthetic contents of the new mass medium and the Left saw it as an opportunity to take its agenda forward in the most popular mass medium. This caught the popular imagination of the educated class, where the Leftists and liberals were ruling the roost. Both Kerala and West Bengal with their film societies and international film festivals bore testimony to this historic tradition of political patronage even today.

THE EXCITEMENT OF THE SUCCESS OF *PATHER PANCHALI*

The excitement of the success of *Pather Panchali*, made in three years with a meagre budget of ₹0.15 million, when it was released in 1955, was a big boost to the spread of the film societies across the country. The film had the government of West Bengal as its primary producer, although Ray began its work before the government stepped in to save the project.

Also, the film, which itself had won many international and national accolades and awards—Best Human Document Award at the Cannes Film Festival 1956 and the Indian President's Gold and Silver Medals in 1955—saw the dawn of a new genre of film-making in

India. Along with the film and the excitement it created across the nation, a new set of audience were also being moulded, though the film societies that vied to show case and appreciate the film.

The worldwide acceptance of Ray's first film captivated the young nation and its pride. The world began to recognise the birth of the New Indian Cinema, in contrast to the dance–drama shows of the existing popular cinema. Seton not only added *Pather Panchali* and its director to her list of *The Art of Five Directors – Film Appreciation*, published by the National Council of Educational Research and Training (NCERT), but also identified an Indian professor who took upon himself the analysis of *Pather Panchali* as a life-long mission. For years, the first professor in the FTII, Professor Satish Bahadur, who was discovered at Agra University by Seton during her lecture tours, remained a specialist in analysing *Pather Panchali*. Professor Bahadur lectured all his life about truly appreciating Ray's first film and similar films, thus establishing a new genre of academic studies on films.

Seton, emphasising on the need for film appreciation, wrote[25]:

> Very few people appreciate the greatest literature or painting the first time they look at an example. The same is true of films. For

Image 2.3 A screen grab still from the film *Pather Panchali*.
Note: This film still remains the toast of Indian Film Society Movement.
Courtesy: The producers and Government of West Bengal.

almost everyone an interest in film appreciation commences with their own film sense being awakened by an exceptional film which produces in them the desire to see more examples.

In his article titled "Everything in the film is Significant," in the British film journal *Sight and Sound*, in 1955, Lindsay Anderson wrote, "*Pather Panchali* is a beautiful picture, completely fresh and personal, which required great courage and perseverance to make."

Akira Kurosova, Ray's contemporary from Japan, who put his country's films on the world map with his production, *Rashomon*, too was excited about *Pather Panchali*. "I can never forget the excitement in my mind after seeing it for the first time. I have had several more opportunities to see the film since then and each time I felt more overwhelmed. It is the kind of cinema that flows with the serenity and nobility of a big river," said Kurosova about Ray's first film.[26]

The film *Pather Panchali* had indeed awakened India and had taken the world of films to a new height, and the Indian cultural enthusiasts were eager to join the bandwagon in the nook and corner of the country. "After *Pather Panchali*, Ray often said that he had learnt film making by seeing films. Some of them he saw a dozen times," Chidanada Das Gupta captured the excitement of the times.[27]

Word was out that if anyone wishes to make meaningful cinema, or be a connoisseur of such films, the first thing to do was to see as many such films as possible. And the only way out to see such films in the 1950s to the 1980s continued to be the film society circuit, unless, of course, one was associated with a film studies organisation. No doubt, film societies increased the awareness of the best of films across the globe and help construct a new film aesthetics and criticism. The new forum through its programme notes, lectures, workshops and journals paved the foundations of film appreciation and film studies in India.

IFSON's first editor, Anil Srivastava, reflected on the entire period as follows[28]:

The film society, *Pather Panchali*, and Nehruvian ethos shaped my being, and I find it difficult to talk about the underlying theme without bias. I believe it is the intersection of these three that contributed to the New Indian Cinema in its various manifestations, whether it was Mrinal Sen's *Bhuvan Shome*; Adoor Gopalakrishnan's *Anantharam*; Girish Kasaravalli's *Ghatashraddha*; Sudhir Mishra's *Hazaaron Khwaishein Aisi*; or, for that matter, New Indian Cinema manifesto authored by Arun Kaul and Mrinal Sen.

TOWARDS A FEDERATION OF FILM SOCIETIES

By the late 1950s, the country was ready for a movement called the film society, and the world for the New Indian Cinema. As Marie Seton was about to leave India after her lecture tours on cinema, the secretaries of Calcutta and Bombay film societies met her and discussed as to how to take the movement forward. She was more than willing to make a note and submit it to the government. That prompted the government to undertake a survey on the Film Society Movement. MV Krishnaswamy, director, film division, prepared a document, and Jean Bhownagary made his own suggestions and submitted them to the government as well. Indira Gandhi, a personal friend of Marie Seton, sent two of her trusted aides, Pupul Jayakar and Pritish Neogi, to Calcutta and Bombay to undertake a fact finding mission on the state of film societies. The seemingly urban spurt of film societies were ready to take off officially and that too with the blessings of the government of the day.

In her article in the first issue of *Indian Film Quarterly*, January–March 1957, Marie Seton featured the increasing enthusiasm in the urban centres of India about the films like *Pather Panchali*. "The reactions evoked by my illustrated lectures on the cinema in Bombay, Delhi, Allahabad, Banares, Patna, Gaya, Calcutta, Madras, Mysore, Bangalore, Hyderabad and Ahmedabad indicate that the time is ripe for the development in India of a film society movement...." Seton defined the aims of the film society:

> (a) to show the best feature and short film from any country, including its own national production of high merit; (b) to encourage a higher level of film appreciation through the development of discussion; (c) when a society or group of societies is sufficiently developed, for example, the Scottish Federation of Film Societies or the Venice Film Society, to publish a magazine of a critical and informative nature.[29]

Years later, the NFAI, in its circular "How to Form a Film Society," expanded the objectives to take the initial momentum, which Seton had observed, as a national movement. The objective as defined by the NFAI was:

> (a) to enable its members to study the history and art of the film by exhibiting films of cultural, artistic and technical merit, especially those which, owning to language difficulties or small box-office

appeal, are not ordinarily shown commercially; (b) to encourage an intelligent and discriminating attitude towards films; (c) to encourage the production of films of artistic values; (d) to promote research on cinema; (e) to co-operate with national and international organizations having similar objects.

Undoubtedly, Seton's lecture tour series of 1955–56 and the success of *Pather Panchali* in 1955 established the film societies as a new arena of cultural activity across the nation.

On 13 December 1959, seven representatives of the existing film societies met at the residence of the secretary of Sahitya Akademi, Krishna Kripalani, and adopted a memorandum of association (MOA) for FFSI. Needless to say, the active involvement of the government meant that the document was vetted by MD Bhatt, an ICS officer, who was the chairman of the Film Advisory Board of the Government of India. The FFSI was registered under the Societies Registration Act XXI of 1860. "Chidu *da* (Das Gupta) had come down from Calcutta and we need to meet at a central place and Krishna Kripalani, who had a house close to the city Centre offered to host our meeting," *Akka* (Vijaya Mulay), who was present there at the meeting of the FFSI recalled.[30]

At the time of adoption of the MOA, the FFSI committee of administration had Satyajit Ray as its president. The vice presidents were Ammu Swaminadhan of the MFS, Robert E. Hawkins of the BFS and S. Gopalan of the DFS. The joint secretaries were Vijaya Mulay and Chidananda Das Gupta. The joint treasurers were D. Pramanick and Abdul Hassan. The members of the committee were R. Anantharaman, Rita Roy, KL Khandapur, Jag Mohan, A Rehman and A Roy Choudhury. The film societies that formed the FFSI MOA were the DFS, Patna Film Society, Roorkie Film Society, BFS, MFS and CFS (see Annexure 2).

Indira Gandhi, who was then a political assistant to her father, Prime Minister Nehru, was also co-opted as the vice president of the FFSI.

Vijaya Mulay clearly remembered the historic day of the FFSI's formation.[31]

I went to Teen Murti house and told Ms Gandhi, that she must become the Vice President of FFSI. She asked me who the President was and I told her it was Satyajit Ray. She readily agreed to be the

VP and she remained on the post till she became the Minister of Information and Broadcasting in Prime Minister Lal Bahadur Shastri Cabinet in 1964.

Summing up the role of the FFSI and the Film Society Movement, Mulay said [32]:

FSM has definitely helped in creating awareness for good cinema and cultivating a discerning audience for good films at a time when there was no Film and Television school to teach film appreciation and discuss films, no Directorate of Film Festivals to showcase good world cinema and hardly any audience for quality films.

Recollecting his association with the historic Agra University Film Club (1960–63), which made him the first professor of film appreciation, Professor Satish Bahadur said in a note:

The most important thing to do was to run the film society as a very 'serious' organisation by giving it the appearance of being a serious organisation, so that when students came to a film society show, they were not going to any film show, but to see a film which deserved more careful attention.

Clearly, the professor was preparing the new generation for a fresh experience of the film as an art.[33]

Indeed, the Film Society Movement created the New Indian Cinema, almost the same time as the Asian cinema got noticed across the globe through the Japanese masters such as Akira Kurosawa, whose Rashomon put Japanese cinema on the world film map. *Pather Panchali* and its director, Satyajit Ray, a film society activist, also put the Indian cinema on the world map. In fact, the initial line-up of New Indian Cinema's pioneers like Mrinal Sen, Ritwik Ghatak, KA Abbas, Adoor Gopalakrishnan, Pattabhirama Reddy in Bangalore were all products or advocates of the budding Film Society Movement.

Adoor Gopalakrishnan, the second batch (1963) student of the FTII, who pioneered the Film Society Movement in Kerala with his *Chitralekha*, recalled those initial days: "the aim of the film society was to spread the culture of the 'new wave' of films, the film literature with publications and then produce films."[34]

THE SPREAD OF THE MOVEMENT WITH THE INSTITUTIONAL SUPPORT FROM THE GOVERNMENT

From Guwahati in the North East, Calcutta (now Kolkata) in the East, Lucknow in the North to Bombay (now Mumbai) in the West and Trivandrum (now Thiruvananthapuram) down South, the quest for a new Indian film culture had taken the shape of film societies, watching, discussing and debating the best of world cinema and creating new films. This ultimately gave India a strong presence in the world film map. With active support and political patronage from the government of the day, the FFSI grew its tentacles across India. The government had no qualms in opening its Central Film Library with the ministry of education to the FFSI network for renting its films for screening. The UGC promoted a UFC to spread film clubs in universities. It allowed the FFSI to import films and access foreign films from diplomatic missions in India, directly, exempting the FFSI network from entertainment tax and censorship. The period of also saw government establishing the Directorate of Film Festivals to organise national and international festivals, FTII, NFAI and FFC, to produce quality films, which the world began to term as "New Wave" Indian films. But for the active patronage of the government of the day, this would not have been possible. Clearly, the film field had taken the challenge posed by the Nehruvians for a new India, giving the spurt of the film clubs the shape of an all-India movement for better film appreciation and acceptance of the new medium as an art form in the cultural milieu.

Over the first three decades, the FFSI has four full-fledged regional offices in the north, east, west and south of the country, situated in Delhi, Calcutta, Mumbai and Bangalore, and there is a sub-regional office for Kerala at Thiruvananthapuram. The National Council of FFSI has 60 members elected through direct voting by the member societies once every two years. The council further elects a 15-member central executive committee to run the FFSI properly. "Federation of Film Societies of India is a body of statute recognised by the Government of India and mostly by all the Provincial Governments of the country as well. It represents in several committees of the Governments related to cinema," the website of the IFFS, of which Mrinal Sen and Francois Truffaut were presidents, states.[35]

NOTES*

1. https://en.wikipedia.org/wiki/Tryst_with_Destiny
2. Chidananda Das Gupta. *The Cinema of Satyajit Ray*, 1st ed. (New Delhi: NBT, 1980), Preface.
3. Chidananda Das Gupta. *Seeing Is Believing: Selected Writings on Cinema* (Delhi: Viking, 2008), Introduction.
4. http://vkcherian.blogspot.in/2012/06/mrinal-sen-at-90-riding-wave-of.html
5. Interview with Pradipta Sen of CFS.
6. Interview with Pradipta Sen of CFS.
7. Chidananda Das Gupta. *The Cinema of Satyajit Ray*.
8. HN Narahari Rao. *The Film Society Movement in India* (Mumbai: Asian Film Foundation, 2009), p. 27.
9. http://cherianwrites.blogspot.in/2016/02/interview-with-yc-halan-past-president.html
10. http://cherianwrites.blogspot.in/2016/02/a-few-notes-for-book-towards-new-film.html
11. http://cherianwrites.blogspot.in/2016/02/national-heald-clip-film-club-of-bhopal.html
12. http://cherianwrites.blogspot.in/2016/02/a-few-notes-for-book-towards-new-film.html.
13. http://cherianwrites.blogspot.in/2016/02/interview-with-govindaraj.html
14. HN Narahari Rao. "Impact of the Film Society Movement (1983)". In *the Film Society Movement in India* (Mumbai: Asian Film Foundation, 2009), 103.
15. Interview with Vijaya Mulay.
16. http://cherianwrites.blogspot.in/2016/02/interview-with-yc-halan-past-president.html
17. http://cherianwrites.blogspot.in/2016/02/interview-with-ms-shyamala-vannarse.html
18. http://cherianwrites.blogspot.in/2016/03/on-fsm-by-anilsrivastava-pioneer-and.html
19. https://en.wikipedia.org/wiki/Marie_Seton
20. http://cherianwrites.blogspot.in/2016/02/interview-with-benegal.html
21. KA Abbas. *I Am Not an Island* (New Delhi: Vikas, 1977), p. 370.
22. HN Narahari Rao. *The Film Society Movement in India*, p. 49.
23. CFS Brochure. *Pather Panchali*'s anniversary, 2012.
24. John W. Wood. *The Essential Mystery: Major Filmmakers of Indian Art Cinema* (New Delhi: Orient Longman), p. 5.
25. Marie Seton. *How to Commence Film Appreciation* (New Delhi: Ministry of Education, 1961).
26. HN Narahari Rao. *The Film Society Movement in India*.
27. Chidananda Das Gupta. *The Cinema of Satyajit Ray*.
28. http://cherianwrites.blogspot.in/2016/03/on-fsm-by-anilsrivastava-pioneer-and.html
29. http://cherianwrites.blogspot.in/2016/02/marie-seton-from-cfs-published-in.html
30. Interview with Vijaya Mulay.
31. Ibid.
32. Annexure 1. MOA FFSI.
33. http://cherianwrites.blogspot.in/2016/02/interview-with-ms-shyamala-vannarse.html
34. http://cherianwrites.blogspot.in/2016/02/adoorgopalakrishnan-on-film-society.html
35. http://www.ficc.info/

---

* All websites accessed on 16 June 2016.

CHAPTER 3

Visionaries of the Film Society Movement and the New Film Culture

Film societies sprang up in the urban centres of India, as an idea of few visionary leaders, and the leader of the pack always managed the group, promoted it and later networked the society on an all-India basis. From defining the very term "film appreciation" to making better world-class films available in India to introducing new technologies, the visionary leadership led the movement and precipitated a new film culture, whether in fiction or documentaries. Just as in Bombay, Calcutta, Patna, Bhopal, Lucknow, Agra or Trivandrum, there were pioneers, mostly English-educated young men and women in all parts of India, to inspire their contemporaries and to push these isolated clubs to an organised national movement.

Whether it was tax or censorship exemptions, the government of the day, extended its patronage encouraging the spread of the movement up to the 1980s. The government also brought in advisors such as a Parisian Jean Bhownagary, a French Indian, from UNESCO to mount the first IFFI in 1952, opening the neorealist films of Italy and mystic traditions of Japan and the new experiments of Eastern bloc countries to Indians. Above all, the first IFFI, which sourced films from various diplomatic missions in India, opened up a new avenue of sourcing films, almost free for the fledging film societies.

The contribution of visionaries like Satyajit Ray, Indira Gandhi, Chidananda Das Gupta, Jean Bhownagary, Marie Seton, Vijay Mulay, KA Abbas, PK Nair, Professor Satish Bahadur and Anil Srivastava led to moulding of a new film culture and growth of the Film Society Movement with their individual interventions, in their respective fields of activity. The exit of the pioneers from their societies and fields saw many of them collapsing, such as CFS, *Chitralekha*, and the Agra film society. Some were revived later, with the support of the pioneers. The CFS was revived and kept alive for its historic role of the launch pad of the pioneers like Ray and Das Gupta. The exit of Bhownagary, who introduced neorealist techniques in non-fiction film-making in India as head of Films Division, saw the end of the government patronage to creative film-makers in documentary.

Pioneers no doubt inspired and created a group of people who took to serious film appreciation and film studies, changing the way films are perceived and made in India. "Should film appreciation, and film-making for that matter therefore remain perpetually split between the masses and their entertainers on the one hand, and the intelligentsia and their artists on the other?" was the question posed by many, a fact often articulated by Das Gupta in his writings[1]. All of them tried to answer the question with their involvement with the Film Society Movement, and Das Gupta even theorised the complex relation between the two streams with his concept of *margi* and *desi* in his last book from his experience of a lifetime settling the initial divides between the two groups once and for all. No narrative of the Film Society Movement can be complete without looking at the contribution of the pioneers, who raised the questions of appreciation and concepts and lived a life of defining them to steer a new path for the film as medium inthe country.

SATYAJIT RAY

If there is any person who can be credited as a true visionary for a New Indian Cinema and its culture and carries the stamp of the emerging new nation called India, in his work, it is the one and only Satyajit Ray. Reams have been written about his films, but there is very little available on record, in English, on his role as a founder of the CFS and as a lifelong mentor of the Film Society Movement of India. The fact that both Chidananda Das Gupta, the co-founder of CFS in 1949, and the film society evangelist Marie Seton were his friends for life explains yet another side of Ray. Satyajit Ray also remained the lifelong president of the FFSI.

Image 3.1 Satyajit Ray speaking at the CFS gathering.
Courtesy: CFS Collection.

Indira Gandhi, who was the president of the Indian National Congress in 1959, agreed to be the vice president of the FFSI, since she was told that the president was Manik *da* (as Ray was fondly called by friends and admirers). "After our decision to form the FFSI, I went to Teen Murti Bhavan and told Indiraji that, I want her to be the Vice President of FFSI." Knowing her personal proximity with Marie Seton and the excitement she shared about the advent of a new film movement, Vijaya Mulay (fondly called as *Akka*) was sure that Ms Gandhi would accept the suggestion. "She asked me who the President was. I said Manik *da* and she readily agreed to be the Vice President under him," said *Akka* pointing out the respect Ray commanded in as early as in 1959.[2]

Ray, unquestionably is the first auteur who put Indian cinema on the world map, with his path-breaking film *Pather Panchali* in 1955. His passion for good films, a new cinematic idiom for the budding nation, was fuelled not just by the renaissance in Bengali culture, but also by exposure to world-class films at London, where he was sent while working as a commercial artist in the British advertisement firm based in Calcutta. He reportedly watched 90 films in three months and films like Italian Victoria De Sica's neorealist classic, *Bicycle Thieves*[3] had a lasting impression on him. Ray's exposure to world classics like Russian classic *Battleship Potemkin* by Sergei Eisenstein,[4] *Nanook of the North* by Robert Flaherty[5] at the CFS and the 90 films at London remained the best-ever education for him as a film-maker. He saw *Battleship* so many times and was smitten by the classic Russian film and its director that he told a visiting Eisenstein archive director just before his death that he wanted to spend a night in the great film-maker's flat in Moscow, said Samik Bandyopadhyay, an art/ film critic from the friend's circle of Ray.[6] The Italian neorealist film-makers such as Roberto Rossellini, De Sica, Luchino Visconti's films, appeared to make a deep impression on the young Ray.[7] "I saw half a dozen Italian films, including Bicycle Thieves. It was tremendous experience," Ray was quoted in his biography, penned by Marie Seton.[8] Enriching this experience with films was his exposure to Jean Renoir's[9] shooting of *The River* in Bengal and the interaction with Russian maestro Vsevolod Pudovkin[10] during his visit to Calcutta.

Ray not only founded the CFS and created a new genre of Indian films with *Pather Panchali*, but also fired up a great interest in the New Indian Cinema across the country. Narrating his entry into the Film Society Movement, Anil Srivastava, founder of the Lucknow Film Society and the Bhopal International Film Club in 1959, described the excitement of getting *Pather Panchali* to be screened in Bhopal those days. "I found Satyajit Ray's phone number and called him. He must have been flabbergasted by the unexpected call from a school kid asking him to screen the film that he asked the distributor (Aurora) to send a 35-mm print of Pather Panchali." Anil was a student of St. Joseph's Convent Bhopal in 1959.[11]

A bio-sketch of Ray reads as follows:

Satyajit Ray was born on May 2, 1921, in Calcutta, to Sukumar and Suprabha Ray. He graduated from the Ballygunge Government School and studied Economics at Presidency College. He then attended *Kala Bhavan*, the Art School at Tagore's University,

Shantiniketan during 1940–1942. Without completing the five-year course, he returned to Calcutta in 1943, to join the British—owned advertising agency D.J. Keymer as a visualiser. Within a few years, he rose to be its art director. In 1948, he married Bijoya Das, a former actress/singer who also happened to be his cousin. Their only offspring, Sandip, was born in 1953. In 1983, Satyajit Ray suffered a massive heart attack. He died on April 23, 1992, in Calcutta after having made some 40 films and documentaries and has numerous books and articles to his credit.[12,13]

The excitement of *Pather Panchali* continued to haunt the film academia across the world. Just as *Battleship Potemkin*, *Pather Panchali*, even today, is a must see for any budding Indian film student. The first professor of film appreciation at FTII, Pune, Professor Satish Bahadur, remained a lifelong expert on Ray's first film, as he taught one batch after another with the example of *Pather Panchali*. Such was the professor's passion in analysing *Pather Panchali* that even Ray wondered how the professor derived various levels of meaning from his films, some of which even he had never imagined as a director.

Such was the excitement about his films and the man himself that when Ray visited Trivandrum in the mid 1980s for the first time, there was an unending reception given to him by competing film societies and institutions, much to his surprise. Ray had transformed his passion for good films as a young man into a movement through CFS and remained the lifelong guardian angel of the "New Cinema" of India, not just with his films, but also with his writings on films and patronage to a whole generation of film-makers. "After every screening of my film at Kolkata, he will call me home and discuss the film in detail and that was an enriching experience," Adoor, who is considered the worthy heir to Ray's school of film-making, recalled.[14] Though, he had difference of opinion with style adopted by the FTII graduates like Mani Kaul[15] and Kumar Shahani,[16] Ray never disowned them as such. "He always believed the film must have a story to be told to the audience and believed he was best at it," Samik Bandyopadhyay, who saw one of the last communication between Ray and Das Gupta, observed.[17]

However, being a busy film-maker, almost a film a year, he could never devote his time for CFS or the Film Society Movement. He never even previewed any of his films at the flourishing CFS, but showed unfinished reels of his film *Devi* at the DFS. "He was busy and totally involved in production of his films and could not spare time to the Film Society Movement," his son, Sandeep Ray,[18] recalled those days from his South Kolkata home. However, his intervention was always sought and taken for the movement, whenever necessary.

Akka, on Ray's active guidance of the Film Society Movement, recalled:

> We had an issue with censoring of foreign films for FS screening. The embassies will not allow us to censor films. So we went to Ms Gandhi, the then Union I&B Minister to discuss the issue. She suggested, getting her—a letter from Manik *da* on this, and Manik *da* was ever obliging as President of FFSI. And Ms Gandhi waived off censorship for film society films.

The flood of uncensored films to the FFSI circuit attracted "undesirable" patrons to the Film Society Movement, much to the disdain of the founder of the movement itself.

However, the flourishing Film Society Movement of the 1960s and 1970s fed vigorously on Ray's works, complementing each other taking "New Indian Cinema" to higher levels. He remained the president of FFSI from 1959 till his death in 1992.[19]

INDIRA GANDHI

It is rare for any prime minister of a country to be featured as one of the pioneers of a Film Society Movement, but the history of the "Indian Film Society Movement" cannot be written without Indira Gandhi (1917–84), the former prime minister. She brought in Jean Bhownagary, a UNESCO film hand to India in 1951, to mount the first IFFI. She was the official hostess of the first film seminar organised under then Prime Minister Jawaharlal Nehru's administration. She was also the hostess and a friend of the evangelist of the Indian Film Society Movement, Marie Seton. She was the first vice president of the FFSI. During her tenure as I&B minister and prime minister, the "New Indian Cinema" registered a robust growth, with the FFC producing a host of such films. After her tenure, no prime minister has ever shown such personal interest in the new film movement of India, leading to the total neglect of this genre of films. The last film enquiry commission was also formed, in the last tenure of Indira Gandhi, as prime minister.

In short, Indira Gandhi remains the true political and administrative visionary behind the new Indian films, which went on to make a place for itself in global film history. From bringing in experts like

Bhownagary for implementing a new Indian films policy to hosting Marie Seton's lecture tour and supporting the scattered film clubs across India for a Federation of Film Societies and formulating a proposal for a Chalachitra Akademi in her last tenure as prime minister, Indira Gandhi's visionary leadership led the new Indian films to newer heights.

In her speech at the presentation of the National Awards for films, on 25 May 1966, Indira Gandhi observed, "Our films seem to be all pervasive. They are brining village and town closer. In numerous other ways also, films have contributed in fostering a sense of oneness in our country." She went on to say, "A film has the quality of a work of art. It depends on the vision of its creator and on the technical mastery with which he communicates this vision in words or sound or colours or images."[20]

Indira Gandhi as a prime minister had clear vision about the quality of Indian films, thanks to her early introduction to film society evangelist, Marie Seton. In her first monograph—*The Film as an Educational Force in India*, published by the ministry of education in 1956, Marie Seton describes an incident involving Gandhi and a party for children at the then prime minister's house. Marie Seton was asked to show films at a children's party Gandhi organised with her two sons and their friends. That was the time when Marie Seton was going around the country lecturing on films as an educational medium and screenings few films to school kids as well. As a concerned mother, Gandhi was keen that her sons and their friends appreciated the best of films.[21]

Indira Gandhi remained a connoisseur of fine arts, including films, and was personally involved even as the prime minister to clear good films from the conservative scissors of the film censors. There is one such intervention that saved a landmark film by MS Sathyu, *Garam Hava*. According to DFS's last president, Gautam Kaul, it was her personal intervention that saw the film getting released.

> I got a call from her saying that, "you are a film society man" come and see what is so objectionable in *Garam Hava*. The film was shown in the basement theatre, at the *Rashtrapati Bhavan*, which was the favourite screening place of the Prime Minister. After the screening, Gandhi looked back and told me, "what is objectionable in this film may be the noble family Muslim girl romancing on the shores of Yamuna at Agra. That we will be able to handle it...is it not?"

A waiting Sathyu asked Gautam Kaul, what her response was. Kaul said, "it is done," ending the long uncertainty over the film's release.[22]

Indira Gandhi had also directed the FFC to treat the script of a film along with the copyright as the collateral, while deciding to finance a film production. The directive went after FFC refused to finance the script of *Bhuvan Shome*, which also received the best script award of the corporation in that year's competition. Mrinal Sen, the writer, approached the prime minister for her intervention. Gandhi seemed to have asked the concerned officials as to what was the most important ingredient of the film, to which they replied that it was the script and later the copyright of the film. She directed the officials to treat both these as collateral while financing a film. Thus, the film *Bhuvan Shome* was financed by FFC and is considered as the film that re-energised the new Cinema of India after *Pather Panchali*.[23]

Not just Mrinal Sen, Sathyu, or Vijaya Mulay, her contemporary and FFSI's joint secretary also had lots to share about Indira Gandhi's personal involvement in the success of the Film Society Movement, whether it was exempting film society films from censorship or import of films for the FFSI network, grant for FFSI functioning or even trying to save FFC Chairman BK Karanjia from Sanjay Gandhi's wrath, Gandhi remained solidly behind the Film Society Movement and good films.

So was the strength of a circular initiated by Gandhi as I&B minister that *Chitralekha* film cooperative in Thiruvananthapuram benefitted from it after four decades in settling the ₹1.5 million loan from the state government. The circular in the 1960s had advised the State governments to grant space for film societies to build alternate cinema halls in each district. *Chitralekha*, which began its operations in the late 1960s, had procured land in the Northern Kerala town of Thalassery for such a cinema hall. The appreciated land value ensured that the cooperative could sell it and pay off its debts by 2010.[24]

Even during the turbulent times through the state of Emergency in the 1970s, when her son Sanjay Gandhi, and the I&B minister VC Shukla were forcing the FFC Chairman BK Karanjia to move out of his chair, Gandhi invited the chairman over tea to hear his version and bargain a compromise. Karanjia described the incident vividly:

> Although I had not met the PM before, I knew her to be a staunch supporter even before she became the Minister for Information and

Broadcasting of what the Film Finance Corporation stood for and what it was trying to do to as a trendsetter and act as a leavening force within the film industry. On one occasion when the Union finance Minister Morarji Desai had questioned the non-return of some of the loans advanced by the FFC, she had written to him: The FFC does not have an investment angle…. Even more important is the promotional aspect…. These words became the FFC's credo.

Even though Gandhi could not save Karanjia from the wrath of the then I&B minister VC Shukla, who was the *Goebbels* of her son Sanjay Gandhi, the former FFC chairman and editor of *Filmfare* magazine gives full credit to Gandhi for her intervention. "In contrast to Shukla, she was extremely courteous and gracious throughout the interview," the veteran editor recalled in his autobiography.[25]

Indira Gandhi kept her commitment to good films till the end of her life. She constituted the last of the film enquiry committees, which helped the government to revise its policies on films. In her speech at the golden jubilee celebrations of the Indian cinema in 1981, Gandhi stressed that "a good film, like any other good art, should be an experience." She also pointed out that "Cinema is entertainment. It is no less important an instrument of social change. And I believe that there is no dichotomy between the two."[26]

Whatever be her political legacy in history, Indira Gandhi remained an ardent connoisseur of good films, who extended political and governmental patronage to the Film Society Movement and good films. No other prime minister, including her own father, Nehru, patronised the new film movement of India, which put the Indian film industry on the world map and transformed the film society initiatives into a movement, the way she had done. Indira Gandhi's name will go down in the history of Indian Film Society Movement as a leading light, among its pioneers.[27]

MARIE SETON

If anyone can be described as a pioneering evangelist/visionary of the Film Society Movement in India and the new India cinema in the 1950s, it is the one and only Marie Seton, the chain-smoking, *saree*-draped, British socialist, film scholar and lifelong *Indophile*. She was not just a film scholar, a family friend of the Nehrus and a coveted guest of Indira Gandhi at Nehru's Teen Murti Bhawan residence, but a true visionary who ignited activists across India, fuelling a new film culture. Marie's relationship with the Nehru–Gandhis and the Indian cinema led her to pen down the biography of both Prime Minister Nehru and new India's cinema giant Satyajit Ray, apart from Paul Robson, the black American musician, and the pioneer of Soviet films, Sergei Eisenstein.

Marie Seton single-handedly evangelised and transformed the scattered interests in film societies in the urban centres of India into a national movement, with her memorandum to the then government. Her suggestions for an FFSI were accepted by Indira Gandhi with political patronage from her father, Prime Minister Jawaharlal Nehru. According to her friend, Pamela Cullen:

> [Seton] had a fascination for India and as a young woman she had been introduced to India's fight for Independence by one of India's greatest political figures, V.K. Krishna Menon, who was then a struggling lawyer in London. She also had family associations with India through her father, who had served as an officer in the British Army in India (during the British Raj) and been seriously wounded during one of the many uprisings of the period.

Professor Satish Bahadur, paying his tribute on her birth centenary in 2010, wrote in an article in The Hindu[28]:

> Marie Seton, the renowned film critic from UK, who played a very important role in promoting Film Society Movement in India, made her first visit to India in 1955–56 on an invitation from the Audio Visual Department of the Ministry of Education, Government of India. After her first visit, Marie Seton developed such an attraction for India, she virtually became a citizen of this country having toured the length and breadth of this vast land and befriended almost every one she worked with.

Whatever be the personal stories of how Marie Seton arrived in India, she remained a part of the Nehru–Gandhi household and one of the closest friends of Prime Minister Indira Gandhi since 1956.

Pamela Cullen, the then social secretary of High Commissioner Krishna Menon, confirms this later emphatically:

> I first met Marie Seton in 1955 when the Indian Ministry of Education, in association with The British Film Institute, commissioned her to lecture on film appreciation at many of India's

flourishing film societies... she was known as a very feisty, formidable lady, who did not suffer fools gladly.... I discovered she was an
extraordinary, stimulating, witty person with words and ideas
tumbling out of her lips with hardly a pause.[29]

In 1959, soon after the formation of FFSI, responding to an
editorial on the Film Society Movement, Marie wrote in the Letters
to the Editor column, which appeared on Christmas Day describing
her advocacy on films in India, as the most satisfying work she did
in many countries. "Of all the work I have done in many countries,
the most rewarding has been in India, because the people are so
responsive in India," Marie noted, while appreciating the *Times of
India*'s editorial on the budding Film Society Movement in the late
1950s.[30]

There was no one in those days in the academic field, media
and film fraternity who had not heard or met Marie Seton. Pradipto
Sen from the CFS credits her with the revival of the then defunct CFS
in 1956. Adoor Gopalakrishnan, the veteran film-maker, remembers
her from his days in the FTII in 1963. Kumar Shahani, veteran film-
maker, remembers Marie screening her version of the Eisenstein's
film *Quiva Mexico*, in FTII, Pune, in the 1960s. In Delhi, Vijaya
Mulay, Marie's contemporary from those days, fondly remembers
the lively chats in her drawing room with Marie along with other
film society enthusiasts.

Marie was the one who ensured *Pather Panchali* got full support of the Government of India. In the words of Ray himself, "there
were some ministers who had taken objection to the film on the
ground for being a so true picture of unadulterated poverty."
According to Ray, "She (Marie) immediately wrote a letter to the
Ministry praising the film and saying if it came to that it fully deserved
to be shown abroad. A few months later Pandit Nehru himself saw
the film."[31]

In 1956, Marie submitted her findings to the Government of
India on how to launch the National Adult Literacy Campaign. Of the
many recommendations she made, one was related to the creation of
film clubs in the urban and semi-urban centres and universities to
quicken the pace of literacy. Her monograph *Film as an Educational
Force in India* was published by the ministry of education in 1956.
The other monographs she published out of her lecture tours with
films from BFI included *The Art of Five Directors, Film Appreciation,*

Image 3.2 Marie Seton speaking at CFS revival function in 1956.
Note: A seminar organized at her behest after the success of *Pather Panchali.*
Courtesy: CFS Collection.

Film as an Art and Film Appreciation. Marie, with her proximity to Nehru and Indira Gandhi, was the key figure in the formation of the FFSI and ensuring the patronage of the Central Government to the Film Society Movement. Marie has also to her credit a monograph of her mentor, VK Krishna Menon, who as the high commissioner in London was instrumental in making her a lifelong *Indophile*. No wonder, she visited the family house (*tharavadu*) of Menon when she was in Kerala as a part of the lecture tour in India. Adoor Gopalakrishnan remembers the incident very clearly, "my colleague at *Chitralekha* Film Cooperative, Bhaskaran Nair, took her to Menon's family house (tharavadu) in North Kerala."

According to Professor Satish Bahadur, she was also the advisor to the UFC, which was set up by the UGC in 1960. However, the project was stuck in the bureaucratic web and was never activated. Despite her falling health, Marie was connected with the production of the film *Gandhi* by Richard Attenborough and even played an important role in the selection of Ben Kingsley to play the titular role in the film.

Marie, according to Cullen, was "deeply upset" with the assassination of her friend and Prime Minister Indira Gandhi in 1984, the year the Government of India honoured Marie with the Padma Bhushan, the third highest national honour, for her contribution to India in its formative years. Prime Minister Rajiv Gandhi, who stayed in Marie's home in London as a student, condoled on her death that "... she was a fine friend who reached out to people, effortlessly crossing the generation gap and any kind of cultural barrier." Marie's estate today is handled by Cullen, says Vijaya Mulay. On her death, she was cremated, on her own request, and the plaque in Golders Green Crematorium reads: "Marie Seton Hesson, Padma Bhushan, and Citizen of the World."[32]

CHIDANANDA DAS GUPTA

Chidu *da*, as Chidananda Das Gupta was fondly called by friends and admirers, was unquestionably the "philosopher visionary" behind the Indian Film Society Movement. Five years after the formation of the FFSI, Chidananda Das Gupta wrote in an article "By screening, discussing, reading, and writing about good cinema all over the world, they create a higher level of artistic taste and thus build up a better and bigger audience for good films within the country."[33]

By 1983, the growth and emergence of two decades of film societies led Das Gupta to write another article listing a few survival models. "If they are to survive, the film societies must therefore turn more to the development of Film Culture on a large scale and provide a stable nucleus for products of the New Cinema in India," the veteran

Image 3.3 Chidananda Das Gupta with daughter Aparna Sen at the premiere of *Chokher Bali*.
Courtesy: CFS.

pointed to the movement already losing its steam of the 1960s and 1970s.[34]

The year 1921 saw the birth of the veteran film critic and historian Chidananda Das Gupta. A writer of over 2,000 articles on cinema, in various periodicals, it was Das Gupta who along with Ray had started the *Indian Film Quarterly* in 1957 and was also one of the prime movers behind the formation of the FFSI in 1959.

Das Gupta has been popularly known for his essays and translations of the works of Rabindranath Tagore, Manik Bandyopadhyay and Jibananda Das. It was Das Gupta who rendered the translation of the famous Bengali poem, *Banalata Sen*, composed by Jibananda Das.

The year 1947 saw the beginning of a new dawn as Das Gupta, along with Satyajit Ray and Hari Sadhan Gupta, founded the CFS. The forming of the film society had a lasting impact on Ray, as well as others, like Mrinal Sen and Ritwik Ghatak, as they were all gifted with an opportunity to view the best of world cinema.

The stalwarts such as Das Gupta, Satyajit Ray, Robert Hawkins, Vijaya Mulay, Ammu Swaminadhan, Diptendu Pramanick, Abul Hassan and A Roychowdury were the pioneers who were responsible for the formation of FFSI in 1959. Das Gupta as the brain behind the movement played a significant role in the growth of the Film Society

Movement in India, through the activities of FFSI and his extensive writing on film appreciation, raising the medium to the level of other traditional arts.

Das Gupta was an eminent film-maker as well. He directed seven films. His contributions to *Sight and Sound,* a British film magazine, have permanent archival value. He even wrote a book on his friend Ray in 1980, *The Cinema of Satyajit Ray,* which houses the most authentic studies of Ray's work.

The year 2004 was a glorious one for Chidananda Das Gupta as he was honoured with a Lifetime Achievement Award at the Osian Film Festival, for writing on cinema. He passed away on 22 May 2011, in Kolkata, succumbing to bronchopneumonia brought on by the Parkinson's disease. Das Gupta will always be remembered as a leading Bengali film-maker, critic, film historian and, above all, the "brain" behind the Film Society Movement in India. The CFS conducts an annual lecture in his name in the city.[35]

VIJAYA MULAY

Akka, as Vijaya Mulay is known to film enthusiasts across India, was the head of the jury of writing on films, in the 2012 National Film Festival of

Image 3.4 Vijaya Mulay.
Courtesy: Author.

India. In her address at the award function at the prestigious Vigyan Bhavan, unlike the other jury heads, she blasted the festival directorate. The reason, according to her, was that they have not yet differentiated between blog writing, traditional writing in journals, forcing the jury to go through thousands of articles to select one article for the award. She ended her speech with an advice, that it was time the festival directorate woke up to new media realities and sort out this confusion, much to the surprise of the audience, which included the President of India.

That is *Akka* for you, rebellious even at 94, frank and straight, and wanting to reform issues she strongly believes in. For the Film Society Movement, she has been as important as Marie Seton, rather she is an Indian Marie. *Akka* worked with Marie Seton to ensure the formation of the Patna Film Society, DFS and FFSI. She was instrumental in the spread of Film Society Movement, as a ministry of education officer in the 1950s and 1960s, in Film Censor Board, in UGC, and in SITE, the first Indian satellite TV experiment. Along with Ray and Chidu *da*, *Akka* in Delhi paved the red carpet of the government, ensuring all patronage to the budding Film Society Movement from the word go. From the formation of two pioneering societies, in Delhi and Patna, to the formation of the FFSI and all important landmarks of FFSI in the growth of the movement, there is nothing that does not have an imprint of *Akka*. After the death of Satyajit Ray, she was also a one-time president of FFSI and earlier was vice president of the FFSI, Northern Region.

Akka recalled her initial days with film societies[36]:

> On my return (from UK-Leeds University) to Patna in 1949 I actively participated in the nascent Film Society Movement of India. Film societies were the only institutions where cinema different from the commercial run of the mill kind could be seen: some of us therefore, started the Patna Film Society. When I was appointed as the Education Officer to the Central Ministry of Education and moved to Delhi in 1954 and found more like minded people to start the Delhi Film Society. Later when eight film societies came together to form the Federation of Film Societies of India in 1959, with Satyajit Ray as its founding President, Das Gupta, the well-known film critic and founder member of the Calcutta Film Society and I were elected as the first joint Secretaries.

In my first sitting with her at her South Delhi residence, she asked me to base my research for the book on the official history book of the Film Society Movement in India.[37] She said there is a book within the official history book of the FFSI and asked me to unearth it. Cheerful, energetic and still with a sharp memory, she shared the snippets of the golden days of the Film Society Movement and the friendly assemblies of people, including Marie Seton at her house. "We were all building the new India and never thought our efforts will lead to a movement or new genre of films. But we did our part," *Akka* told me during the four long sittings.

Akka's reflections gave me the sense of the period and history to the Film Society Movement. Indeed, it was all a patriotic act of a generation that saw the transition from colonial to self-rule of India. The Film Society Movement for her and her friends were a search for new Indian idiom in Indian films, separate from the mythological and melodramas of the nascent film industry of the British Raj and early days of the new republic.

Akka wrote[38]:

> I was fortunate to be in England at a time when the performing arts were reflecting new ideas and techniques. The Unity Theatre of workers played to full houses. Films from Soviet Union and Eastern Europe were running in repertory theatres... I also gained a better perspective and understanding of cinematic art, by joining the Leeds University Film Society. Thus film viewing, which was just a pastime before, became a serious passion.

She had returned to Patna, in 1949, where she went to work actively in the local film society. However, in 1954, Mulay shifted to New Delhi as she was appointed as an education officer by the Government of India. It was her love for cinema that made her stick to her passion and, eventually, in 1959 she was instrumental in the formation of the DFS. Soon after, eight film societies came together and the initiation of the FFSI took place, with Vijaya Mulay and Chidananda Das Gupta as its joint secretaries. Her visionary position in the movement was evident, when she was nominated as the president of FFSI as the worthy successor of Satyajit Ray, after his death.[39]

KHWAJA AHMAD ABBAS

KA Abbas (Khwaja Ahmad Abbas) may be best known as the director who introduced Amitabh Bachchan to Indian films or the script writer of Raj Kapoor in popular film history, but his body of work is much

Image 3.5 Khwaja Ahmad Abbas (KA Abbas).
Courtesy: Dr Zoya Zaidi (niece of KA Abbas).

more serious than just the popular ones. As a member of Indian People's Theatre Association (IPTA), promoted by the CPI, Abbas has been active in the film field as a film critic and directed the film *Dharti Ke Lal* even before the country got its political freedom. He was also one of the key figures behind the film society Film Forum in Bombay, along with the fellow journalist and script writer VP Sathe, film-maker

Basu Chatterjee, Bikram Singh, a civil servant-turned film-maker, and Arun Kaul, who produced Mrinal Sen's *Bhuvan Shome*. Film Forum was a film society of the film technicians and trade union members, unlike other thriving societies that were either too elitist or too star stuck, arranging receptions for film stars.

"Our industry is suffering from certain handicaps to general development and I said we need all-around general development and progress to have those handicaps removed," Abbas said at the first government seminar on policy on films, in 1955.[40] He had no hesitation in telling the seminar he had the brief of no less a person than the Prime Minister Nehru in arguing for a new vision for Indian films.

He had also bitterly complained about the lack of cinema halls for Indian films and domination of English films in movie halls in Mumbai and other cities, calling for an Indian resurgence in films at the 1955 seminar. A long-standing film critic, Abbas was an active member of the IPTA and had directed a few films and had even organised film technicians of Bombay under a trade union by 1955.

Abbas was the first president of the Film Forum, the film society that inherited the mantle of India's first film society, the Bombay Film Society. He had established Film Forum in 1965 with film trade unions and others. They were the ones connecting Bombay with FFSI and had 2,500 members at one point of time. Film-maker Govind Nihalani was a member of the Film Forum, so was Khalid Mohammed, a film critic and now film-maker. Film Forum was the most active film society showing up to seven films a month. Amol Palekar, the star director-actor, too was groomed at the Film Forum.

Born on 7 June 1914, Abbas was a noted director, novelist, screenwriter and a journalist in all three languages: Urdu, Hindi and English. He was the maker of many popular and nationally acclaimed Hindi films such as *Saat Hindustani* (1969) and *Do Boond Pani* (1972), which bagged the National Film Award for the Best Feature film on National Integration. His movies *Pardesi* (1957) and *Shehar Aur Sapna* (1963) were even nominated at the Cannes Film Festival, which won the National Film Award for the Best Feature Film. Abbas is considered the harbinger of the neorealistic Indian cinema, for he not only penned films catering to the parallel Indian cinema, but also was the one who initiated such films in India with pre-independence production *Dharti Ke Lal*.

It was in 1945 when Abbas made his debut as a director with the film *Dharti Ke Lal* for IPTA. Naya Sansar was the production company that he founded in 1951, and which consistently produced films that were socially relevant, such as *Anhonee*, *Munna*, *Rahi* (1953), *Shehar Aur Sapna* (1964), *Saat Hindustani* (1969), which also bagged the Nargis Dutt Award for the Best Feature Film on National Integration.

Abbas was a prolific writer and novelist and during his illustrious career; he wrote 73 books in English, Hindi and Urdu. His best-known work, *Inquilab*, was based on communal violence, which made him a leading light among the writers of his generation. Many of his works have been translated into Russian, Italian, German, French and Arabic. He also wrote the script for many Raj Kapoor films, including *Awaara*, *Shri 420*, *Henna*, and the most famous of them all *Mera Naam Joker*.

Khwaja Ahmad Abbas will always be known as one of the greatest producers, directors, scriptwriters and journalists of international repute. As an IPTA activist, his support to the Film Society Movement will remain etched in golden letters as he, with the Film Forum, brought the Bombay film trade unions to the fold of better cinema. Film Forum gave Indian films a few good directors like Basu Chatterjee, Basu Bhattacharya, Bikram Singh, Govind Nihalani and Khalid Mohammed, who fondly recalls his days at Film Forum screenings with excitement.[41]

If there is a true visionary of new Indian films among the pioneers, even under the British Raj, it was KA Abbas. From his writings to film-making to organising trade unions and film societies, he led the Indian film culture to a new level, making a mark for himself and Indian films with his unique contributions.

AMMU SWAMINADHAN

I had heard about Ammu Swaminadhan, a freedom fighter and a member of Parliament from the Indian National Congress Party, hailing from Tamil Nadu in the year 1952, while I was searching for the origins of the MFS. She was the patron of the MFS, carrying the Film Society Movement to the south of Vindhyas and the first vice president of the FFSI, along with Indira Gandhi.

"The Madras Film Society was formed on October 30, 1957. It was at the laps of the American Consulate, MFS took its birth on that day. Ammu Swaminadhan, mother of Advocate General Govind Swaminadhan, was the founder President of the Society," narrated AG Raghupathy, one of the founding members of the FFSI and general secretary, the MFS, Chennai.

Image 3.6 Ammu Swaminadhan.
Courtesy: Mrinalini Sarabhai (daughter).

Her name was also thrown at me as I progressed in my research, when I was trying to seek the speed at which the Kerala film societies were being patronised by the southern FFSI. They were all buzzing about a Malayalee lady with a sweet name Ammu Swaminadhan. Later, I was in for a big surprise as I found out that Ammu was the mother of the famous danseuse, Mrinalini Sarabhai, and the historic

INA freedom fighter, Captain Laxmi Sehgal. Ammu was also the maternal grandmother of the much admired danseuse and social activist Malika Sarabhai and Suhasini Ali, a trade unionist and a Politbureau member of the CPI(M).

"My mother (Kamala Sharada Prasad) says that Ammu Swaminadhan was extraordinarily beautiful and vivacious. She was later to become a member of the Constituent Assembly and the Rajya Sabha," recounted Ravi Prasad, an IITian friend of mine. Kamala was in the legal team that prosecuted Gandhiji's assassin Nathuram Godse, and the wife of Sharada Prasad, who served as the long-time information advisor to the prime minister, Indira Gandhi.

Ammu Swaminadhan (1894–1978) belonged to a Nair family from the Palghat region, a northern border town between Kerala and Tamil Nadu, then Madras Presidency. She was married to a Tamil Brahmin, Swaminadhan, a leading lawyer. He was the product of the family's largesse in promoting young intelligent men in education. After her marriage, Ammu was taken to Madras by her husband, where he made a successful career in law.

She took an active part in India's struggle for freedom and became a close disciple of Mahatma Gandhi. Her political entry was during the 1942 Quit India Movement, when along with Manjulakshmi, Kuttimalu Ammal and others, she was arrested and sent to Vellore Jail with a sentence of about two years.

She was elected member of Parliament in 1952 and was associated with many cultural and social organisations. She went to Ethiopia, China, the United States and the USSR, as a goodwill ambassador. She was also selected as the "Mother of the Year" in 1975, on the inauguration of International Women's Year.[42]

ANIL SRIVASTAVA

Evangelist is a term that is often used in IT technology, which, I am sure, has roots in the Christian belt of the United States. In the technology field, evangelists illustrate innovations by promoting an idea or a product for getting attention of the market. Much before such terms came to India in the public narrative, Anil Srivastava, one of the founders of NASSCOM, the IT industry body of India, can truly be described as an evangelist, for the Film Society Movement. He organised film societies as a student in Bhopal and Lucknow and went to edit the film society's journal *IFSON*. He even got Prime Minister Nehru to visit his film club at Bhopal.

Image 3.7 Anil Srivastava.
Courtesy: Shampa Srivastava.

My interview with Gautam Kaul, Anil's film society mate at Lucknow, opened my eyes to Anil as a film society activist. After re-establishing contact, I sent him a questionnaire on his involvement with the movement, as I had heard about him from his other former colleagues of the Film Society Movement, PK Nair and Vijaya Mulay. Let me give Anil's own version of his initial involvement with his first love as a lifelong evangelist of the new phenomenon, in his own words:

My involvement with the Film Society Movement started with the International Film Club in high school (St. Josephs' Convent, Bhopal) in 1959. The father of two of my classmates, Saleem and Parvez Romani, had a used Bell & Howell 16 mm film projector. We used this and started showing films and started a film society on 4th August 1959. We began with 16mm film distributors like MGM, Columbia and NEIF Film Club. Tagore's birth centennial (1961) was coming up and from the newspapers we learnt about Satyajit Ray and his Teen Kanya based on Tagore's stories and Tagore's documentary.

Jaya Bahaduri Bachchan was a couple of years junior, and her father writer, journalist and stage artist Taroon Bahaduri, was a well-known personality in Bhopal and well known for his writings on dacoits of the Chambal Valley.

Tapan Sinha was coming to Bhopal to shoot *Kshudita Pashan* (*The Hungry Stone*). If I remember correctly, Taroon Bahaduri was the host (or had something to do with Tapan Sinha's film) and that is when the idea of getting Satyajit Ray's film for screening in Bhopal was born.

Prime Minister Jawaharlal Nehru was coming to visit Bhopal. So we decided to write to 'Chacha Nehru' telling him about the International Film Club and the wonderful work we were doing and asked him to gift us a film projector.

Marie Seton, as I had learnt later, was Nehru's house guest at Teen Murti Bhawan in Delhi. Nehru passed on our letter to Marie. We were surprised by a long letter from Marie Seton telling us about the Film Society Movement in UK; Vijaya Mulay and the film societies in Bombay, Calcutta and Delhi; and the formation of the Federation of Film Societies of India (1959).

This was the beginning of a long correspondence over the years. I have always marveled at Marie's dedication to the Film Society Movement and her effort to bring together everyone she got to know, from Indira Gandhi and Satyajit Ray, at one end, to a kid like me, who just happened to share her interest in film.

In course of my correspondence with Marie, I had mentioned to her about the film we were working on. We called it *Together We Learn*. She promptly responded with the information about *News Chronicle* in London about a competition on films made by children, suggesting that we should enter the competition, which we did.

Marie's letters were amazing; they were usually several pages long and full of news, ideas and connecting to interesting people with similar interests. Her letters talked about the film festivals that FFSI was planning; films she was getting for private screening for Prime Minister Nehru; NIAVE (National Institute of Audio Visual Education) of NCERT (National Council for Educational Research and Training) where she was helping with the Central Film Library, written couple of monographs on film study and the wonderful man, Satish Bahadur, at Agra University whom I must meet.

For me, in a faraway Bhopal, Marie's letters were my window to the wondrous world of cinema. Each letter was like a tutorial telling me about all the wonderful people and films and in between, she talked of contemporary India—Nehru, Indu (Indira Gandhi) and Krishna Menon.

I had finished my High School. My father's two year posting in Bhopal was coming to an end. We were going back to Lucknow, I told Marie. I was very unhappy about having to leave Bhopal. She told me about Professor Kailash Nath Kaul, director of the National Botanical Gardens (now it is called National Botanical Research Institute) and suggested that I should meet him about starting a film society in Lucknow.

For Anil, from then onwards, life was about films and new technologies. Marie, the film society evangelist at the national level, found a child prodigy "evangelist" in Anil. She, in turn, brought this to the notice of Vijaya Mulay, Chidananda Das Gupta and Satyajit Ray. His involvement with the Film Society Movement led to his co-founding the Lucknow Film Society and later a close collaboration with Professor Satish Bahadur and PK Nair at both the Film Institute of India and the NFAI. He edited *IFSON*, and went on to edit Satyajit Ray's issue of *Montage* and *Movement* published by *Suchitra* Film Society, Bangalore.

Anil's interest in cinema has continued through his work with the Centre for Development of Instructional Technology (CENDIT), where he led a National Film Heritage Programme, building the Indian film collection at the US Library of Congress and introduction of colour broadcasting in India. Anil collaborated with Richard Leacock on the use of 8-mm film for broadcasting. He later served as a technical advisor of UNESCO at the FTII on use of small band film and video for broadcasting.

He co-authored with Shampa Banerjee the book *One Hundred Indian Feature Films: An Annotated Filmography* and led the team which included PK Nair to create the International Federation of Film Archives (FIAF) guidelines for cataloguing of films and allied material in the film archives, using computers.[43]

Anil remains a true visionary of new Indian films, always looking for ways and means to marry new technologies with films. After all films are a product of the technological inventions of 19th century.

PK NAIR

He had retired in 1991, but the first director of the NFAI, Prameshwaran Krishnan (PK) Nair lived in Pune, not in his Laurie Baker-designed house in his native place Thiruvananthapuram, Kerala. Despite his difficulties in moving around after a road accident, Nair *saab* (as he was popularly called), was around NFAI till he died (1933–2016), just as he has been from 1961, when he joined the FTII as a research assistant. The reason is simple. His life is all about films and its

Image 3.8 PK Nair.
Courtsey: Sasi Kumar, TVM.

preservation for future. For him, preservation of this cultural format and its true appreciation, and development of discerning audience is the mission of his life. He remains a true visionary of the film appreciation, which the Film Society Movement is all about.

Nair *saab*'s life itself is a testimony to the emergence of an Indian film culture. Under his leadership, the country has a film archive that capsules the first film to the latest for history. "In Pune, between Film Institute and National Film Archive, only two of them (PK Nair and Prof Satish Bahadur) had complete knowledge and view about films. Others were mostly specialists in their fields," Anil Srivastava, who was associated with them from the early 1960s, noted. He is credited with spotting *Raja Harishchandra*, the first Indian film by Dadasaheb Phalke, bought it and restored the film to be shown across India and to preserve for the future.

Together, Nair *saab* and Professor Bahadur built a repository of systems, institutions and people for a new film culture over the years, which the film-makers and even the government is dependent upon now. This fact is best explained by an incident involving legendary film-maker Mrinal Sen. A few years ago, Mrinal Sen was invited to Cannes film festival for a retrospective of his films and found that most of the prints of the films are not in a good condition. As a member of the Parliament, he was wondering how he could go ahead. "Prime Minister Manmohan Singh heard about my plight and sanctioned funds to restore and digitise all his films through NFAI," Mrinal Sen said, recounting the historic service that NFAI has now undertaken.[44] A massive digitisation programme is ongoing in NFAI, converting all films in its earlier formats to digital formats.

As for the film societies across the country, NFAI and PK Nair were the prime sources of film classics from across the world. One of my early shocks in the *Chitralekha* Film Society during the 1976–79 period was seeing the Ingmar Bergman films, *Wild Strawberries, The Seventh Seal* and *Silence*; the three black-and-white films remain etched in my mind even today. Little did I know that it was an NFAI package that was put together by PK Nair for the film societies then! Along with the archiving of films, Nair *saab* had taken on the responsibility to fill the spreading appetite for good films from international circuit, other than from Hollywood.

Since he could preserve the dance maestro Uday Shanker's 1944 film *Kalpana*, we in *Chitralekha* could see that too. In fact, Nair *saab* had developed NFAI into an alternate film circuit source to the diplomatic missions of various countries, which were then not easily accessible for those in places other than the four metro cities of India.

Looking back, it is now evident that Nair *saab* introduced the international film-makers Ingmar Bergman, Akira Kurosawa, Andrzej Wajda, Miklós Jancsó, Krzysztof Zanussi, Vittorio De Sica and Federico Fellini to the film society circuit. The NFAI screenings at FTII, Pune, in the 1970s and 1980s, and the annual film appreciation course were events themselves for the film society enthusiasts and film buffs. By the 1980s, the films of Indian stalwarts like Satyajit Ray, Ritwik Ghatak, Mrinal Sen, V Shantaram, Raj Kapoor and Guru Dutt were made available to the FTII students, film society members and other film study groups in the country.

By the turn of the 1990s, the NFAI had spread its screening and study centres to Mumbai, Kolkata, Bangalore and Thiruvananthapuram, catering to the increasing space for good international and regional films, which were adjudged as best in national and international film festivals. Even today, all these centres have developed yearly international film festivals of their own, catering to the appetite for latest and acclaimed films across the world. Apart from establishing a film circuit, NFAI under Nair *saab* advised and helped establish film societies across India with the required paper work and advisories. When the government tried to establish film clubs in universities, UGC was asked to coordinate with NFAI.

Nair *saab* is often described as Henri Langlois of India considering his dedicated life for archiving films in India. Henri Langlois was a French film archivist and *cinephile*. A pioneer of film preservation, Langlois was an influential figure in the history of cinema. *Celluloid Man* is a 2012 documentary film directed by Shivendra Singh Dungarpur, who had documented the life and work of the legendary Indian archivist.[45]

In three decades, he built the NFAI from scratch and collected films both from India and abroad. His dedication to films ensured that NFAI now has in its collection most of the early films, including the first film of India, Dadasaheb Phalke's *Raja Harishchandra*. Some of the noteworthy films in the NFAI collection included *Kaliya Mardan*, Bombay Talkies films such as *Jeevan Naiya, Bandhan, Kangan, Achhut Kanya* and *Kismet*, SS Vasan's *Chandralekha* and Uday Shankar's *Kalpana*.

PK Nair was born in the capital of erstwhile Kingdom of Travancore, now Thiruvananthapuram, Kerala. Tamil mythological films in the early 1940s, such as K Subramaniam's *Ananthasayanam* and *Bhakta Prahlada*, flamed his early interest in films. Although his family was not appreciative of his interest, he was determined to get into films soon after his graduation in science from the University of Kerala in 1953. He proceeded to Bombay to pursue a career in film-making, realising little that he was among the few graduates pursuing such a career at that time, though he had the good fortune of working with directors such as Mehboob Khan, Bimal Roy and Hrishikesh Mukherjee.

Nair *Saab* recalled those days[46]:

In Mumbai, I realised that academically I had a different bent of mind, may be my degree in science led me to look at the emerging opportunities in the film establishment as suggested by SK Patil committee. I heard about Jean Bhownagary, a French Indian and advisor to the Ministry of Information and Broadcasting and went to meet him. It was he who advised me to wait and apply for the post of a researcher/archivist at FTII, which they planned to convert into a film archive.

It was here that PK Nair along with Marie Seton, Professor Satish Bahadur, started the annual film appreciation course in 1967. The programme continues even today.

The independent NFAI was established in 1964, and PK Nair was appointed assistant curator in November 1965. He was promoted as the director of the archive in 1982. When he retired in April 1991, he had collected over 12,000 films, of which 8,000 were Indian. He had also established NFAI as an institution worthy of its stature in the international film archive circuit, in three decades of his service.

Unquestionably, his contribution to the Film Society Movement is a pioneering one. He was a supporter of the "minority cinema," as he later called it, against the majority, more popular one, though he never made any differentiation while archiving films. "Why do you buy all these trash films," asked a secretary at the I&B ministry, in an interaction to convince them on the annual budget. Nair *saab* kept quiet there, but later wondered aloud, "why do you allow such trash films to be made at all!" That is Nair *saab* for you.[47]

The clash of the "majority" and "minority" films and its impact on quality films were always in his mind. The article he wrote in 2000 reveals it all.[48]

Let us not assume everyone wants to see the same kind of Cinema. The market forces would naturally dictate the filmmaker to cater to the majority for his very survival. But we have to create the necessary climate for the Other Cinema also to survive. The one which does not cater to the majority. For a healthy society, all shades of views and expression should be allowed to flow. Just because someone doesn't want to talk to the majority but just shares the views with a minority who would like to listen to him? Should he be prevented from doing so? It would be a sad day for the society if all its resources are earmarked only for the majority and doesn't care what happens to the minority.

No one has to be told where the author's heart is, after reading this article.

A life dedicated to promoting, archiving and supporting the quality films, that is PK Nair.[49]

PROFESSOR SATISH BAHADUR

Image 3.9 Professor Satish Bahadur.
Courtesy: Apurva Bahadur (son).

If someone can truly be called the guru of film appreciation in India, it is Professor Satish Bahadur. He was not just the first academician to become a professor of film appreciation in the FTII, Pune, but was a lifelong promoter of film appreciation. With the one-month-long course at FTII, along with the National Film Archive from 1967 till his death in 2010, he nurtured many batches of academicians and film buffs from all walks of life and diverted them into the aesthetics of cinema.

"Nothing in the film is accidental. Everything that you experience is 'put there' by the makers of the film," were his often-repeated words, recalls one of his students, Arun Khopikar. Recounting his days in the classroom presided over by Professor Bahadur, Arun wrote:

Bahadursaab made us understand how a film is 'made'. To concen-
trate on that, we needed to be denied the pleasure of sitting and

staring hypnotized at the screen. Like a mother who applies bitter medicine to her breasts for weaning, Bahadursaab used cruel methods to shake us up from the somnambulist state of a film spectator. Sometimes, he would tell you the story of a film before he showed it, ruthlessly killing the pleasures of anticipation and surprise. At other times, he would project the film in half-lights and comment with his pointer at its compositional highlights. Occasionally, the film would be projected without sound and sometimes only the sound track was kept on for to you to analyze it.[50]

The professor defined Film Appreciation also as Film Criticism.

A film maker makes a film. A spectator receives the film. These are two segments of the communications process. The critic also a spectator, but of a special kind. What critic does has a special significance for the lay spectator and for the film maker, as also the development of the Art of the film.[51]

Professor Bahadur began his career as a lecturer in economics at DAV College Kanpur and later continued at Agra's St. John's College, where he found the first university film club in India. The Agra Film Club was one of the early film clubs of India and Professor Bahadur was its secretary. As an academician, he encouraged debate on a film after every screening, and this led to further debate on the film from various angles. This caught the attention of Marie Seton, the British film expert evangelising film appreciation in the late 1950s in India.

When FTII began its operations, Professor Bahadur was persuaded by Marie Seton to join there as the professor of film appreciation, and he remained there till he retired in 1983. His close associates in the field were Vijaya Mulay and PK Nair, who later became the curator of the Film Archive. "Prof Bahadur remains the initiator of serious film appreciation in the country," said Adoor Gopalakrishnan, his student from the second batch of FTII.[52]

"Satish was not only the lifeblood of the film appreciation but he greatly contributed to the development of the filmmakers like Adoor who led the new cinema movement," says Anil Srivastava, who worked with the professor to bring out the first journal of FFSI.[53]

Because Bahadur was a professor of film appreciation, it was under him that the one-month-long film appreciation summer residencies were conducted at the FTII, along with the Film Archive. From 1967 onwards, the summer residency had been an annual feature at Pune, attracting film buffs from all shades of the academic fraternity and Film Society Movement for years.

Professor Bahadur wrote about his pedagogy, as far as film appreciation is concerned, as follows:

> I have shaped myself through my conscious decision of using the classroom as a space for live interaction with young minds. My entire being as teacher depends on the obvious fact that I am face to face with live young persons who are hoping to learn from what I do in the classroom. This unrelenting practice over the years has built in my system a natural respect for young students who are willing to learn. Such teaching-learning interaction in the classroom builds up confidence in a student that he can go beyond the mere understanding of the subject and discover his own path to learn more and more.

The one-month residency over the years had spread to other centres on a yearly basis. Many of the institutions and film societies have been hosting film appreciation courses of a shorter duration in various cities of India over the years.

Comparing films and literature, he insisted that there is no film culture without a film criticism, just as there is literature without literary criticism. Professor Bahadur theorized in his Notes on Film Criticism, "Literary Culture is not merely Literature. It is Literature plus Literary Criticism. It is Criticism which completes the communication process and makes Literature a social entity. Likewise Film Culture is not merely films. It is Films plus Film Criticism."[54]

The Moradabad-born professor had numerous publications to his credit, but he is best known for his analysis of Satyajit Ray films. His last writing was the textual analysis of the *Apu Trilogy*. He wrote and taught Ray's early films so much that even Ray was quoted about how critics find meanings in films which sometimes even the film-makers have never thought of while making it.

Though he taught Film Appreciation for about four decades, he has not left his teachings as a textbook and his writings remain scattered. Shyamala Vanarse, his long-time associate, remarked:

> He loved to lecture and discuss films, but he was almost averse to writing. The only book he saw through was posthumously published, *A Textual Analysis of Apu Trilogy*. He wrote his lectures for AIR and wrote papers for seminars, but never really bothered about

getting into print... and his hands were full with lecture tours, courses and routine teaching at the Institute. Many people had urged him, but he would just freely pass on his notes.[55]

Professor Satish Bhadur took over and continued the serious academic studies into films, which Marie Seton and Chidananda Das Gupta initiated in India. He will be known as the first Indian professor of film studies in the history of academic film studies in India. By initiating film society leaders and academics into serious film appreciation through the annual film appreciation workshop of FTII and NFAI, Professor Bahadur also contributed immensely to the Film Society Movement, which is all about serious film appreciation. His visionary approach to film studies paved the way for Indian universities to initiate academic studies about films. Now many a university in India has graduate and postgraduate studies in films.[56]

JEAN BHOWNAGARY

Image 3.10 Jean Bhownagary.
Courtesy: Janine Barucha (daughter).

Jean (Jehangir Shapurji) Bhownagary may not be in the long list of activists and organisers of Indian Film Society Movement, but his visionary role in promoting the alternate film culture, especially the governmental institutions like IFFI, FTII, NFAI, FFC and making Film Division a creative hub of documentaries cannot be written off, while chronicling the development of films as a medium.

The institutions he promoted as an advisor in the ministry of I&B of the Government of India, in the early 1950s, extended the political and administrative push to the Film Society Movement as well in creating the new Indian films. He was the trusted advisor to Indira Gandhi, who even wetted the Mari Seton's plan for the formulation of FFSI in 1959.

Bhownagary, a half French Indian of Parsi origin, started his career with the British predecessor of Films Division, Information Film India, in the early 1940s and went on to work in UNESCO in Paris. It was at Paris where Ms Indira Gandhi, then the daughter of Prime Minister Nehru, met him only to be enamoured by his vision for a new Indian films in 1950, including that of establishing an IFFI to show case the best of world films to Indians.

Gautam Kaul, who was a cousin of Ms Gandhi and an insider at Teen Murti Bhavan, the official residence of Prime Minister Nehru, recalled[57]:

> On her return from Paris, Indiraji gave a note to her father Prime Minister Nehru who was busy building India from the scratch. A true democrat Nehru, passed on the note to his Information Minister R.R. Diwakar. Minister Diwakar, found out who was behind the note and approached Indiraji for help to implement the vision behind the note. Indiraji in turn directed the Minister to Jean, who was the brain behind the note. He was made an advisor in the I&B Ministry to prepare for the first International film festival.

The first IFFI was inaugurated by Prime Minister Jawaharlal Nehru on 21 January 1952. Twenty-three countries and the United Nations participated in the festival with 40 feature films and about a 100 short films. The main festival was held in Bombay from 24 January to 1 February 1952. The festival later travelled to Madras, Delhi and Calcutta.[58]

The man behind the festival, indeed, was the advisor in the ministry of I&B, confirmed PK Nair, who was then an assistant director in the Bombay film industry. According to PK Nair, Jean was known as the point man of the government in setting up new film institutions, and he went to meet him at his office in Delhi. Nair was given an overview on the government's plan for films by Jean, who advised him wait and apply for the film curators join at FTII, which he was engaged in setting up. Nair joined the FTII and went to set up the NFAI.

The International Film Festival of 1952, the first of the sort in Asia, also came as a boon for the spurting film societies in the metro cities of India. The societies like CFS were already starving for films in the early 1950s. The international film festivals and involvement of the various embassies in it with the supply of films through governmental channels was a new opening to source films from those countries. As the commercial charges for one-time screening of many of the films were very expensive for even the Government of India, Prime Minister Nehru had involved the embassies of target countries to get films. Most embassies obliged the government by bringing their films free through the diplomatic channels. This arrangement continued with FFSI in the years to come, as various countries found it the best way to promote their films and culture in India.

However, it took almost a decade to make the IFFI an annual feature, the credit for initiating the IFFI goes to Bhownagary. Inaugurating the festival, the prime minister hoped that, "Indian film industry, which has made such great progress in the past, will make every effort to improve the quality of our films also."[59] Recalling the impact of the first IFFI, Marie Seton wrote, "There is no doubt that the International Film Festival of 1952 came as a happy revelation to those who saw the films submitted by various countries, especially the Italian and Japanese films.... The festival certainly prepared the way for a new attitude towards the cinema."[60]

The period was before Marie Seton and Satyajit Ray's *Pather Panchali* and also the establishment of institutions like the FTII, FFC and IFFI directorate. Bhownagary, as advisor, was responsible for implementing the SK Patil committee report on films of 1950, along with the then I&B secretary, whom he shared a good rapport, apart from Indira Gandhi and the prime minister himself. In short, India's trust with its new films and films culture started with Jean Bhownagary's tour de force in organising the first IFFI.

Later, in 1959, Ms Indira Gandhi referred the note submitted by Marie Seton for the formation of FFSI to Bhownagary and MV

Krishnaswamy, the then director of Films Division for their opinion. Both of them wholeheartedly supported the move, and FFSI was incorporated in December 1959.

His daughter wrote Janine in a profile as follows[61]:

> My Papa was a man of great vision. His talent in discovering, choosing and trusting film-makers became legendary. He encouraged a cross-fertilisation of talents, inviting artists from different fields, musicians, painters, sculptors, dancers to join the creative process, resulting in the production of one masterpiece after another, bringing home many national and international awards for films by historical names such as Sukhdev, K.S. Chari, M.F. Husain, S.N.S. Sastry, Shanti Varma, Shanti Choudhury, Prem Vaydia, N.V.K Murthy, to name but a few.

Bhownagary was appointed as the director of Films Division of India twice, first from 1954 to 1957 and then from 1965 to 1967, a period that inaugurated the golden age of experimental short films from Films Division. His tenure at Films Division saw the entire organisation getting converted into a hub of new documentary, with creative people from all across the country making films on various burning issues of growing India.

Peter Sutoris, author of *Visions of Development*, recalled[62]:

> Bhownagary is credited with turning the film propaganda wing of the Government of India, a world war relic of the British Raj, into a world class documentary unit, reflecting the issues of India of 50s and 60s. He brought in the neo-realist techniques of film making in non-fiction films. The series of documentary on the occasion of 25th anniversary of India, mirroring the ground level issues of India was shown all over the world.

The book features the emergence of non-fiction films with a development angle in India.

Dilip Padgoankar, in his obituary of the pioneering film-maker and policy man in 2004, wrote.[63]

> Jean was also a ceramist, a potter, a lithographer, a painter and, above all, a gifted documentary film-maker. The films he directed or produced all over the world for UNESCO, which he served for more than three decades, won awards at prestigious film festivals.

Under his leadership, India's documentaries began to be noticed internationally. Names like Sukh Dev, artist MF Hussain, Pramod Pati emerged as iconic figures in the field. Bhownagary is credited with mentoring Sukh Dev's critical films of India's development process, which sparked off a debate, as to why the government must fund a film critical of its policy implementations. *India 67*, a documentary of Sukh Dev on the silver jubilee of India's freedom, was viewed across the world and was hailed as the coming of age of Indian documentary. Bhownagary brought in Marie Seton and even John Grierson, the British documentary maestro, to discuss and debate on the issue of future of Indian documentary as early as in 1960.[64]

Parallel to promoting the new wave in Indian films through the Film Society Movement and other institutions like FTII and FFC, the government of the day also brought about resurgence in Indian documentary film-making. Just as Marie Seton evangelised the need for a meaningful film appreciation, Bhownagary worked behind the governmental system and headed Film Division to create the new Indian documentary and improve its techniques and content. His role as advisor in the ministry of I&B to initiate IFFI, FTII and FFC places him as one among the pioneering visionaries of the Indian Film Society Movement.

There are other pioneers who worked as secretaries of FFSI, such as AK Dey and Arun Kumar Pramanik, Arun Roy from Patna, Amitabh Ghosh from Jamshedpur, John Joshua of the DFS, Jag Mohan of the Film Forum and DFS, Muriel Wasi of the DFS, Arun Kaul and Gopal Dutia of the Film Forum, Mumbai, and contributed to the growth of the Film Society Movement. However, one is forced to limit to the present list to keep the focus on the visionaries of the movement, whose contribution were unparalleled.

NOTES*

1. HN Narahari Rao, ed., *The Film Society Movement in India* (Mumbai: Asian Film Foundation, 2009), p. 71.
2. Interaction with Vijaya Mulay by the author.
3. https://en.wikipedia.org/wiki/Bicycle_Thieves
4. https://en.wikipedia.org/wiki/Battleship_Potemkin
5. https://en.wikipedia.org/wiki/Nanook_of_the_North
6. https://en.wikipedia.org/wiki/Samik_Bandyopadhyay
7. http://www.bfi.org.uk/news-opinion/news-bfi/lists/10-great-italian-neorealist-films
8. Marie Seton, *Preface of Portrait of a Director: Satyajit Ray* (New Delhi: Penguin Books, 2003), p. 55.

9. https://en.wikipedia.org/wiki/The_River_(1951_film)
10. https://en.wikipedia.org/wiki/Vsevolod_Pudovkin
11. http://cherianwrites.blogspot.in/2016/02/a-few-notes-for-book-towards-new-film.html
12. Dilip Basu. *Biography of Satyajit Ray* (Santa Clarita, CA: Ray Film and Study Center). Available at: http://satyajitray.ucsc.edu/biography
13. http://www.satyajitray.org/
14. Interview with Adoor Gopalakrishnan.
15. https://en.wikipedia.org/wiki/Mani_Kaul
16. https://en.wikipedia.org/wiki/Kumar_Shahani
17. Interview with Samik Bandyopadhyay, art/film critic. https://en.wikipedia.org/wiki/Samik_Bandyopadhyay
18. https://en.wikipedia.org/wiki/Sandip_Ray
19. http://www.satyajitray.org/
20. *Selected Speeches of Indira Gandhi: Jan 1966–69.* (New Delhi: Publication Division), 279.
21. http://cherianwrites.blogspot.in/2016/03/marie-setons-first-book-let-edited.html
22. Interview with Gautam Kaul.
23. Ibid.
24. Based on interview with Kulathoor Bhaskaran Nair, MD, Chitralekha Film Cooperative.
25. BK Karanjia. *Counting my Blessings* (New Delhi: Viking 2005).
26. *Selected Speeches and Writings of Indira Gandhi.* (New Delhi: Publications Division, Ministry of I&B, GOI, 1975), p. 378.
27. https://en.wikipedia.org/wiki/Indira_Gandhi
28. http://www.thehindu.com/arts/article148630.ece
29. Marie Seton. *Preface of Portrait of a Director: Satyajit Ray* (New Delhi: Penguins, 2003), Preface.
30. http://cherianwrites.blogspot.in/2016/02/marie-setons-letter-to-editor-published.html
31. HN Narahari Rao, ed., *The Film Society Movement in India*, p. 228.
32. https://en.wikipedia.org/wiki/Marie_Seton
33. HN Narahari Rao, ed., *The Film Society Movement in India*, p. 72
34. Ibid., p. 102.
35. https://en.wikipedia.org/wiki/Chidananda_Dasgupta
36. Vijaya Mulay. *As Others See It* (NFAI project), p. 3.
37. HN Narahari Rao, ed., *The Film Society Movement in India.*
38. Ibid., p. 19.
39. https://en.wikipedia.org/wiki/Vijaya_Mulay
40. RM Ray, ed., *Indian Cinema in Retrospect: Speeches of the 1955 Seminar* (New Delhi: Sangeet Natak Academy, 1955).
41. https://en.wikipedia.org/wiki/Khwaja_Ahmad_Abbas
42. https://en.wikipedia.org/wiki/Ammu_Swaminathan
43. http://cherianwrites.blogspot.in/2016/02/a-few-notes-for-book-towards-new-film.html
44. Interview with Mrinal Sen.
45. https://en.wikipedia.org/wiki/Celluloid_Man
46. Interview with PK Nair.
47. Ibid.
48. http://cherianwrites.blogspot.in/2016/02/from-nfai-collection-national-cinema.html
49. https://en.wikipedia.org/wiki/P._K._Nair
50. http://www.academia.edu/957386/White_chalk_and_Blackboard_On_the_occasion_of_Prof._Satish_Bahadurs_book_release

51. http://cherianwrites.blogspot.in/2016/02/interview-with-ms-shyamala-vannarse.html
52. Interaction with Adoor Gopalakrishnan.
53. Interactions with Anil Srivastava.
54. http://cherianwrites.blogspot.in/2016/02/a-personal-note-onscreen-education-work.html
55. http://cherianwrites.blogspot.in/2016/02/interview-with-ms-shyamala-vannarse.html
56. https://en.wikipedia.org/wiki/Satish_Bahadur
57. Interview with Gautam Kaul.
58. Government of India. *Collected Works of Jawaharlal Nehru* (Publications Division: Ministry of Information and Broadcasting), p. 311.
59. Ibid., p. 58.
60. http://cherianwrites.blogspot.in/2016/03/marie-setons-first-book-let-edited.html- Chapter-2.
61. http://cherianwrites.blogspot.in/2016/04/daughter-of-jean-man-behind-nehruvian. html
62. http://www.petersutoris.com/visionsofdevelopment
63. http://timesofindia.indiatimes.com/home/sunday-times/all-that-matters/Jeans-magic-spell/articleshow/653690.cms
64. Ezra Mir, John Grierson, James Beveridge, Akira Ivasaki, John Heyer, Richard Griffiths, Paul Zils, Jean Bhownagary, Herbert Marshall, and Paul Rotha, "What Is a Good Documentary Film?" *Marg*, 13, no. 3 (June 1960): 65–70.

*   All websites accessed on 16 June 2016.

CHAPTER 4

The Networks of Films and Film Buffs

Although India became politically independent in 1947, until the late 1950s the Hollywood films were hot favourite of the best of cinema houses in urban centres of the country, despite the country emerging as a major film production centre. A rough estimate indicated that 80 per cent of the films shown were of foreign origin and Indian-language films were not so popular with the system, although the people were willing to lap them up.[1]

Film-maker KA Abbas, "invoking the authority of no less a person than the Prime Minister of the country who asked us to consult among ourselves," on the first day of discussion at the film seminar organised by the Sangeet Natak Akademi in 1955, lamented[2]:

> In Bombay all big cinemas (almost all the air-conditioned cinemas) located in the finest, best and hygienic parts of the city, run pictures belonging to the foreign exhibitors. Indian films are shown in these picture houses, once a year or once in two years or three years…. This is against our national pride and self-respect that you cannot see Indian pictures in certain Indian cinemas.

Little did Abbas realise that even after years of political freedom, the country was following the policies and practices of the Indian Cinematograph Act, 1918. The Rangachariar Committee on films during the British Raj (1927–28) had dictated that "Every characteristic of cinema industry makes it unsuitable for provincialisation."

It went on to suggest that the policies to favour English films from the UK follow a strict regime of censorship.

No wonder, Jean Renoir, the French director, advised Satyajit Ray back in 1949, while shooting in Calcutta for his film 'River, that "If you could only shake out Hollywood out of your system and evolve your own style, you would be making great films here."[3]

In the 21st century, the world film map shows that there are only few countries, notably India and France, which still have their own film industry and films, depicting the social and cultural issues of its people and are popular in their cinema houses. Both India and France have been able to counter the onslaught of Hollywood with in-house film productions. Even in the metro cities, and most regional centres, all movie theatres treat Hindi films or regional language films as being more important than the English films, as the viewers prefer their own cultural products.

The annual report of the ministry of I&B of 2014–15 listed a total of 12,977 films censored during the period, out of which only 222 were foreign films.[4] Clearly, over the six decades of free India, the country has been able to grow its film industry into a formidable force.

The story of how this resistance in films mounted from 1955 to 2015 is also the story of a young nation's quest for its own idiom in films, guided and patronised by two Indian Prime Ministers, Jawaharlal Nehru and Indira Gandhi.

The Film Society Movement, an alternate film circuit, which they (the PMs) promoted for their goal in the film field, may not be in a good shape today, but they seemed to have achieved their goal through "Bollywood" films,[5] the popular term for the Hindi film industry. Bollywood films give Hollywood films a run for their money in India and wherever Indians are across the globe. Some of the star directors, technicians and stars of Bollywood are either from FTII or the products of the Film Society Movement, which the founding fathers of India supported wholeheartedly for the development of Indian films.

It is said that Satyajit Ray saw over 99 films during his short stay at London, before making his first film, and among them the Italian neorealist films made a deep impression on him. "He learnt most from Italian films (in London). During his voyage home, he worked on the script of 'Pather 'Panchali and thought of ways he could raise money to make the novel into a film," Marie Seton, his biographer, described the Ray's London education in films as a young art director of a British advertising firm.[6]

A writer takes to reading like a fish to water, and for a film-maker seeing films is his/her *raison d'etre*. Film societies have been filling this role of exposing film buffs and film-makers to the best of cinema from across the world now for decades as an exclusive channel, till the advent of videos and digital versatile discs (DVDs) in the 1990s. India is perhaps the only nation that has not seen a takeover of the imported (Hollywood) films of its screens till today. This is something that India can be rightly proud of, especially in these days of globalisation, when Hollywood cinema has virtually dominated the world screen. The first two decades of cinema in the country saw the imported films, mostly from Europe, occupying the bulk of our screen. The figures at the end of the silent era were 80 per cent imported and only the balance 20 per cent being indigenous. The beginning of the "Talkies" made it possible to see, hear and enjoy films in one's own language. This brought in a dramatic change with the imported films (by this time mainly American) getting pushed out and cinema in various Indian languages taking over.

Slowly, the ratio reversed; it became almost 98 per cent Indian and the rest foreign films (2014–15). Since then, Indian cinema has never looked back.[7] It continues to have a hypnotic hold on the Indian masses, both within and outside the country. This continues despite the heavy onslaught of the dominant cinema from the mighty Hollywood.

PK Nair, analysing the foreign films in India, observed[8]:

They tried to dub their films in Hindi and other Indian languages to penetrate the Indian market barring exceptions like Jurassic Park or Titanic, they could not make much of a break through. But with costs soaring sky high and diminishing returns and a crumbling economy, can we hold on for long? This should be a matter of concern for all of us.

FILM AS AN ART AND ITS APPRECIATION

In a country where the literacy rate is still 64 per cent,[9] the political leadership from the first prime minister onwards has been identifying deeper influence of visual medium and films, compared to books and print media, to take their literacy campaigns forward. Maybe television has taken over the role of films, but cinema remained a major influence on people throughout the 20th century. Identifying the influence of films over other means of communication, Prime

Minister Nehru had clearly set out to draw a line. "... What is presented should mould the public taste, action and reaction," Nehru's policy direction on films was clear from the word go.[10]

Nehru did appreciate the growth of the film industry over the three decades prior to 1955. "Nevertheless, they have made progress (film industry) ... of course, many people criticise the quality of many of their films from their rather highbrow point of view, and their criticism from that point of view is justified, highbrow or not,"[11] the scholar statesman made his point clear to an audience that included film industry giants such as Devi Rani, KA Abbas, SS Vasan and Prithviraj Kapoor and his sons. Nehru bluntly told them that the melodrama, which was the hallmark of films those days, put him to sleep. He stopped short of saying that the government had some interest in setting the agenda for the film industry, though by 1960, he was exercising it through institutions like FFSI, FTII, FFC and NFAI.

Paul Rotha, the eminent British film historian, did not consider such a criticism as highbrow and went on to say, "Almost the whole potential of the cinema as an instrument of public education has been neglected by the industry's controllers in their pursuit of big returns." He emphasised that, "film appreciation is concerned with these films and enabling people to separate the chaff from the grain in cinema."[12]

"Film appreciation aims to cultivate a taste for the grain," Marie Seton, the British film scholar wrote.[13]

The Film Society Movement pioneer, Chidananda Das Gupta, went a step further to emphasise on the need for appreciation of quality films as a precursor for making good films. In his introduction to his book *Cinema of Satyajit Ray*,[14] he wrote:

> In a country fed mostly with imported escapist films and their inept local imitations, the exposure to *Battleship Potemkin, Nanook of the North, Night Mail* and *Un Carnet de* bal brought about a burning desire to tell what a great art cinema was and to prove in the shortest possible time, that great films could be made in India— films that would shake the world and change our own country.

Earlier during a review on the Film Society Movement, in 1965, Das Gupta further explained[15]:

> Without wishing away the difference between the art audience and the mass audience, it is still possible to direct film appreciation at two objectives: to inject more cinematic technique and attitude into

the commercial cinema and to make it raise its sights within reason: and to create the urge for and the climate in which genuine artistic expression becomes possible on a wider scale.

All of them were pointing towards the emergence of film as an art, a serious vocation aimed to positively influence viewers, just as any other art form, be it painting, theatre or music. The art that developed as a by-product of industrial Revolution in the West came to India when there was no industry here, hence the science and art of film-making was seen as an extension of the country-side dance dramas in its initial years. However, the new nation, out to industrialise itself through huge public sector units, was ready to explore the art and its technology seriously, with inputs of contemporary sensibilities of the West where the medium originated. The yearning for film appreciation through the Film Society Movement was the vehicle identified for it, by the connoisseurs of the culture and the government of the day.

SOURCING GOOD FILMS: PRE-FFSI AND NFAI DAYS

The success of a film society was dependent on its ability to screen a varied number of films, Indian or foreign, not necessarily English, as Hollywood films were abundantly available in India from the colonial times.

The acquisition of Sergei Eisenstein's *Battleship Potemkin*, by CFS by 1948, opened up a new avenue for the film societies as far as sourcing of films for their screening was concerned. *Battleship* ended up being shown as the first film in most of the early film societies, such as the Lucknow and Patna film societies. Even today, there is hardly a film society member who has not seen the Russian film of an early revolutionary struggle at Odesa[16] harbour steps. It was the first film of the circuit, and its classical position in film history had made it a must see.

Chidananda Das Gupta, while discussing the parallel history of Indian cinema, observed[17]:

> India's doors and windows had started to fly open. In 1948, the CFS imported a copy of *Battleship Potemkin* and showed it, dodging police restrictions, to stunning effect of its viewers. Hard on the heels of this event came Jean Renoir's visit for a recce in 1948 and for the shooting of *The River* in 1949…. The shooting of The River was observed by many who were later to turn famous practitioners,

such as cinematographer Subrata Mitra, art director Bansi Chandra Gupta, documentarist Harisadhan Das Gupta and so on. Roberto Rossellini came a few years later and so did John Houston, Frank Capra, V Pudovkin and Nikolai Cherkassovall names to reckon with in cinema, popular or unpopular.

The erstwhile Soviet Union-produced film *Battleship* also gave a big boost to other films from the entire Eastern bloc, where film-making was identified as a political act to promote their ideology. The Eastern bloc sensed the appetitive for non-English films in the film society circuit and was ever ready to pump in their films as part of their spreading the influence over Indian intelligentsia under Prime Minister Nehru, who loved to be identified as a left-leaning socialist. Ray had seen *Battleship* over and over again and even scored his own music for this silent film, with a collection of the LP records, when he saw it 22nd time.[18]

The story of *Pather Panchali* being shown in Bhopal by the students led by Anil Srivastava, in the late 1950s is yet another land-mark in the history of the films that excited the societies. Marie Seton came to India with seven films from the British Film Institute: Charlie Chaplin's *The Immigrant*, Alexander Dovshenko's *Earth*, Vsevelod Pudovkin's *Storm over Asia*, GW Pabst's *Kameradschaft* (*Comradeship*), Rene Clair's *Le Million* (*The Million*), Luchiano Emmer's *Sunday in August*, John Ford's *They Were Expendable* and *Children of Hiroshima*. The collection was from the British Film Institute to which Marie was associated. This unique film-package travelled with her to various metro cities of India and some chosen non-metro cities too, giving an opportunity to the increasing film societies and select academics a glimpse of emerging film scenario in the West.

After her lecture tour with the films, Marie wrote: "The films illustrating Film Appreciation stressed that the feature film at its best is an educational force and that dramatic films can be based upon real situation as in *They Were Expendable, Kameradschaft* and *Children of Hiroshima*."[19]

Some of the films shown by the CFS in the first two years included the Mexican film *Portrait of Maria*, *A Cage of Nightingales* (France), *Brief Encounter* (UK, David Lean), *The Way Ahead* (UK, Carol Reed), *This Land Is Mine* (Jean Renoir, France), *Counter Attack* (Hungary, Zoltan Korda), *Nanook of the North* (Robert

Flaherty, USA).[20] Most of these films were either procured from the regular circuit or granted by embassies of the respective countries or obtained from the Central Film Library of the ministry of education.

With the formation of the FFSI in 1959, a plan with the active involvement of the film bodies of the Central government was put into place and submitted to the government. "To begin with some Government organisations—the Films Division or the Board of Film Censors—should be asked to act as the importer and distributor of film societies," the first Five-Year Plan of the FFSI suggested.[21] FFSI was allowed to import 16 films a year without the mandatory customs duty, provided they had enough foreign exchange to do so. Indeed, FFSI could import a few films during the period 1963–64. The federation did get a package of films from the Colombo Film Society of Sri Lanka. The package included films such as *Passion of Joan of Arc, The Last Laugh, Le Million, The Italian Straw Hat, The Cabinet of Dr Caligari, The Blue Angel* and *Metropolis*. In 1965–66, few films were directly imported from London. Three films were obtained from the Swedish Embassy. All of them were procured with the generous grant of the Government of India, to promote the availability of quality films for the FFSI network.

However, over a period of time, FFSI ended up being dependent on the Central Film Library of ministry of education and the diplomatic missions in India, as the government grants dried up. The censor restrictions further restrained them from getting more films. In 1964, Indira Gandhi as the information minister exempted film society screenings from censorship, and there was a flood of films from all diplomatic missions, especially the Eastern bloc. Films from Poland, Hungary, Czechoslovakia, Bulgaria and Russia remained the toast of the film society circuit for a long-time.

In the first five years before the formation of NFAI, FFSI was able to circulate over 70 feature films in its network.

Das Gupta, in his assessment of first five years of FFSI, recalled[22]:

Direct import and an exchange through UNESCO have accounted for all of these films, the rest having been arranged with the cooperation of various foreign missions in India, notably those of France, Sweden, Mexico, Japan, West Germany, Poland, Hungary, Bulgaria, Czechoslovakia, UK, Yugoslavia, USSR and East Germany.

The meagre membership fee charged by the film societies did not allow them to hire cinema halls for 35 films and pay a screening fee from the normal film distribution circuit. Hence, they were mostly dependent on 16-mm film prints. Most of the cultural and educational institutions had the 16-mm projector as part of the educational tools. Since the growth and spread of film societies were around educational or cultural bodies till the advent of video and DVD projectors, 16mm films suited the fragile economics of running a film society.

THE CENTRAL FILM LIBRARY TO NFAI

The Central Film Distribution Library had 16-mm print of 20 classic films of Sergei Eisenstein, Robert Flaherty, Vittorio De Sica, David Lean, Henri Georges Clouzat, Jean Vigo, Mark Donoskoi and Charlie Chaplin. Documentary films of John Grierson, Basil Wright, Paul Rotha and Humphrey Jennings were also available at the library, whose membership was accorded to the film societies affiliated to FFSI. The founders of the FFSI, had access to these films through their contacts in the government, such as Vijaya Mulay and Marie Seton, both of whom were attached to the Central ministry of education in Delhi.

All these films were later transferred to the NFAI in the 1960s. The I&B ministry took over the functions of the Central Film Library, and the films were housed at NFAI attached to the ministry and remained available for distribution to film societies. The NFAI's Distribution Library had over 25 active members in 2014, throughout the country, and it also organises joint screening programmes on weekly, fortnightly and monthly basis in six important centres. NFAI has over 17,000 films, 25,000 books, 10,000 film scripts and more than 125,000 photographs. Various educational institutions, cultural organisations and film societies are members of the NFAI Distribution Library. "To start with the Archive's distribution library had about 20 film classics. This unit started expanding gradually, and by 1980s it reached a figure of over 100 titles that included both Indian and foreign classics," PK Nair wrote in *IFSON*, the official journal of FFSI in 1981.[23]

NATIONAL FILM ARCHIVE OF INDIA, PUNE

As many as 739 film societies across India were affiliated to NFAI from 1994–95 onwards to source their films for screenings. Most of them were not even affiliated to the FFSI going by the numbers. On an average 30 film societies per year were registered with NFAI and PK Nair, its director, satisfied himself with the conduct of each of these film societies and transported the films from the NFAI library.[24]

NFAI has also taken upon itself the promotion of film appreciation as envisaged by the founders of the film societies. The annual one-month summer course at the FTII, organised by NFAI, is a big draw even today. In 2015, over 40 film enthusiasts from across the country participated in the summer one-month long course. At the international level, NFAI supplied several Indian classics for major screening programmes to those interested in Indian films, ensuring a two-way exposure of films.

The Distribution Library despatches films by railway, surface courier and air, throughout the country. It is also responsible for sending films abroad with a view to popularise Indian cinema in foreign countries. Hence, booking of films may be done well in advance.

A number of classics like *Bicycle Thieves, Pather Panchali*, documentaries like *Nanook of the North* feature in the Distribution Library list of NFAI. All the national award-winning films are to be procured by the NFAI, apart from the panorama films of IFFI.

As a part of its activities under dissemination of film culture, NFAI, with its headquarters at Pune and three regional offices at Bengaluru, Kolkata and Thiruvananthapuram, extended distribution library facilities to the members throughout the country. The Distribution Library caters to the special screenings of films from the NFAI collection. NFAI also conducts joint screening programmes at Mumbai, Kolkata, Bengaluru, Hyderabad, Thiruvananthapuram, Kochi, Jamshedpur and Pune.

FFC and its contemporary version, National Film Development Corporation (NFDC) was also a source of films for film societies. Various diplomatic missions continue to be another source for most recent films from non-English-speaking countries.

The grey market too has emerged as a major source for film buffs. At Thiruvananthapuram, I saw a list of over 5,000 films with a film critic. He told me that such films or any new films in the international circuit are available for a throwaway price in the city. A whole new grey market operates outside the city. I saw the same on a visit to Dhaka, where I could buy a collection of Ray and Ghatak movies at throwaway prices. The arrival of DVD and CDs has completely changed the availability of films and the very need for film societies just to see film for serious film buffs.

ENTRY OF EASTERN BLOC AND OTHERS: NON-ENGLISH FILMS

In my early days in Delhi during the 1980s, I used to receive letters from film society friends from Kerala. All of them were asking me to help them to procure films from diplomatic missions of Eastern bloc countries of Poland, Hungary, Czechoslovakia, Cuba, Yugoslavia and Bulgaria. Since India was with the Eastern Bloc during the Cold War, the diplomatic missions saw the films from their countries as a good way of getting to reach the cream of the Indian society. It gave them and their ideology acceptability and entry to the upper strata of the society.

The films of Germans, French and Japanese were also eagerly awaited in India. Although these films never got into the regular cinema houses, they had become a hot property in the film society circles. In the 1980s, there was hardly anyone in the film society circuit who was not seen or excited about the films of Jean Luc Godard,[25] Werner Herzog,[26] Ferderico Fellini,[27] Ingmar Bergman,[28] Miklos Jansco,[29] Krzysztof Zanussi[30] and Akira Kurosawa.[31] Bergman, Kurosawa, Fellini, Godard, Jansco and Zanussi became cult figures among the film societies and film students. An added attraction was that these films were not censored and portrayed female nudity artistically, much to the surprise of the Indian audience.

The fact that the government establishments and Leftists supported the Film Society Movement wholeheartedly, as a part of their wider political agenda made the acceptance of the Eastern Bloc films easier. The IFFIs always had a good package of films from these countries. Most of these film-makers were invited to visit India during the film festivals. As a journalist, I remember meeting Polish film-maker Zanussi and Cuban film-makers Humbarto Solas and Thomas Alea while they were on an official tour in India. Indian film critics too feasted on their films and wrote extensively for the mainline and regional media. Most of the film festival entries were detained by the diplomatic missions for a wider circulation through the film societies those days. This opened up a huge film library, which was mostly available free for screening films of film societies. This arrangement also suited the fragile economics of the film societies and attracted more members to the societies.

"The initial selection of the films was done by the cultural attaches of the different embassies and programme officers of the consular offices/cultural centres. The selection followed pattern like tributes to film eras, important film directors and illustrious actors

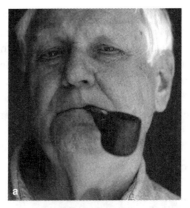
Miklos Jancso

Federico Fellini

Ingmar Bergman

Zoltan Fabry

Krzysztof Zanussi

Image 4.1 Popular western film-makers in the film society network in 1970s and 1980s.

Courtesy 4.1a to 4.1d: Wikipedia Creative Commons.
Courtesy 4.1e: James Joseph.

95

and actresses," pointed out Abhijit Ghosh Dastidar in his note to this author, a Kolkata-based film writer and a retired Indian postal service officer, who made it a habit to travel to all major film events in search of good films across India and the world. He writes his column in the Kolkata-based English weekly *Frontier*.[32]

The French, Canadian and Netherlands embassies were also equally supportive of the film society movement. According to Adoor Gopalakrishnan:

> The French embassy with a special audio visual section (they had a great collection of both classic and contemporary films in 16 mm which was freely available). Canadian High Commission(National Board of Canada which produced highly experiments films, prominent among them being Normal Mc Laren's unique creations exploring new frontiers in cinematic expressions). Netherlands (the Dutch) Embassy again with a large collection of documentaries significant among them being, *Mirror of Holland, Zoo, Glass, Rembrandt-Painter of Man* etc. by Bret Hanstra was another attraction for film societies. The Czech Embassy and their consulates with a large collection of the Czech New wave films in 16 mm was another source.[33]

FTII AND FFC FILMS MAKE AN ENTRY

The FTII, which was established in 1961, had started producing a line-up of well-trained and well-exposed film technicians and directors to the field. The FTII along with NFAI had also started a one-month summer film appreciation course, exposing film buffs to world cinema and starting a film appreciation course, which kicked off as the pioneer for the academic film studies in India.

The FFC had started funding some of the FTII graduates to make films. This circuit then began to throw up a new set of film-makers. This was in addition to film-makers such as Satyajit Ray, Ritwik Ghatak and Mrinal Sen who had been making waves in national and international film circuits. Ghatak even served as the vice principal of FTII, influencing a fresh set of young film-makers. Adoor Gopalakrishnan, Mani Kaul, Kumar Shahani, John Abraham, Girish Kasaravalli and a host of others were joining the ranks of Ray and his colleagues from Bengal. Most of these FTII graduates made their first film with FFC funding, giving an official stamp of the government of the day to "New Wave" films.

Kumar Shahani

G Aravindan

Girish Kasaravalli

Image 4.2 Popular Indian film-makers in film society network in 1970s and 1980s.

Courtesy 4.2a and 4.2c: Sasi Kumar, TVM.
Courtesy 4.2b: NM Kabir.

However, there was no governmental avenue for release of many of these films, and for some like Kumar Shahani and Mani Kaul, the film society circuit remained the only outlet for their FFC-produced films. Although Adoor, John and Girish Kasaravalli got theatre releases for their films, in their regions, Shyam Benegal, with his refreshingly new Hindi films, and G Aravindan, with his esoteric films, also began to excite the film society circuit and film festivals in India and abroad. Pattabhirama Reddy, Girish Karnad, BV Karanth, AK Kaul with his film *27 Down* carried forward the New Wave to their regions.

By 1975, the crowd of film-makers had captured the annual national awards and many an international award at Cannes, Berlin and Moscow, jettisoning the regular mass appeal films. A new set of technicians, actors and film-makers entered the regular film industry from FTII, giving it a fresh outlook and technical quality. Many of them totally rejected the popular style of film-making, and with government patronage, they were placed as the new face of Indian films. FFC Chairman BK Karanjia, who patronised New Wave films with lavish funding, was later removed during the Emergency, as the few in the government did not agree with the way New Wave was discrediting the glamorous popular films. However, Ms Indira Gandhi reaffirmed her commitment to new wave when she came back as prime minister after a three-year break by appointing a new Film Enquiry Committee under the Karnataka cultural icon Dr Shivarama Karanth.

There was also a new set of film-makers popularised by the film societies at its peak of popularity in the late 1970s and 1980s. They included Mani Kaul, Kumar Sahani, Saeed Mirza, Shyam Benegal, AK Kaul and Govind Nihalani in Hindi; Ritwik Ghatak, Mrinal Sen, Budha Dev Das Gupta, Gautam Ghosh, Aparna Sen and Utpalendu Chakravarthy in Bengla; Pattabhirama Reddy, Girish Karnad, BV Karanth and Girish Kasaravalli in Kannada; Adoor Gopalakrishnan, G Aravindan, John Abraham, TV Chandran, KR Mohanan and Shaji N Karun in Malayalam; Jabbar Patel in Marathi; Jhanu Barua in Assamese; and Nirad Mohapatra in Odiya. Most of them were trained in film-making in FTII and were award-winning film-makers either at the national or at international film festivals. They all took the film society network and its members as their basic audience, as the films were made with aesthetic appeal and not on a box office formulae. Film Society membership in the 1960s, 1970s and 1980s was a connoisseur's prized possession in most urban centres of India and they feasted on these New Wave films, making their arrivals as happening events in the media as well as in public, although the box office response to most of these films was lukewarm.

Mrinal Sen, a contemporary of Satyajit Ray, explained the philosophy and economics behind his kind of film-making, which, he believes, is best appreciated by the minority audience in and outside India as follows[34]:

> You cannot expect large number of people to see your films. Any sensible film maker, when he makes films, his films are not that reachable to everyone.... For instance take fiction.... If you read novels.... Popular novels are very different.... Even then I want to

be popular…. But I am a popular failure most of the time…in the box office. But then that is why my arithmetic is very simple…. I make low budget films. People say film making is an expensive process. I do not agree with them…. Not all agree with them (repeat). Films can be made low cost. I have been making low cost films…. If you make low costs films and if you can get to the larger minority audience scattered across the world. The larger minority audience … who would be seeing your film and that way I keep going. That is in spite of the fact that I am a popular failure at the box office, I keep going.

Sen and Arun Kaul of the Film Forum (Bombay) had come out with a manifesto for the New Indian Cinema, when they collaborated for the film *Bhuvan Shome*, which is considered the first film that ushered in the new wave in Hindi films. The budget of the film financed by the erstwhile FFC was ₹0.15 million and was totally shot on location introducing actors like Utpal Dutt and Suhasini Mulay to Hindi films.

The New Wave films challenged the approach of the popular film-makers to the film-making itself and also brought about a change in the taste among the viewers. The impact was manifold. The studio-based films became a thing of the past, just as New Wave films, the good old Bollywood began to adopt to outdoors to foreign locations and technology. The FTII-trained actors, cinematographers, audiographers and editors ventured into Bollywood, giving even the popular films a fresh look in approach, content, technology and even financing. Shyam Bengal received funds by Amul Milk Cooperative to make a feature film on the cooperative. By the 1990s a film-maker Sudhir Misra,[35] son of a Lucknow Film Society activist, began to make films that were in mainstream but totally different and still popular. FTII-trained actors like Jaya Bhaduri Bachchan,[36] Shatrughan Sinha,[37] Naseeruddin Shah[38] and Om Puri[39] established themselves as mainline Hindi film actors, and most of them were introduced by the New Wave film-makers. Though the New Wave film-makers and actors got into the mainstream film circuits, the film society films were still out of the normal film screening circuit.

CREATION OF ALTERNATE NETWORK OF FILM SCREENING

I visited Bharat Bhavan in Kolkata to see what was left of the CFS and met the president, Pradipta Shanker Sen, in 2012. The one hour I spent at the CFS office, under the gaze of a huge portrait of Satyajit Ray, gave me an idea about the present state of affairs of CFS and many existing film societies across India.

Most films are now on DVDs and a projection system makes it possible to hold a film screening in a house. This is the transition of not just CFS but most existing film societies, from the regular 35-mm cinema houses and 16-mm projectors, now to the digital projectors.

In Kozhikode, Kerala, I was told the oldest *Aswini* Film Society, frequented by film-makers G Aravindan and John Abraham, survives on a gift of a digital projector by some well-wishers from the Gulf countries. A majority of the film societies turned to digital projections, and only booked theatres if they had a film festival, that too supported by local governments or similar agencies with huge funds.

Very few film societies have a screening theatre and cultural complex of their own, such as *Suchitra* in Bangalore, Ritwik Sadan of the Berhampore Film Society, Midnapore Film Society in West Bengal and the Karimnagar Film Society owned Film Bhavan in Andhra Pradesh. All of them too had come up on government allotted land.

The *Suchitra* Film Society promoted the *Suchitra* Cinema Academy Trust, the first of its kind in India, and construction of the auditorium was inaugurated by Satyajit Ray on 8 January 1980. The first phase of the project was completed in September 1981 and the second phase in August 1986.

In Kolkata, Nandan[40] Film and Cultural Complex built by the then Left Front government were the by-product of the fledgling Film Society Movement of the city. In Thiruvananthapuram, the two cinema houses, Kairali and Kala Bhavan, were also established by the state government catering to the film society culture of the city. The Kerala government has taken its role in creating alternate film screens and went on to build 11 cinema houses across the state under its Kerala Film Development Corporation (KSFDC) for the promotion of alternate cinema, although they are also available to popular film releases.[41]

Throughout the years, film societies were using small halls or academic institutions and their 16-mm projectors for their screenings. In Delhi, as the Central government was involved in the movement, the auditoriums of Films Division, Sapru House and ministry of education were made available for screening for the DFS. In Kolkata, the Sarala Mandir School and other halls were the favourite screening places of the film societies. In Mumbai, the hall of the National Centre for Performing Arts was the hot favourite of the film societies. In Thiruvananthapuram, a supportive Chief Minister C Achuta Menon, in the 1970s, asked the public relations department to install a 35-mm projector at the Tagore Centenary Hall to promote screenings by the film societies. "The chief minister was himself in the audience, many times," says *Chitralekha*'s Managing Director, Kulathoor Bhaskaran Nair. For 16-mm shows, the Museum Hall and Engineers Hall in the heart of the city were all available to the film societies.

The largest bill for any film society screening was the theatre/hall hiring charges, and hence with the fragile economics of the societies, most opted for 16-mm screenings at the local friendly educational institutions, with a 16-mm projector to screen the film loaned from NFAI. The archive had a good library of 16-mm films.

As the 16-mm projector and its musical sound vanished from the background of the film society screenings, film society activist KR Manoj made a film, in video, on the projector and its role to popularise the film society culture in Kerala. Such was the emotional association of 16-mm film format and the projector itself for the film societies. In the early days of *Chitralekha*, Adoor Gopalakrishan himself operated the 16-mm projector, to avoid confusion in loading rolls of the film.

In 1983, reviewing the Film Society Movement, Chidananda Das Gupta noted:

> Paris has some 50 art house theatres, constantly showing film classics from all over the world. India has 216 film societies, but no art theatres. If 150, even 50, art theatres are established in the major cities in India and if censorship standards are somewhat relaxed, will the film societies survive?[42]

Clearly, despite Indira Gandhi's (as information minister of India) indulgence in giving an instruction to the state government to provide government land for art house theatres across India, very few film societies could ever afford to utilise it effectively.

ORGANISING THE RIGHT AUDIENCE

Who were these people out to make a difference in the film culture of India? Dr Pathy, the noted documentary film-maker, D Jefferies, AQ Jairazbhoy and A Padamsee were among those who founded India's first film society, the Amateur Cine Society of India, Bombay in the late 1930s, according to Chidananda Das Gupta. The CFS was started by Das Gupta and Satyajit Ray and his friends who had a deep interest in films. Later, Calcutta University vice chancellor was to become the president of CFS, attracting the cream of intellectuals and artists to the movement. The Patna Film Society was again formed by an educationist, Vijaya Mulay, and her friends. The Lucknow Film Society was the pioneering contribution of Professor Kailas Nath Kaul of Lucknow Botanical Gardens and father of Gautam Kaul, the present FFSI president.

The DFS was formed more or less by the officers associated with the ministry of education. The Roorkie Film Society was, of course, formed by the academics of the town, particularly the Central Road Transport Research Organisation. In Bangalore, the film societies were flagged off in various public sector units and Indian Institute of Science. In Madras, it was more of an offshoot of an involvement of the upper strata of society and the cultural centres of consulates of countries like the United States and Canada, with local politician Ammu Swaminadhan leading the torch of Film Society Movement in the already film-crazy city.

In Thiruvananthapuram, it was Adoor Gopalakrishnan, an FTII graduate, and his literary friends who formed the film society. They could carry the entire literary and academic crowd of the city, and later the professionals from the Indian Space Research Organisation (ISRO) in the outskirts of the city started a second unit. In Chandigarh, the PG Medical institute witnessed the formation of the film society. In Bhopal, it was again the students with the help of their teachers who formed the International Film Society.

In her document recommending the formation of FFSI, Marie Seton wrote in 1957:

> An incomplete survey of the film societies in India shows that there is a spasmodically active society in Bombay. In Calcutta, a film society has been inaugurated as a result of my six-day seminar in that city. In Madras the British Council has been running an excellent film society, which will become independent as soon as there is a reasonable possibility of it being able to survive on its own. In Bangalore the Indian Institute of Sciences has been running a Scientific Film Society. In Hyderabad the Central Laboratories are planning to form a film society, while various people in Ahmadabad and Delhi hope to create their societies in the near future.[43]

Noting the enthusiasm of the academics to take film appreciation in India to a different level Marie Seton along with Children's
Film Society of India had proposed UGC to organise university film
clubs, which could have led to a long-term development of the Film
Society Movement. However, the heavy bureaucratic set-up of the
UGC scuttled the move. Sashidharan, the NFAI director, who succeeded PK Nair remembers a Delhi University lecturer being posted
at NFAI to work out the programme for university film clubs. Vijaya
Mulay too remembers her consultancy arrangement with UGC on
this project. However, today the NFAI has no such coordination with
UGC, although many universities have started film studies in their
mass communications curriculum across India.

FILM APPRECIATION AS A CLASS ACT

The British Raj, along with many of its faults, also gave India much
needed modern education. Many bright young Indian minds gained
an English education, and many in India found English education to
be a window to the world, opening up new possibilities of the indus-
trialised and fast-changing world outside India.

Vijaya Mulay wrote about her entry into film society as
follows[44]:

> I learnt about language and grammar of cinema when as a student
> I joined the University of Leeds in UK in 1946 and after a steady diet
> of good cinema, found it difficult to digest the stuff that was then
> being shown in commercial cinemas (back home).

She along with like-minded people went on to form the Patna
Film Society on her return to India.

Commenting on the growth of the DFS, eminent film critic
Amita Malik, wrote: "Its membership was initially confined to civil
servants, people in involved in cultural activity, people from universities, both academics and students and usual sprinkling of upper
classes in search of culture."[45] A look at the other early film societies
also points out this fact of the "aspirational class" of independent
India, out to prove a point with films. CFS was full of early film enthusiasts, just as Bombay Film Society, Lucknow Film Society education-
ists, so were the Roorkie Film Society and Patna Film Society.

With the ministry of education and Marie Seton playing a lead
role, many educational institutions jumped on the bandwagon of film
societies progressively. "Enthusiasm for cinema became respectable,

and a wide range of people rushed to film societies," summed up Chidananda Das Gupta, in his introduction to his book.[46]

Commenting on the art of film appreciation, the first professor of film appreciation at FTII, Professor Satish Bahadur, said in an interview:

> Distinction of quality already existing on other arts. Cinema being the product of 20th century is always been popular entertainment. Out of 100 films may be one or two could be put in the criteria of a good books are being made.

The professor had made a 15-part television series under the UGC's country-wide classroom series on how to appreciate films.[47]

The professionals working in public sector units and scientific establishments in Bangalore led the Film Society Movement, and in many non-metros, the academia and literary crowd joined the movement. In Mumbai, the film technicians and film-makers like KA Abbas carried the torch. In the state of Kerala, the Library Movement and the Little Magazine Movement of the 1960s and 1970s added to the interest in film societies, leading to its spread across the state, many of which are still continuing in various forms and shapes. The political support from the Left parties ensured that wherever they had a foothold, they looked upon film societies as part of their cultural sensitisation. The regional branch of FFSI in Kerala is run by the activists associated with CPI (M). The same is the case of those associated with the societies in Kolkata.

The 1966 government decision to exempt film society films from censorship brought yet another kind of members into the movement. The European films itself reflected the sexual permissiveness of the continent, and nudity of female characters was part of films from France, Sweden or Eastern bloc. Till the time of the "video revolution," the lure of uncensored films also brought in a set of people into the film societies.

PK Nair observed as follows[48]:

> By the seventies societies had sprung up in every nook and corner of the country, even in some remote places one never heard of before. The misguided proliferation brought all sorts of people to the movement. People who had never heard of a Flaherty or Ozu,[49] or could distinguish between Einstein and Eisenstein, emerged as

the new breed of film society organisers. Presumably, their only aim was to climb up the social bandwagon or getting invited to an Embassy cocktail party. The craze for watching uncensored films gave a membership boost to number of societies and even some of the organizers went out of the way to schedule such films in their programmes and take pride in the fact they have the largest viewer ship, using the same yardsticks as that of a commercial exhibitor, equating the two and thereby defeating the very purpose of a film society.

From finding out of a new meaning and giving class dimension to the films and its appreciation and also a route for uncensored films, the Film Society Movement began to redefine the way Indians looked at films. The FFSI, NFAI, and diplomatic missions never allowed themselves to be vehicles of crass films and only class films allowed were in the Film Society Movement, making it yet another class act of the aspirational society of a young independent nation. With active patronage from the government, the academia and professionals, Indians and their films moved away from the clutches of Hollywood and began to experiment with its own film aesthetics, some inspired by the European, Latin American and Japanese films, which were freely available in the film society network.

NOTES*

1. http://cherianwrites.blogspot.in/2016/02/from-nfai-collection-national-cinema.html
2. RM Ray, ed., *Indian Cinema in Retrospect: Speeches of the 1955 Seminar* (New Delhi: Sangeet Natak Academy).
3. Marie Seton. *Preface of Portrait of a Director: Satyajit Ray* (New Delhi: Penguin Books, 2003), p. 58.
4. http://mib.nic.in/
5. https://en.wikipedia.org/wiki/Bollywood
6. RM Ray, ed., *Indian Cinema in Retrospect: Speeches of the 1955 Seminar.*
7. Marie Seton. *Preface of Portrait of a Director: Satyajit Ray.*
8. http://cherianwrites.blogspot.in/2016/02/from-nfai-collection-national-cinema.html
9. https://en.wikipedia.org/wiki/Indian_states_ranking_by_literacy_rate
10. RM Ray, ed., *Indian Cinema in Retrospect*, p. 29.
11. http://cherianwrites.blogspot.in/2016/02/from-nfai-collection-national-cinema.html
12. NFAI Library Notes.
13. Marie Seton. *Film Appreciation* (New Delhi: NCERT, 1956).
14. Chidananda Das Gupta, *The Cinema of Satyajit Ray* (New Delhi: Viking, 1980).
15. HN Narahari Rao, ed., *The Film Society Movement in India* (Mumbai: Asian Film Foundation, 2009), p. 71.
16. https://en.wikipedia.org/wiki/Odessa
17. Chidananda Das Gupta. *Seeing Is Believing: Selected Writings on Cinema* (Delhi: Viking, 2008), p. 85.

18. Interaction: Samik Bandyopadhyaya. https://en.wikipedia.org/wiki/Samik_Bandyopadhyay

19. Mari Seton, "The Film Movement in India", *Indian Film Quarterly*, 1956. http://cherianwrites.blogspot.in/2016/02/marie-seton-from-cfs-published-in.html

20. HN Narahari Rao, ed., *The Film Society Movement in India* (Mumbai: Asian Film Foundation, 2009), p. 21.

21. Ibid., p. 35.

22. Ibid., p. 73.

23. IFSON-1981-NFAI library.

24. RTI reply from NFAI.

25. https://en.wikipedia.org/wiki/Jean-Luc_Godard

26. https://en.wikipedia.org/wiki/Werner_Herzog

27. https://en.wikipedia.org/wiki/Federico_Fellini

28. https://en.wikipedia.org/wiki/Ingmar_Bergman

29. https://en.wikipedia.org/wiki/Mikl%C3%B3s_Jancs%C3%B3

30. https://en.wikipedia.org/wiki/Krzysztof_Zanussi

31. https://en.wikipedia.org/wiki/Akira_Kurosawa

32. http://cherianwrites.blogspot.in/2016/02/soruce-of-films-and-film-programs-of.html

33. Interaction with Adoor Gopalakrishnan.

34. http://vkcherian.blogspot.in/2012/06/mrinal-sen-at-90-riding-wave-of.html

35. https://en.wikipedia.org/wiki/Sudhir_Mishra

36. https://en.wikipedia.org/wiki/Jaya_Bachchan

37. https://en.wikipedia.org/wiki/Shatrughan_Sinha

38. https://en.wikipedia.org/wiki/Naseeruddin_Shah

39. https://en.wikipedia.org/wiki/Om_Puri

40. https://en.wikipedia.org/wiki/Nandan_(Kolkata)

41. http://www.ksfdc.in/html/cinematheatres.php

42. Chidananda Das Gupta. *Seeing Is Believing: Selected Writings on Cinema*, p. 99.

43. http://cherianwrites.blogspot.in/2016/02/marie-seton-from-cfs-published-in.html

44. Chidananda Das Gupta. *Seeing Is Believing: Selected Writings on Cinema,* Introductory Note by Vijaya Mulay.

45. http://cherianwrites.blogspot.in/2016/03/the-role-of-film-societies-by-amita.html

46. Chidananda Das Gupta. *The Cinema of Satyajit Ray* (New Delhi: NBT, 1980), Introduction.

47. https://en.wikipedia.org/wiki/Satish_Bahadur

48. http://cherianwrites.blogspot.in/2016/02/havefilm-societies-lost-their-relevance.html

49. https://en.wikipedia.org/wiki/Yasujir%C5%8D_Ozu

* All websites accessed on 16 June 2016.

Prime Minister Jawahar Lal Nehru inaugurates the first film seminar held in February 1955 by Sangeet Natak Akademi.

Courtesy: Sangeet Natak Akademi.

PK Nair, Professor Satish Bahadur and Professor Shyamala Vanarse at the annual FTII–NFAI Film Appreciation Course, which continues to be an annual feature even today at Pune.

Courtesy: Apurva Bahadur (son of Professor Satish Bahadur).

Prime Minister Indira Gandhi with the FFSI delegation, 1982.
Courtesy: FFSI/Asian Film Foundation, Mumbai.

Shooting still of *Piku*—A Shoojit Sircar film starring Amitabh Bachchan and
Deepika Padukone. *Piku* is the best example of the Margi integration into
Desi, by a director who is a product of the film society culture of Delhi.
Courtesy: Mr Sircar's unit.

Kairali Theatre, first of the 11 cinema houses of the Kerala State Film Development Corporation (KSFDC) to promote alternate films in the state.
Courtesy: Author.

A Film Appreciation Course at FTII–NFAI.
Courtesy: NFAI.

Mrinal Sen at his South Kolkata flat, 2012.
Mrinal *da* was the President of the IFFS
and also FFSI, a rare honour for any
film-maker from India.

Courtesy: Author.

The then Vice President of India
S Radhakrishnan and Indira Gandhi at the
inaugural ceremony of the Indian Film
Seminar, the first major consultation of Nehr
Government with film industry in
February 1955.

Courtesy: Sangeet Natak Akademi.

Pradipta Shanker Sen (centre) and colleagues at the CFS office in 2012.
Courtesy: Author.

CHAPTER 5

The Driving Forces Behind the Film Society Movement

WHO WERE THE FILM SOCIETY MEMBERS? A PERSONAL ACCOUNT

Looking back, as a degree student, I ask myself what made me join the *Chitralekha* and *Chalachithra* film societies in 1976. Clearly, my interest in the literature and arts led me to the film societies. The fact that one could see films from various countries of the world, just as one could read books from various countries in a library, drove me to film societies. The library movement that had taken root in almost all the villages in Kerala had already put me onto the library circuit as a high school student. For me, it was a natural progression that I moved from books on to films.

There was no television in Kerala's capital those days, and films were the only medium of mass entertainment. Slowly, I found myself among various groups of people discussing literature, films, art and politics. I also found myself in the esteemed company of writers, theatre personalities and film-makers. One of the most rewarding memories of those days was being in a queue at the city's Sreekumar Cinema house, where the English film *One Flew Over Cuckoo's Nest* by Milos Forman was being shown. I found myself standing and waiting behind the ace film-maker Adoor Gopalakrishnan and his wife, Sunanda, in the queue. After his first two films, Adoor had already become a celebrity in Kerala.

When I was in the second year of my degree course, I began to spot film-maker G Aravindan, writer Padmarajan, who had entered film-making, and theatre activist Professor Narendra Prasad (became a popular film actor later) among the film society crowd at Tagore Centenary Hall. There were my lifelong friends like film writer MF Thomas, who was the secretary of *Chitralekha*, and Vijayakrishnan, the film critic, and an entire group of students from Trivandrum Fine Arts School to hang out with.

HOW DID THEY BEGIN IT?

Adoor, recounting the formation of the *Chitralekha* Film Society in 1965, said[1]:

> I am an academically and professionally trained filmmaker. I have studied cinema at the Film Institute in Pune (second batch). I was very clear about what I wanted to do. In fact, I went on to start the movement in Kerala because firstly, I wanted the intelligentsia in Kerala to become aware of a cinema of high caliber that existed in the world outside. Also, I wanted to continue watching international cinema after leaving the Film Institute. The Film Society Movement is not a mass movement. It is aimed at a small, niche and discreet audience, good critics and passionate film lovers.

Chitralekha was inaugurated by the then governor of Kerala, Bhagawan Sahay, in July 1965, with the city's literary figures witnessing the event organised by Adoor and his friends from the theatre and literary fields.

The film society crowd was a mix of the literary people, students like me, state and Central government officials, college lecturers, bank employees, officials from ISRO and Keltron, the fledging public sector electronic company of Kerala till the 1980s. I recall Keltron's first chairman, the iconic KPP Nambiar, who rose to become the secretary of the Central Electronics Department, as a member of the *Chitralekha* Film Society. Nambiar often used to come with his wife to the screenings. KN Raj, a former Delhi University vice chancellor, who had established the Centre for Development Studies (CDS) near the *Chitralekha* film cooperative complex, was another celebrity member of *Chitralekha*. The membership of the society promoted by Adoor was a coveted one in those days, with the elite from all circles of the city vying for it, recalled MF Thomas, who was the secretary of the film society in its last years.

Thiruvananthapuram, being the capital of Kerala, was not just the seat of the state's political power but was the favourite centre of the academia and literary figures, as well as many a Left leaning institutions. Malayalese had come to accept films as a serious art form, with film-makers Adoor and Aravindan winning national awards. Film societies began to be seen as charmed circles of cultural, political activists and intellectuals, who thronged them in numbers in the 1970s and 1980s. "After the screenings, we used to walk to the bus stop and discuss the film as routine act, till we got our respective buses home," recalled Vijayakrishnan, the noted Malayalam film critic.[2] The "we," he described, were Gopi, the *Bharat* award-winning actor of Adoor's film *Kodiyettam* and MF Thomas, who became the secretary of *Chitralekha* and a film critic. *Chitralekha* was the cradle of emerging new medium as well as many future celebrities, like Gopi and a host of new actors, technicians and directors in Malayalam films.

Watching films from various countries made me curious about journals like British Film Institute's journal *Sight and Sound*, which was available along with various British newspapers at the local British Council Library. They helped me track the developments happening in international cinema. I also found American film publications in the university library and books like *Films As An Art*.

There were many like me, in other cities, getting initiated to the world of films, beyond what was available in the usual cinema houses. TV Chandran, the National Award-winning Malayalam film-maker, recalled his days with the film society. "I used to jump the gates of USIS in Bangalore and later in Chennai to see films. I used to make detailed notes of each film." Just as film societies, the screenings of the United States Information Service (USIS), the Alliance Française and the Max Mueller Bhavan in metros had also become the favourite haunts of film buffs in the 1980s and 1990s, and continue to be so even now.

Abhija Ghosh, a JNU scholar, stated as follows[3]:

Film societies signified different initiatives in different locales and among different groups, ranging from selective and alternative cultural groups, cooperative communities to powerful pedagogical and political forces generating discourses on cinema. Among other things, the movement witnessed productive collaborations, long-lasting friendships, debates on cinema, censorship and membership, internal fissures, and problems of sustenance. However, these aspects involving the members of the societies and cinephiles have been overwhelmed by institutional discourses on 'good cinema' and auteur studies of preferred filmmakers.

The brain behind the movement, Chidananda Gas Gupta, too defines the Film Society Movement as "homogeneous groups which attracted people with certain common cultural backgrounds." It is well known that Das Gupta's CFS drew a huge crowd from the academia. Calcutta University Vice Chancellor Nirmal Kumar Siddhanto was its president when CFS restarted in 1956.

Pradipta Sen, who was a member from those days, recollected the golden days of CFS as follows[4]:

> The membership grew from 250–300 to 2500. Apurva Kumar Chanda, DPI Education, of West Bengal also got associated with CFS. BN Sircar of New theatres and the Eastern India Motion Pictures Association, secretary were all patrons of CFS. *Prachi* Cinema-all Bengali cinema house allowed free shows. In early 60s we organised an, Eisenstein film festival at the Academy of Fine Arts to full house and even Ray, who came to see the Russian Maestro's film had to sit on the stairs, such was the rush.

The act of seeing films was treated with such a passion that even Ray could not resist creating his own compilation of music for *Battleship Potemkin*, when he saw it for the 22nd time. "To the surprise of the visiting Eisenstein archive curator from Moscow, Ray described the incident," recalled Samik Bandyopadhyay,[5] formerly of Seagull books. Ray was playing the long playing records (LPs) of music he compiled at the show and could not produce a track to the excited curator. *Battleship* was the prized procession of CFS in the late 1940s itself and the 16-mm print continued to be the very first film of pre-*Pather Panchali* days of the most film societies and remains one of the most screened film of most societies even today.

The DFS's biggest draw was the vice president of FFSI, Indira Gandhi, who became the I&B minister in Lal Bahadur Shastri's Cabinet and later prime minister. In 1964, Gandhi, as I&B minister had to sit in a room adjacent to the projection room at Sapru House Hall, where the Ingmar Bergman's *Wild Strawberries* was shown. Freedom fighter Aruna Asaf Ali and the then Defense Minister VK Krishna Menon were patrons of DFS, apart from the officials of various ministries, academia from Delhi University and the city's elite. *Akka* (Vijaya Mulay) recalls Krishna Menon rushing in to see Satyajit Ray's film *Devi*, which was previewed at DFS. IK Gujral, who succeeded Ms Gandhi, as I&B minister, and later became prime minister of India, was a treasurer of FFSI during the 1960s.

It seems that the BFS was the most elite of the lot. Led by RE Hawkins, the general manager of OUP, BFS had ST Berkeley Hill, VM Vijakar, VN Raiji, Padma Raiji, MP Strimpel, J Farbtein, A Bhaskara

Rao and KL Khandapur of the Film Division. By 1962, Jag Mohan, MV Krishnaswamy was also in the committee. The BFS was closed in 1962 and its funds amounting to ₹1,500 were transferred to the Film Forum. According to a note by RE Hawkins, "The first Indian film to be screened by the society was *Uljhan* produced and directed by NR Acharya. The Director and the cameraman were present during the discussions (which followed). In the same year Chetan Anand's *Neecha Ghar* and *Ishara* were shown."[6]

Adoor recalled the initial growth of the movement in Kerala as follows[7]:

> *Chitralekha* was not only the first film society to be formed, but it served as the nucleus of the movement. We were promoting and supporting enthusiasts in each town to form Societies and we shared the films we sourced for screenings and supplied relevant literature with them to be distributed to their members. We became a virtual voluntary agency to coordinate the film societies in Kerala, much before FFSI actively began to undertake it. We also motivated the University Students Unions to conduct film appreciation camps and enlightened them on the new culture of cinema.

In Mumbai and Bangalore, the professionals of various public sector units, such as Babha Atomic Research Council, Bharat Electronics and ISRO, found the booming Film Society Movement an attractive place to groom their interests in films. "The scientists from BARC were regulars at our screenings," recalls V Sasikumar, who was then working at the department of telecommunications, in Mumbai. In Bangalore, Nara Hari Rao, an engineer with the Bharat Electronics started the *Suchitra* Film Society and rose to become the FFSI president. In Thiruvananthapuram, *Chalachithra* was floated by the engineers of ISRO. George Mathew of *Chalachithra* and VK Joseph, who is the secretary of Kerala FFSI (2015), were employees of ISRO. Soorya Krishnamoorthy, who later parted from *Chalachithra* to begin his own cultural outfit, *Soorya*, was also from ISRO.

A NEW NATION'S YEARNING FOR A PLACE UNDER THE SUN

While the individual film societies were blooming in the metros of India, the government of the young nation too woke up to the immense possibilities that films as a medium had thrown up.

Setting the agenda for the 1955 Sangeet Natak Akademi seminar on films, its Chairman Dr Rajamannar, while addressing the inaugural meeting attended by Prime Minister Nehru, said, "The film should also be judged by the standards which we employ to judge any other work of art. The film is a new art form, which is in a continuous state of development.... India must and will make its distinctive contribution to the film art of the world and I am confident it will."[8]

The seminar directors were Prithviraj Kapoor and Devika Rani, and the seminar was attended by the vice president of India, S Radhakrishnan, and Indira Gandhi, along with a host of film-makers from across India. Admitting that the influence of films in India was greater than that of newspapers and books (due to literacy levels in 1955), Prime Minister Nehru went on to say that films have to be "treated realistically as something of the highest importance in the life of a country." Nehru ruled out the government setting the agenda for the film industry, but went on to say that negative tendencies like war mongering through films would be stopped and the government itself would produce films for children and other films without competing with the industry as such.[9]

Nehru's daughter and successor, Indira Gandhi, too emphasised on the need for quality work of art for films in her speech presenting the National Awards of 1966. "Quality comes from intellect, technical mastery, and the determination to be honest. Above all quality comes from courage, courage to be different, to be non-conformist," Indira Gandhi pointed out.[10] The statement of the first vice president of FFSI and ardent admirer of Satyajit Ray remained self-explanatory.

Both Jawaharlal Nehru and Indira Gandhi had clearly set their agenda for films, extending all official patronage to film as an art and also the development of an audience for it. Prime Minister Indira Gandhi, even after relinquishing her post of the vice president of FFSI, lent her social secretary Usha Bhagat as its joint secretary, thus keeping a close eye on the Film Society Movement.[11]

THE POLITICAL PATRONAGE

Prime Minister Nehru, the Oxford-educated scholar statesman, had clear plans for a mass medium like cinema. In 1950, he formed an expert committee of films for a new policy regime on films under SK Patil, which made far reaching recommendations. In 1951, he had appointed a French Indian, Jean Bhownagary, as the advisor to the I&B ministry for flagging off the first IFFI. He also invited Marie Seton from the British Film Institute to evangelise films for educational purpose across India and to precipitate arrival of the budding film societies into an organised movement. A fact confirmed by Shyam Benegal, a veteran film-maker of the new cinema of India, who became the president of FFSI in 2009.

> When India became Independent in 1947, the leadership of the time felt that Cinema had a role to play in the film development of the country. People like Jawaharlal Nehru and others felt that Cinema, an important component of popular culture, had great potential in terms of supporting the development of the country.... In addition to this it set up a high level committee under SK Patil in 1951–52 to look into the problems of the film industry itself. This resulted in formulating a film policy that included:
>
> (a) A Film Finance Corporation for financing of feature films.
> (b) A film school to train filmmakers in all disciplines.
> (c) A children films society to encourage the making of films for children.
> (d) Re-organisation of the film certification policy (which until then followed the British Censor Code).[12.]

However, since a policy on films was implemented later, Adoor Gopalakrishnan, Benegal's contemporary does not give full credit to Nehru for that. He prefers to give credit to Indira Gandhi for bringing Marie Seton to spread the Film Society Movement. Answering the same question, whether the FS and new cinema were a result of Nehruvian policy initiative, Adoor said; "I can't say if it was a planned initiative by the Nehruvians." But the SK Patil Committee appointed by the Nehru Government had recommended many measures to improve the standards of the Indian film industry, such as setting up a film institute, institution of National Awards, a film financing institution and the National Film Archive."[13]

The sequence of activities by the Government of India indicates that without the political and personal patronage of the country's first Prime Minister Jawaharlal Lal Nehru, there should not have been any Film Society Movement in India at all. Prime Minister Nehru and his trusted aide VK Krishna Menon brought in Marie Seton to advise the government on how to promote films as an "educational tool." While in India, she wrote a book called *Film Appreciation*, which was published by the ministry of education. Few other monographs on film appreciation written by Marie were also published by NCERT during those days.

The formation of FFSI in 1959 was followed by a report by Marie Seton to the ministry of education after her lecture tour of the various Indian cities. Gandhi, herself, became associated with FFSI as its vice president. The government allowed FFSI to import 16 films for circulation from its affiliated members. It also provided an exemption of censorship for FFSI-circulated films. States were asked to provide entertainment tax exemption for screening by the film societies.

Indira Gandhi even intervened personally from time to time with state chief minister's to ensure the exemption of taxes was not a deterrent for the smooth running of the film societies. The only other film expert committee constituted by the Government of India, after the committee of 1951–52, was in 1980, when Indira Gandhi was the prime minister. The committee was headed by Dr K Shivarama Karanth, an eminent Kannada literary figure. No other prime minister, after Gandhi, showed any particular interest in films, and the film field was left to fend for itself. The political leaders are content with being seen with film stars and film personalities at India's International Festivals and National Film Award functions over the years. In his first review of the FFSI in 1965, Das Gupta wrote: "The Union Minister for Information and Broadcasting has requested all State Governments to exempt all member societies of Federation from entertainment taxes and other levies. The Federation has so far received a total of ₹10,000 from the Union Government, ₹5,000 from Sangeet Natak Academy and ₹3,000 from Sangeet Natak Sangam, Madras, as grant-in-aid.[14]

The Central Government's grant for FFSI continues even today, though FFSI has not received the annual grant of ₹0.6 million it was allocated sometime back.[15]

THE ACADEMIC, ARTISTIC INTERVENTIONS

For any work of art to flourish, it needs appreciation and criticism; appreciation to encourage the artist and criticism to look at the form and structure of the work of art. Film appreciation was seen as more of amazement with starry eyes, by the actors and artists, and there was hardly any film criticism in India in the 1950s till the 1960s. Though the likes of KA Abbas started off as a film critic, the genre as such was more of stories about the films and not analysing the film with its technical and aesthetic tools. This was one of the reasons films were not yet accepted as a mainline art, like writing, theatre or painting or music, though the films had all these in it. The absence of literature on films, its technicalities and its developing aesthetics added to the problem in the 1940s and 1950s. That is why Vijaya Mulay talks about creating *rasiks* through film societies, and the late K Bikram Singh,[16] erstwhile Film Forum activist and a film-maker, talked about the needs to have classic approach in appreciating films. "Classic," he defined as in music or painting.

Chidananda Das Gupta wrote over 24 pages explaining the concept of *Margi* and *Desi*, the traditional 'classical and folk' divide in his last book.[17] He went on to defend this classification and pointed out that, "One advantage of accepting the age old division between *Margi* and *Desi* or classical and folk (more correctly pop, in the urban context) is that neither category can then demand the non-existence of the other." All of them were emphasising the need for the classic approach to film as an art, which the film societies promoted by their screenings, publications and discussions.

The first editorial of the *Film Quarterly* of CFS, in 1956, too emphasised the need to bring in the *Margi* aspect to Indian films through informed criticism and literature on films. "As a journal of the Calcutta Film Society, it represents and becomes an instrument of a new movement to promote the growth of a better cinema and better audience. Its objects are to develop the two elements which are so lacking in our cinema and film criticism; thought and sensitivity."

In her memorandum to the Government of India for the formation of FFSI, Marie Seton addressed the issue of film appreciation and criticism. "In order that a film society should be dynamic and serve its fullest purpose, it is essential to have discussions and lead the members into its fullest participation. Further, it is essential that any central film institute keeps in constant dynamic contact with film societies and the real desires of the public so that both can grow." Seton was equally keen that India promotes university film clubs to enlist a new generation to the Film Society Movement.[18]

THE UNIVERSITY FILM COUNCIL AND FTII–NFAI SUMMER RESIDENCY AT PUNE

The suggestion found an immediate welcome at the UGC headed by CD Deshmukh (1896–1982), a distinguished civil servant who had resigned from Nehru's cabinet as finance minister and was appointed UGC chairman for five years (1956–61). Deshmukh, who was also the first chairman of the Reserve Bank of India (RBI) and had held other important positions, appeared to be an enthusiastic votary of Film Society Movement, as he established a UFC, and headed by former I&B minister at Nehru's cabinet RR Diwakar (1894–1990), another politician scholar from Karnataka.

On new year's eve (1959–60), the Film Council was inaugurated by the UGC chairman. Inaugurating the first meeting of the UFC, UGC Chairman CD Deshmukh said, "the Film Society Movement in Universities and colleges would definitely bring about a healthy trend in the production of feature films. The film medium could be utilised to act as a positive and corrective force in shaping a balanced view of life among the youth," as he was quoted in the Times of India's reportage of the event.[19]

The UGC had approved the scheme to start film clubs in affiliated universities and 14 of the individual universities had already approved the proposal. The UGC appointed Marie Seton as the technical advisor and instituted a grant of ₹5,001 for those institutions under it to form film clubs.

In his inaugural speech, chairman of the council RR Diwakar said that the council would make available 16 outstanding films of the times, both Indian and foreign to the University Film Clubs. The films were those which the students did not have a chance to see at "commercial theatres." Mahendra Nath, the member secretary of the Film Council, said that the British Film Institute had promised to support the initiative.

The Times of India reported as follows[20]:

As things are today, the students have no opportunity to see any of the avant-garde films or experimental films for documentary. The result is that most of them have never seen a picture from countries like Japan, France, Italy and Poland, which have produced some of the most expressive films in the last fifteen years.

This was a period that recorded the emergence of Akira Kurosawa in Japan, Victoria De Sica in Italy, Godard and Truffaut in France and Andrzej Wajda in Poland. "All that a University has to do is to buy a projector, reserve a large hall in one of its buildings for the showing of films in the evenings, and appoint a person for correspondence and other work," the report pointed out.[21]

In a letter to the Times of India, published on Christmas day 1959, Marie Seton added: "The idea of film societies in Universities was brought to the University Grants Commission by the Children's Film Society and it is the Children's Film Society which suggested my name for nine months to commence this valuable scheme." Marie also mentioned that FFSI was formed with six

Image 5.1 Marie Seton with Professor Satish Bahadur at one of the annual film appreciation courses at NFAI–FTII.
Courtesy: FFSI/Asian Film Foundation, Mumbai.

film societies earlier in December 1959, noting the "ever growing interest in better films."[22]

Vijaya Mulay, who was then Joint Secretary of the FFSI and worked with the ministry of education, said that the UFC became entangled in the bureaucratic web of the UGC and did not finally take off. It was, indeed, a big loss to the Film Society Movement. However, from 1967, the establishment of the National Film Archive saw an annual summer film appreciation course that was organised by NFAI and FTII. This continues even today and remains the only healthy annual engagement on serious film studies. The one-month summer course is for film society members, academia, and government servants handling cinema, researchers and film critics from media.

The credit of starting and maintaining this summer residency goes to Professor Satish Bahadur, who started one of the first University Film Clubs at Agra University along with PK Nair, the director of NFAI. Recalling the first film appreciation course of 1967, KV Subbanna, of Ninasam,[23] the eminent rural theatre personality of Kannada noted:

Marie Seton was the programme organizer and director for the first six week film appreciation workshop at the FTII, Pune, in 1967. Working in association with her was the young Prof. Satish Bahadur. We were about 40 participants at the workshop. The course which included classes, lectures, debates and movie screenings, used to beginning in the morning and would go on for 12-13 hours, beyond midnight. There were several guest lecturers at the workshop, but the two permanent people there Marie Seton and Satish Bhadur.[24]

PK Nair and Professor Bahadur defined film appreciation, formulated the curricula and conducted the course, setting the basis for film studies in India as a serious vocation. The summer residency remains a much-awaited annual event for film buffs across India up-till now (2016).[25]

Together with the first professor of film appreciation, Satish Bahadur at FTII, PK Nair created an army of film *rasiks* across the country, over the years. The one-month summer residency of Film Appreciation remains a big draw even today. "Looking back, Prof Bahadur and Nair created and nurtured new regime of film appreciation, across the country through these summer courses," Anil Srivastava, their contemporary recalled. From government servants to university lecturers, film society members and media rushed to Pune for the summer course over the years.

The Film Society Movement along with the appreciation courses threw up a generation of film critics and new cinema writers across India in all languages: from Amita Malik, who criticised DFS for limiting its membership to 250 and forced them to raise it to 500, to Hamimuddin Mohammed, who later joined the Film Festival Directorate, Vasant Sathe, Muriel Wasi, Jag Mohan, Iqbal Masood, Khalid Mohammed, John Dayal (social activist now) Anil Saari, Deepak Roy, Shanta P Choudhary, Sadanand Menon (ACJ–Chennai), Ravi Vasudevan (CSDS), Ashish Rajadhyaksha (author of *Indian Cinema in the Time of Celluloid*), Rashmi Doraiswamy and my friends from Thiruvananthapuram, MF Thomas and Vijayakrishnan, who taught me the basics of film aesthetics.

There are a special set of film writers such as Chidananda Das Gupta and Sudhir Nandgaonkar who are also full-time film society activists. Chidu *da* held CFS flag high from the word go. Sudhirji is doing that at Mumbai and the rest of Maharashtra even today. "Prabhat Chitra Mandal was established in 1968 by group of five film critics. Vasant Sathe, English writer on cinema was its President and Sudhir Nandgaonkar, the General Secretary. All the film critics with Sathe–Sudhirji's team were professional writers and regulars with various Marathi newspapers. The Film Society was named 'Prabhat' to cherish the memory of Prabhat Film Co. lead by V Shantaram in

John Dayal

Deepak Roy

Vijayakrishnan

MF Thomas

Sudhir Nandgoankar

Image 5.2 The group of film critics emerged along with film society movement across India, interpreting the new film culture and its appreciation.

Courtesy 5.2a: From his pvt collection.
Courtesy 5.2b–e: Photo by the Author.

early 30s and 40s," Sudhirji recalled the origin of PCM and his involvement with the Film Society Movement.[26]

The names are endless if you compute all regional language writers. The list of National Award winners in the category, books on films and writers on films, includes most of these names. They exhorted the readers into a new culture of films as an art with their writing, helping a generation to see films in a more aesthetic manner.

Film critic-turned film-maker Khalid Mohammed[27] remembers seeing Godard's *Breathless* at the Film Forum in the 1960s. "It changed my outlook towards films," he said. No wonder the period made the JNU scholar Abhija Ghosh write:

> The trajectory of the Film Society Movement was affected by a period of cinephilia that was sincerely invested in the aesthetic possibilities of cinema, and equally informed by the celluloid materiality of the form they engaged with…. And, on the other hand, the rare opportunities of watching international and art cinemas combined with the consciousness of the transitory nature of the celluloid image, significantly transformed the viewer/member's temporal and spatial relationship to cinema.[28]

Indeed, it was the combined assault of the political leadership, government of the day, film-makers, cultural icons, academia and media on the existing film sensibilities through the vehicle of the Film Society Movement, triggering far-reaching positive changes of the popular films itself.

UNCENSORED FILMS

It was in the period 1964–66 that Indira Gandhi exempted the FFSI network films from censorship. The reason was that the embassies willing to give their country's film did not want the films to be put through the conservative scissors of the Indian "Censor Board." Satyajit Ray, as the FFSI president, wrote to Gandhi on the issue. Ms Gandhi, the then I&B minister, conceded to the request for exception of censorship, for FFSI screenings, ensuring a steady source of films to screen on minimum expenses for the film societies. The final official order was out in 1966. The order empowered an FFSI committee to preview films and recommend to the government for censorship exemption and showing in FFSI-affiliated film societies for three years.

The step facilitated the rush of non-English films, from Europe and Latin America to the FFSI network of societies, many of which were with explicit female nudity, which made film societies attractive to a new group of people, who were not necessarily connoisseurs of films with aesthetic quality. The period was when uncensored films were strictly illegal and sex in films were a taboo, not to speak of nudity per se. Naturally, there was a rush to join film societies in the 1970s and 1980s till the arrival of video, DVDs and the Internet. I remember the DFS in the 1980s was overflowing with such members and had locked its membership. The reason: from the limit of 500, DFS reached 1,500, as a new set of members other than the "margis," as Chidu *da* described, entered the circuit. The very same phenomenon spread to all the urban centres where film society membership had become a status symbol by the 1970s.

The craze for watching uncensored films gave a membership boost to the societies. Some of the film societies even scheduled such films in their effort to increase the membership, using the same yardsticks as that of a commercial exhibitor, thereby bringing undesirable elements to the network, defeating the very purpose of a film society screenings for a better film culture.

"No wonder such gate crashers could not thrive for long. They had to have their natural exit," pointed out PK Nair, in an article he wrote in 2004.[29] This also made the film societies a totally male dominated movement and women kept off from the crowd "enjoying uncensored films."

In his review of the Film Society Movement, in 1983, Chidu *da* too noticed this populist trend in the movement which he heralded. He also noted that it was a deliberate decision of FFSI to go all out and expand membership on a large scale, a decision made by the All-India Conference of Film Societies at Calcutta in 1967, to address the issue of economic liabilities of individual societies.

Chidu *da* observed as follows[30]:

> The harm done should not be measured in terms of shows of films with nudity and sex, because the notion that they corrupt adult audiences is in itself highly questionable. What was lost in the process was the interest in good cinema on the part of the large majority of the film society members.

The new kind of members had choked the film societies across the country, a fact I personally found out in Delhi in 1981. This may have put off many young entrants in the 1980s and contributed to their lack of interest when the movement was in crisis by the end of the decade. The crisis was mainly due to the advent of national television, video and later DVD, making the film society circuit less attractive as uncensored films began to flood the grey market of video and DVDs. This, of course, made the movement fall back on its original supporters from other streams like the academics and literature and the film industry itself.

EXTENSION OF OTHER MOVEMENTS: LITERARY, LIBRARY AND LEFTIST

Image 5.3 The journals of FFSI and film societies.

Note: These journals had academic articles on films of the film society network and also of Indian film-makers along with the emerging aesthesis of Indian films.

Courtesy: Author.

Out of the 293 film societies affiliated to FFSI in 2014 (as submitted to the I&B ministry), 118 are in Kerala alone. Kerala has been unique in the spread of the film societies from the 1970s. The reasons for this unique phenomenon are manifold. However, one of the most compelling reasons can be the other parallel movements that were already there: the Library Movement of the 1950s and 1970s along with the little magazine groups that sprang up across Kerala.

When the Library Movement celebrated its silver jubilee in 1971, the Film Society Movement was taking off in the state. Kerala had 4,000 libraries spread across the state, and half of them had their own buildings, with good reading halls. The libraries had a membership base of 650,000 and stocks of over 7 million books (Kerala Library Movement: Silver Jubilee Souvenir 1971). Just as the Film Society Movement, the Library Movement in Kerala had its own crisis following the arrival of the multichannel television, which beamed captivating tearjerkers. Unlike the little magazine groups, which were more of a Leftist cultural renaissance, the Library

Movement ran parallel to the freedom movement and was led by a visionary activist, PN Panicker.[31]

"Read to Grow" was the motto of the Library Movement. When the Kerala Film Society movement celebrated 50 years of its existence in 2015, marking 50th anniversary of *Chitralekha* Film Society, which was formed in July 1965, the founder of the society attributed the spread of the movement to a festival they organised for the all-India literary festival at Alwaye, near Kochi, in January 1966.

Gautaman Bhaskaran described the emergence of the Film Society Movement parallel to the literary one, in the authorised biography of Adoor Gopalakrishnan, as follows[32]:

> The fifth All India Writers Conference at Alwaye, Kerala, in January 1966 provided a wonderful opportunity off the ground. They organised screenings of fifteen world classics – to coincide with the conference–in the state's nine districts as well as the bordering Nagarcoil in Tamil Nadu. Vans carrying prints (of films) criss-crossed the region pushing and promoting a novel cinema culture and arousing public interest in different genres.

The collection of films included Ray's *Devi* and Ritwik's *Mege Dhaka Tara* along with Russian, Polish, French and Hungarian films. Adoor strongly believed that the film festival of 1966 made a deep impression on the viewers across Kerala, that films were an aesthetic art object and created a hunger for such films in a population who were already exposed to quality literature through the Library Movement. The libraries also organised discussions on new books and held at least an annual function with a writer participating in it. This was almost the way film societies organise festivals of films with screenings and discussions with film-makers.

The period also saw the Kerala Peoples Arts Club (KPAC),[33] promoted by the CPI, successfully staging its production—You made me a communist—throughout the state. The KPAC was an affiliate of the IPTA, which had already produced films with KA Abbas. Within a decade, Kerala had the largest number of film societies in the southern region, with over 100 units spread across the state. "Each town had a film society and they not just screened the films, but organised serious film discussions," recalled Vijayakrishnan, one of the early film society evangelists. Vijayakrishnan travelled across the state evangelising a new kind of cinema and wrote extensively on films in Malayalam journals. He was the first to be given the National Award for the best book on cinema in 1983 for *Chalachitra Sameeksha*, published by Current Books, a popular Malayalam publishing house.[34]

Though the Left Front governments in Kerala and West Bengal have been supporting the Film Society Movements, and even established centres like Nandan, Kariali and Kalabhavan art house theatres to screen quality films, there was not a full-throttled direct support to the new cinema. In West Bengal, the then information minister Buddhadeb Bhattacharya, who later become the chief minister, was the force behind Nandan, the film and cultural complex. His department also promoted many a young film-maker and is credited with the promotion of Ritwik Ghatak's film packages across India. His department organised a Ritwik film festival in 1981, with a workshop with the late film-maker's celebrated students such as Kumar Shahani and Mani Kaul, when the late Safdar Hashmi was head of the information office of the West Bengal government in New Delhi.

Professor Mihir Bhattacharya, who introduced film studies as a postgraduate course at Jadavpur University (first in any university in India) in Kolkata, listed the contribution of the Left in films and culture in those glorious days of the IPTA.[35]

> If you look back on the years marked by the vital presence of the Indian People's Theatre Association in Bengal – the nineteen forties and fifties in particular, though the movement started earlier and lasted longer – you may find that the mental map of culture you have prepared needs considerable revision.... Therefore, what looms large in my mapping happen to be Nabanna of Bijan Bhattacharya, Raktakarabi of Shombhu Mitra, Angar and Tiner Talwar of Utpal Dutt, Ebang Indrajit of Badal Sircar, the novels of Manik Bandyopadhyay, Satinath Bhaduri, Samaresh Basu, Sulekha Sanyal and Nani Bhowmik, the poetry of Bishnu Dey, Arun Mitra, Samar Sen, Subhash Mukhopadhyay and Sukanto Bhattacharya, the music of Ravi Shankar, Jyotirindra Maitra, Hemango Biswas, Binay Ray and Salil Chowdhury—and the incomparable Harindranath Chattopadhyay who composed largely in Hindi—the choreography of Uday Shankar, Shanti Bardhan and Shombhu Bhattacharya, the paintings and sketches of Somenath Hore, Jainul Abedin and Chitta Prasad, the photography of Sunil Jana, the graphics of Khaled Chowdhury, the cinema of Nimai Ghosh, Satyajit Ray, Ritwik Ghatak and Mrinal Sen, and the like. Much of what I have listed has endured and a good many of the texts have achieved the status of modern classics.
>
> The ideological projection of my mapping is obvious; most of the texts had deep links with the organized cultural movement inspired, aided and propagated by the Communist Party of India.

The professor, who is associated with Left in West Bengal, also pointed out that, "there are some exceptions, though. *Raktakarabi, Ebang Indrajit* and *Pather Panchali* and a few others had no manifest links with the Party or the movement."

In Kerala the CPI-M had floated its own film production unit named Janashakthi Films and even produced one of John Abraham films *Cheriyachante Kroora Krithangal (Cruel Deeds of Cherian)* in the1970s. However, they have been openly supporting the Film Society Movement and their local units have been the strongest supporters behind the Kerala FFSI's regional activities from 1990 onwards. The Left and Democratic Front government in 2010 even allotted ₹5 million for the film societies as a onetime grant for the FFSI Kerala unit. Though, there are occasional allegations of partisan attitude in the activity of the Kerala FFSI unit, the Left parties must be given full credit for sustaining as many as 119 film society units across the state and even celebrating 50 years of the Kerala Film Society movement in July 2015. "In Kerala unlike earlier days, when the entire movement was identified with few film societies, FFSI is a strong entity, which is engaged in spreading a better film culture," FFSI Keralam's general secretary VK Joseph, a former ISRO employee, explained. FFSI Keralam actively supports the International Film Festival of Kerala (IFFK) with its Open Forum and organises a short film festival, *Signs*, every year.[36]

Despite all their involvement, the Left have always been caught between the mass and aesthetic appeals in cinema. In a note to the then chief minister and Politbureau member of CPI(M) Buddhadeb Bhattacharya, veteran actor and theatre activist Utpal Dutt explained clearly the predicament of the Left parties on the films and Film Society Movement. He pointed out:

> At present the so-called "good films" are totally alienated from the masses. They are explicitly directed at a petty-bourgeois elite and these elitist directors proudly proclaim that the masses are too backward to understand their masterpieces.... Typical of this is these elitist directors demand for "alternate channels" of release, a cowardly admission that they do not even dare to challenge the commercial cinema in its own circuit.[37]

Gautam Kaul, president of FFSI (2015), acknowledged the support by the Leftists to the Film Society Movement over the years. According to him, the Left's support to the Film Society Movement stemmed from former Soviet leader VI Lenin's identification of cinema as a medium of great influence on masses, as far as back in the 1920s. Socialist realism was the key word for the Left in culture, which both KPAC and IPTA upheld. The films from Eastern Bloc and Latin America too upheld the Leftist thought in films wholeheartedly until 1991. "Until the middle of 90s Film Society Movement in Kerala was kept completely free of any political colour or character even as we were regularly screening films from countries like Soviet Union, Czechoslovakia, Hungary, Poland, Cuba, etc.," Adoor recalled the political influence over the movement in the State.

Till the 1980s, the mainstream cinema was treated as "not so cultural" and was viewed as an essentially "black money laundering" investment by dubious businessmen. However, with a series of government interventions through institutions like FFC, FTII, NFAI and support to Film Society Movement, the sector became respectable. The national and international awards, celebrity status of the filmmakers and artists made it even glamorous, though money laundering continues to plague the field. Many national and international corporates and media houses have their film companies producing and distributing films today.

The Film Society Movement did create an excitement in the urban centres of India, and in places where the parallel literary and political movements took the excitement seriously. It received the official patronage of the government of the day, and the National Awards encouraged the movement, giving it a larger-than-life image.

Chidananda Das Gupta observed as follows[38]:

> The movement (FS) has an impact far in excess of its size. It prepared the foundation for India International film festivals and built and audience for the new cinema. At its peak in the late 1960s and early 1970s, the FFSI has about 300 film societies affiliated to it. Many societies had as many as 2000 members.

Clearly, the Film Society Movement was the need of the times, a yearning of the new republic to look for a place for its own films in the world film map and giving respectability to the evolving art form, along with other traditional arts in the field of culture.

The official FFSI website claims that the significant achievement of the Film Society Movement is perhaps the great opportunity it provided to millions of cinema lovers to watch and appreciate non-Hollywood world cinema. Without the tireless efforts of FFSI, classics of great masters like DW Griffith, Sergei Eisenstein, Vittorio De Sica, Roberto Rossellini, Federico Fellini, Jean Renoir, Francois

Truffaut Jean Luc Godard, Ingmar Bergman, Satyajit Ray and Akira Kurosawa would have remained inaccessible to the cineastes in India.

The FFSI accessed and circulated films from most of the film-producing countries in Asia, Africa, Latin America and Europe. Promoted by the FFSI, the Film Society Movement inspired generations of Indian film-makers to create a cinema different in texture and feel from the mainstream cinema in India.

Starting with Satyajit Ray and Mrinal Sen, film-makers like KA Abbas, Ritwik Ghatak, Shyam Benegal, Basu Chatterjee, Basu Bhattacharya, Govind Nihalani, Adoor Gopalakrishnan, Aparna Sen, Girish Kasarvalli, Amol Palekar, B Narsing Rao, Ketan Mehta and many others are products of the Film Society Movement. The movement also succeeded in bringing about a qualitative change in style of film criticism in India: it brought a greater understanding of film criticism. "It also worked as the basic inspiration to include film studies in curriculums of several Universities," the FFSI website noted.[39]

In its report, the Film Enquiry Committee headed by Dr Shivarama Karanth in 1980 also took stock of the role of the Film Society Movement:

> While the Film Society Movement has made a distinct contribution in the propagation of film consciousness, the movement has remained largely confined to major urban centres. Its expansion has been handicapped on account of non-availability of exhibition facilitates and lack of awareness on the part of the Government to appreciate the crucial role which this movement can play in creating audience for good cinema by changing audience taste through regular exposure of good films to a cross section of people.

The report had also noted that in 30 years the movement only had 200 societies with about 75,000 members, though it acknowledged that 300 other societies had applied for affiliation with FFSI.[40]

In 2015 as well, the number of FFSI-affiliated film societies remains almost the same, with 293 of them affiliated to FFSI, but has no larger-than-life image, not even a credible pull among the target audience and is limited to the film academia and students. Even in its reduced profile, the Film Society Movement supplies the largest resource pool of film academia, which the government and all decision makers draw their strength to take forward, their agenda's in this sector. Clearly, the Film Society Movement over the years attracted the people of sound academic minds to examine the aesthetics of films and its impact on society, through exposition and analysis of best of films from India and the world.

NOTES*

1. http://cherianwrites.blogspot.in/2016/02/adoorgopalakrishnan-on-film-society.html
2. https://en.wikipedia.org/wiki/Vijayakrishnan
3. Abhija Ghosh. *Celluloid in Transit: Film Society Cultures in India*. MPhil Thesis, JNU.
4. Interview with Pradipta Sen of CFS. http://cherianwrites.blogspot.in/2016/03/cfs-cine-central-interviews.html
5. https://en.wikipedia.org/wiki/Samik_Bandyopadhyay
6. HN Narahari Rao, ed., *The Film Society Movement in India* (Mumbai: Asian Film Foundation, 2009), p. 26.
7. http://cherianwrites.blogspot.in/2016/02/adoorgopalakrishnan-on-film-society.html
8. RM Ray, ed., *Indian Cinema in Retrospect: Speeches of the 1955 Seminar* (New Delhi: Sangeet Natak Academy), p. 23.
9. RM Ray, ed., *Indian Cinema in Retrospect: Speeches of the 1955 Seminar*, p. 28–29.
10. *Selected Speeches of Indira Gandhi: Jan 1966–69* (New Delhi: Publication Division), p. 279.
11. http://cherianwrites.blogspot.in/2016/02/interview-with-benegal.html
12. http://cherianwrites.blogspot.in/2016/02/adoorgopalakrishnan-on-film-society.html
13. HN Narahari Rao, ed., *The Film Society Movement in India*, p. 73.
14. http://cherianwrites.blogspot.in/2016/02/reply-from-ministry-of-i-ffsi-funding.html
15. https://en.wikipedia.org/wiki/K._Bikram_Singh
16. http://cherianwrites.blogspot.in/2016/02/interview-with-benegal.html
17. http://cherianwrites.blogspot.in/2016/02/marie-seton-from-cfs-published-in.html
18. http://cherianwrites.blogspot.in/2016/02/press-report-of-film-council.html
19. Ibid.
20. Ibid.
21. Ibid.
22. http://cherianwrites.blogspot.in/2016/02/typical-film-appreciation-course-by.html
23. http://www.ninasam.org/
24. Pages-751-2, KV Subbanna, Areshatamaanada Alebarahagalu, 2004.
25. http://cherianwrites.blogspot.in/2016/02/interviewwith-sudhir-nandgoanker.html
26. https://en.wikipedia.org/wiki/Khalid_Mohamed
27. Abhija Ghosh. *Celluloid in Transit: Film Society Cultures in India*. MPhil Thesis, JNU.
28. http://cherianwrites.blogspot.in/2016/02/havefilm-societies-lost-their-relevance.html
29. HN Narahari Rao, ed., *The Film Society Movement in India*, p. 101.
30. http://www.pnpanicker.org/aboutpnp.html
31. Gautam Bhaskaran. *Adoor Gopalakrishnan* (New Delhi: Penguin–Viking, 2010), p. 66.
32. https://en.wikipedia.org/wiki/Kerala_People%27s_Arts_Club
33. https://en.wikipedia.org/wiki/Vijayakrishnan
34. http://cherianwrites.blogspot.in/2016/03/cinema-and-bad-new-times.html
35. https://www.facebook.com/public/Ffsi-Keralam
36. *Utpal Dutt on Cinema* (Kolkata: Seagull, 2009), p. 149.
37. Ibid., p. 84.
38. https://en.wikipedia.org/wiki/Federation_of_Film_Societies_of_India
39. Ministry of I&B. *Report of the Working Group on National Film Policy* (New Delhi: Ministry of I&B, GOI, May 1980), p. 13.3.23.
40. Ibid.

* All websites accessed on 16 June 2016.

CHAPTER 6

The Great Fall and Resurgence Through Digital Mode

I n 1980, as a student of the IIMC[1] in New Delhi, I tried to become a member of the DFS. As a member of *Chitralekha* and *Chalachithra*, I thought it would be easy to get into DFS. I still remember the huge crowds at the Federation of Indian Chamber of Commerce and Industry (FICCI) auditorium, at Mandi House, where the screenings were held. I was new to the city with no friends in the DFS. My friends discouraged me from joining DFS, as they said, "it was full of people who just wanted to see uncensored films."

They, instead, prompted me to attend the diplomatic mission screenings at the Soviet Cultural Centre, Hungarian Information Centre, Marx Mueller Bhavan, and the USIS to keep my appetite for good films going. I became friends with many of the organisers at these diplomatic mission centres as a student of IIMC, and the Hungarian Information Centre even invited me to join them as the editor of their journal *News from Hungary*, making me stay put in the capital. Graduates from IIMC were welcomed in most newspapers then, as the institute had a good reputation in media circles.

The IIMC too had a good collection of documentaries. I remember seeing most of the Dutch documentary films by the film-maker Bert Haanstra at the institute, and I was the only one who had already seen *Battleship Potemkin* among the students. Professor DN Choudhary, the son of the famous writer Nirad C.

Choudhary, and Professor Viswanathan, from the Tamil film industry, encouraged me to undertake a diploma project on video, while
most of my colleagues had written projects. My diploma project was
a documentary on OV Vijayan's cartoons, with an interview with the
cartoonist at our studio.

I had invited film-maker Kumar Shahani to a lecture at the
Institute, after I met him at one of the seminars in Delhi and that
should have promoted my professors to push me to make a video
project. The writer in me was active with occasional dispatches for
Kalakaumdi publications on films and film seminars, back home at
Thiruvananthapuram. By the end of the decade, my occasional writings in English publications in Delhi and Malayalam publications got
me into the hallowed circles of film critics and film festival circuit of
Delhi. I was mighty pleased when Anil Saari, the eminent film critic,
asked me to write an obituary on the film-maker John Abraham for
The Hindustan Times in 1989.[2]

After I joined the Hungarian Information Centre in April 1981
and found myself among the organisers of the evening film screenings, getting many friends to fill in the empty seats last minute. I had
forgotten to join the DFS, whose reputation had begun to decline
considerably as the membership composed of enthusiasts for "uncensored" films. This put off many like me from showing any more
interest in DFS, and it took some time to dawn onto me that DFS was
going down; it finally shut down in 2006.

A similar fate was being faced by the film societies in other
metros too. During the 1970s, Mumbai had 18 film societies. Film
Forum was the strongest with 1,500 members. However, after the
departure of Basu Chatterjee and Arun Kaul, its membership started
dwindling.

> The Film Society Movement in Bombay has lost the kind of hold it
> had few years ago. It has now to find a way out of the problems that
> keep mounting, rising costs, dearth of theatres, and as Khalid
> Mohammed has observed in its assessment, the general apathy of
> the people towards better cinema.

Wrote Amrit Gangar, regional secretary of FFSI, to *The Times
of India*, reacting to an article on the plight of film societies of the city
by Khalid Mohammed.[3]

However, there was at least one society that was taking shape even in those days. "We started our full-fledged office so that we could serve our members better. This resulted in getting more members. Of course in strong programming and participation in film festivals, Prabhat stood first." Sudhir Nandgaonkar of Prabhat Chitra Mandal (PCM), and the FFSI activist who had kept the movement alive in Maharashtra during the difficult times, recalled.[4]

Pradipta Sen of CFS, who also saw this period, confirmed the fall. By the early 1960s, CFS had over 2,500 members on its rolls but, sadly, today it has been reduced to a mere 250. "The success of CFS made others too venture into organising film societies. Three other film societies sprang up in Calcutta, Cine Club, Cine Central and Cine Institute," Sen pointed out.[5] Over the years, Ray and the pioneers of CFS lost interest in the functioning of the society. Though Ray pre-viewed his film *Devi* in New Delhi at DFS, no such privilege was given to CFS in Kolkata. "The uncensored films had brought in such an undesirable crowd to the film society circuit that even Ray distanced himself from the Movement he pioneered," noted the Kolkata-based film critic Abhijit Ghosh Dastidar.[6]

In many cities, the pioneering societies were seen as highbrow elite zones, and getting a membership was difficult; however, it was easy to get a membership in the new ones. Cine Central, which was established in 1965, organises a children's film festival and an annual festival at Nandan, the cultural centre, in association with UNICEF and the West Bengal government even today. It also participates in the annual Kolkata Book Fair and sells DVDs and scripts of famous films through its stall.

CHITRALEKHA: THE BEST EXPERIMENT OF THE FILM SOCIETY MOVEMENT FAILS

In Trivandrum too, *Chitralekha*'s screenings came to a halt in the 1980s. *Chitralekha* had an impressive membership over the years, but with the active support of the city's ISRO and the banking sector employees, *Chalachithra* emerged as the biggest film society of the city, as *Chitralekha* was perceived as too exclusive. The waning inter-est of Adoor, *Chitralekha*'s founder, in the regular activities of the society as he was busy with his film productions, and his growing differences with the Film Cooperative's managing director Kulathoor Bhaskaran Nair, added to the society's woes. The cooperative and the film society had an umbilical connection and trouble in its leadership broke this unseen cord leading to the collapse of both the pioneering organisations.

Although it was successful for a limited period, the *Chitralekha* Film Cooperative remains the best highlight of the New Indian Cinema, as well as the Film Society Movement of India. A bold experiment that will remain as a unique milestone in the history of world art house cinema.

The Film Cooperative started with a loan of ₹1.5 million from the state Government in the 1960s; since then, it has repaid the amount to the exchequer, after a negotiated interest cut. The Film Cooperative produced three feature films, *Swayamvaram, 'Kodiyettam* and *'Prathisandhi*, a commissioned film on family planning for the Government of India, all directed by Adoor.

The cooperative also produced 25 documentaries for various organisations from 1965 to the early 1980s. "*Swayamvaram* was made for a small budget of ₹2.5 lakh and it earned a revenue of ₹5–8 lakhs and *'Kodiyettam* was even more successful. We had planned not just the Film Studio at Aakulam, in the outskirts of Thiruvananthapuram, but an entire artists' village, where cultural icons from various fields could live together," Kulathoor Bhaskaran Nair, who is still the managing director of the "paper organisation," recalled the film cooperative's golden times.[7]

Adoor's biographer Gautaman Bhaskaran wrote as follows[8]:

> The *Chitralekha* Film Cooperative – which built a full-fledged studio, including a recording theatre, a processing laboratory and editing facilities – helped produce, a different kind of cinema. Gopalakrishnan's first two works, *Swayamvaram and 'Kodiyettam* and several documentaries. Aravindan's debut work *'Uttarayanam* and many other ground-breaking movies emerged from the studio or with the help of its equipment.

The erstwhile *Chitralekha* Film Studio Complex is now the headquarters of Southern Air Force Command. The complex that ran into issues was taken over by the government and given to the Indian Air Force. The picturesque complex was designed by the famous architect, builder, the British-born Laurie Baker,[9] who was a resident of Thiruvananthapuram.

Image 6.1 *Chitralekha* film studio complex at Thiruvananthapuram.
Courtesy: Meera Sahib, first assistant of Adoor Gopalakrishnan.

Image 6.2 A still from open house of the 20-year-old International Film Festival of Kerala (IFFK), conducted by the government and run by Chalachitra Akademi of the State. Seen in the picture are (L to R): MS Sathyu, Girish Kasaravalli, KR Mohan and Rajiv Nath, all film directors.
Courtesy: Author.

"Sadly, the *Chitralekha* Film Society faded into oblivion in the 1980s. So did the *Chitralekha* Film Cooperative, and the most important cause of this was Gopalakrishnan's disassociation from both. His differences primarily with Mr Nair (Kulathoor Bhaskaran Nair) led to Gopalakrishnan's exit, and like many other institutions in India which weaken and wind up after that one man bids adieu, *Chitralekha* too floundered after its very spirit and soul left," Adoor's biographer described the failure of the experiment that was once watched with envy by film-makers across India and the world[10]

Together with the other Laurie Baker-designed institution, the Dr KN Raj promoted CDS.[11] Film Studio Complex, built in 1975, remains an important landmark of the capital of Kerala even today. *Chitralekha* complex stands as a memorial to one of the failures of the most prestigious experiment in world film history.

THE EMERGENCE OF NATIONAL TV, VIDEO LIBRARIES, SATELLITE TV AND FALL OF EASTERN BLOC

I recall seeing Godard's film, *Week End*,[12] on the impact of live TV on people, much before TV as a live medium arrived in India. It was like a fairy tale in the 1970s for India. But looking at the infiltration of television as a medium in all spheres of life with their "breaking news," live coverage and sting operations, one can easily say that we are more in an Orwellian world. Big Brother is watching you, commenting and sometimes interfering in your life too. Films, which re-create the world in time and space, have no chance in all these live shows. It helps you only to reflect on the past, if you still find the time to do so, in the present.

The growth of television in India was in a controlled fashion by the government until 1991. In fact, an experimental television service had started in Delhi in September 1959, and was boosted with the introduction of the colour television in 1982, when the Asian Games was held in New Delhi. The national network of terrestrial channels in the metros and few capital cities had the newscast in the evening from the Asiad days. By 1984, most state capital TV stations were connected to Delhi and thus national programming started with news, current affairs and serials.

Hum Log, depicting Delhi's middle-class life, became a pioneer and was soon taken over by Ramayana and Mahabharata serials in the latter part of the 1980s. The situation continued until 1991, when the Gulf War brought in satellite television channels to India. The 1990s saw national and international television channels getting launched in India. An early private Indian channel like Sun TV started its programming with only films in 1992. They showed Tamil films continuously, mesmerising the already film-crazy population of the state. Weekend films and weekly musical shows, such as *Chitrahaar* aired on Doordarshan, had made a huge impact on television viewers, deflecting their attention from cinema houses.

In 2015, the government statistics show that Doordarshan operates 33 satellite channels, has a vast network of 67 studios and 1,416 transmitters of varying powers and provides TV coverage to about 92 per cent population of the country. The cable and satellite television market in India emerged in the early 1990s, spurred by major international events like the Gulf War and the growth of home-grown media companies. The industry has experienced robust growth, with the number of subscribers increasing from just 0.41 million in 1992 to more than 161 million by the end of 2013. India today has a large broadcasting and distribution sector, comprising around 790 television channels, 6,000 multi-system operators (MSOs), up to 60,000 local cable operators, seven direct-to-home (DTH)/satellite TV operators and several Internet Protocol Television (IPTV) service providers.[13]

The world was also undergoing major changes during the 1980s and 1990s. The authors David Page and William Crawley wrote as follows[14]:

> Three important developments underpin the media revolution, which has changed the way South Asians see the word—the demise of Communism, the increasing integration of world markets, and very rapid advances in communication technology. In the aftermath of the collapse of the Soviet bloc, free trade and the free flow of information became dominant philosophies of the late twentieth century, with the United States the chief protagonist of both.

For the film society movement, these developments turned out to be a double-whammy effect, onslaught of television taking away its audience and fall of the Soviet bloc drying up the easy flow of films to their screenings.

FILM SOCIETY MOVEMENT AT THE CROSSROADS

All of these developments happened from 1984 to 2000, when the fledging Film Society Movement was undergoing a crisis due to the new-found attention of the middle and the educated class of India. The sudden spur of visual entertainment through television took away the major chunk of the film society visitors. The national network of Doordarshan showed almost all FFC-financed films, and even produced films with Satyajit Ray, Mrinal Sen, Adoor Gopalakrishnan and Shyam Benegal. State governments such as West Bengal with its enlightened leadership of I&B minister Buddhadeb Bhattacharya, who later became the chief minister, got into film-making with the new cinema protagonists. Most of these films of even the old maestros were telecast on the national television network, including several award-winning films. Doordarshan itself began to patronise such films, along with the popular Hindi films and regional films in regional language channels. I remember viewing a Ritwik Ghatak film festival in early 1989 on Doordarshan National channel, aired with subtitles. Doordarshan, during that period, became another patron of the Film Society Movement, by airing New Wave and award-winning films, although its main obsession was Bollywood films and serials like Ramayana and Mahabharata.

The period also saw many international film festivals springing up in cities like New Delhi, Kolkata, Bangalore, Mumbai and Thiruvananthapuram. These festivals were organised by the leading film societies of the region in collaboration with the state governments, or even directly by the governments. These festivals were in addition to the IFFI that was anchored at Goa. Thus, the exclusivity of the Indian Film Society channel, which was once the only oulet to show case new cinema and uncensored foreign films, especially from non-English-speaking countries, was seriously challenged.

The period also saw the inflow of films from Soviet bloc countries drying up. The fall of the Soviet and the entire Eastern bloc countries also affected their State-owned system of film-making. Film-makers who enjoyed State patronage for their creative activities disappeared. It took another decade for films to re-emerge from these countries. The economies of these countries went upside down and the cultural field was thrown open to the market forces. The Russians closed their huge network of cultural centres across India. In Delhi, the Soviet Information Centre at Connaught Place was closed, and the property was sold off to a corporate house. The bubbling Soviet Cultural House, which was a hub of Russian culture, began to be known as a beer guzzlers' paradise with a pub coming up there. The cultural centres of Soviets in other cities also faced closure.

THE FORMAT CHANGES: VIDEO, DVD AND THE INTERNET

It was during the same period that the advent of new technologies happened in India. First, it was the video technology as television networks demanded it. Films began to be converted into video films to be played on TV sets. Video films substantially reduced the cost of making films and hence most documentaries took to that format. Private viewing of even feature films through video format and television became the order of the day.

The worst was yet to come for the traditional film formats. There were global developments in IT, and India became a major back-end service station for the world. This put the film formats upside down. Today, there are no films as they existed in pre-1990s formats and there is a massive digitisation programme even in NFAI. The world leader of celluloid film Kodak closed its shop in 2012.

Kumar Shahani, the eminent film-maker, observed as follows[15]:

> The world of films will be different now, with each image being captured and seen through the aesthetics of the person who shoots it. A photograph can never be the reflection of reality as such, as it can be modified in umpteen numbers of ways through digital technology.

Kumar, who refused to work in digital format, and insisted on his old 35-mm film format, found himself outdated and almost stopped making films during this period.

A look at the number of films censored by the Censor Board of India reveals it all. In 2014, the annual report of the I&B ministry documented that it censored a total of 12,977 films for viewing in India. Out of the total number of films censored, those in celluloid format numbered just 74, 5,098 were in video format and the digital format dominated with 7,805 films.[16]

The emergence of video and digital formats also turned the Film Society Movement upside down, as they had to bid farewell to the 16-mm and 35-mm film prints and adopt new technologies. Recently, when Cine Central got a film from Swedish Film Institute for their annual festival in Kolkata in the old format, they found themselves spending a huge amount of money to courier the prints, upsetting their fragile economy. Obviously, they will not want such huge expenditure in any future festivals, as DVD and Blue Ray format can be transported across the globe with minimal charges.

The period of 1984–94 was the worst for film societies across India. The period also saw the tremendous growth of satellite and television channels, beaming numerous films daily. Every major network has a few movie channels today. Film-makers have now found a good revenue model in selling their film's television rights to these channels. FICCI, an industrial body that conducts an annual media and film industry meet at Mumbai commissioned a study by the global consultants KPMG. The last of the published study observed:

> Television is the largest medium for media delivery in India in terms of revenue, representing around 45% of the total media industry. The TV Industry continues to have headroom for further growth as television penetration in India is still around 60% of total households and increasing to 161 million in 2013. The number of Cable & Satellite (C&S) subscribers increased by 9 million in 2013 and touched 139 million. Excluding DD Direct, the number of paid C&S subscribers is estimated to be 130 million. This C&S subscriber base is expected to grow to 181 million by 2018, representing 95 percent of TV households. Of this, paid C&S base is expected to be 171 million in 2013, representing 90 percent of TV households.[17]

Television's spread brought a video revolution. Satellite and cable television added to the video programmes. The late-night television films and shows opened up an entirely new legal avenue for Indian viewers to access soft porn without the conventional censorship, just like the uncensored films of the film society circuit. There were a few channels known more for their late-night films, than any other programmes till the government came down heavily on them with conservative guidelines. The immediate impact on Film Society Movement was that those in its circuit, those who were there for the uncensored films, lost interest in the membership of the societies.

Following the economic reforms in 1991, the Indian film industry emerged as the world's largest, despite Hollywood's glamour, fame and financial muscle. The nickname "Bollywood" for the Indian film industry may be an accident, but reveals the association the city of Bombay has with the industry, with the largest number of films produced in Hindi. In 2012, Bollywood produced 1,602 films, compared to a mere 476 from Hollywood. India also beats Hollywood hands down in ticket sales. In the same year, Bollywood transacted an impressive 2.6 billion in ticket sales as against the United States, whose number was just 1.36 billion. However, Hollywood does have more financial clout and leads the way in terms of box office revenue. American films grossed $10.8 billion in 2012. Even though India produced more films, the Indian film industry could only manage $1.6 billion.[18]

The impressive growth of the film industry did not find a parallel in the Film Society Movement during the period. Till the arrival of DVDs and now Blue Ray and other technologies, the video format and television made almost half of the 300 film societies perish. The changing media formats and the flood of television channels took away people's attention span too, leaving the film societies to the most serious film buff.

Opender, a Western region FFSI activist, put the issues of the decade and its solutions in the best way.[19] According to him, the biggest problem was finding a theatre for screening of the 35-mm films, as 16 mm had become obsolete. The absence of a cheaper and handy format was yet to arrive (the DVDs had not arrived then). The lack of a credible second line of leadership was also becoming an issue. Foreign films got undue importance in matters of film appreciation, as against Indian films, among film societies. International directors Bergman, Fellini, Kurasova and Zanussi became more popular than Indians like Girish Kasaravalli, Adoor Gopalakrishnan or Mani Kaul in the film society circuit. The elitist nature of the film societies of big cities and their lack of effective positioning with the new middle class that emerged following the 1991 economic reforms, took away the glamour and status quotient from the movement. Above all, the failure to take the movement to the universities affected its sustainability.

Though the decade marked a crisis period for the movement, it was during this period that *Suchitra* Film Society built and inaugurated its complex in Bangalore. Prabhat in Mumbai and MFS continued to organise their activities. The stars at the height of the movement like CFS, DFS and *Chitralekha* in Thiruvananthapuram were sinking.

This was also the period when the veterans of the Film Society Movement were passing the baton to a new leadership, as they themselves were overwhelmed by the fast-paced changes which video, television and fall of Eastern bloc and economic reforms brought in.

Chidananda Das Gupta observed as follows[20]:

It has become necessary now to treat the FFSI as a major instrument of the development of film appreciation, professionalise its management and cleanse it of the elements that have drifted into it for doubtful pleasures of purveying uncensored films or finding their way into diplomatic cocktail parties.

A list of film societies in different regions over the years clearly shows the rise and decline of the movement. The FFSI started with six film societies in 1959, and had an impressive growth for the next two decades. By 1964, there were 23 film societies and, in 1967, there were 108 film societies affiliated to FFSI, the eastern zone dominated the activity with 63 film societies. In 1971, the FFSI had 111 units across India. By 1980, when the Film Society Movement peaked across India, there were total of 216 film societies with FFSI and with 95 units South India dominated the movement.

The crisis period of 1984–94 brought the FFSI units down to 98 in 1994. In 2014, the count had improved to 292 units, with more than half in the southern region, Kerala leads the pack with 113 units.[21]

Recording the crisis in the Film Society Movement, U. Radhakrishnan, the FFSI, northern region secretary, wrote:

The decade of 1984–1994 was the period during which the Film Society Movement in India, in all the regions, with no exception, suffered a severe setback and activities almost came to a standstill. The number of Societies in the Southern Region reduced from 140 to 70, Northern region came down from 41 to 18, Western zone which was the worst hit, suffered a big slide from 25 to 10 and the Eastern region, though there was no reduction in number, the activities slumped to the lowest level.[22]

ADVENT OF THE INTERNET: ONLINE DATING SITES TO PORNOGRAPHY

By 1995, India also allowed the entry of the Internet in public arena, and by 2000 various Indian and foreign websites began to open up new vistas for the urban Indian population. The "dotcom boom" changed the media industry landscape, including that of films. There was a dotcom for everything, be it films or people involved in films.

The Amazons of the world began to sell films from all over the world, online. Slowly, some of these films began to be uploaded on the net for free downloads, though the quality of such films was not always predictable.

The Internet always had a driver in carnal feelings of humans. Dating, sex chats, porn sites were all part of it. Interpersonal relationships went global and the much-cherished privacy went for a toss. Nudity is no longer a taboo, with Internet access providing a gateway to the underbelly of the human culture as never before. Over the years, there has been a replication of everything human in the digital world. Today, there are a large number of Indian and foreign porn websites catering to netizens, despite an occasional crackdown by government agencies. The Internet has thus removed the people who, Chidananda Das Gupta described as "elements that have drifted into it for doubtful pleasures of purveying uncensored films" from the film society movement.

By 2000, with the emergence of regional film festivals organised by the state governments, the FFSI and its units lost its prime position as the exclusive venue of "uncensored" films, which it had from 1966. The reason was the continued squabbling by the leadership about giving such sanctions to individual societies and their festivals. The government appointed a committee headed by film-maker Shyam Benegal to examine the issue. They favoured a one-time grant of exemption to any registered body with the government to screen uncensored films, as against the three-year grant for "uncensored" films in the FFSI circuit. This effectively ended the prime status of FFSI being the exclusive channel of 'uncut' films in India and the status of a second censor board of India.

ENTER THE DIGITAL MODE

The arrival of video CD (VCD) and DVD is also seen as a watershed in the crisis-ridden Film Society Movement. VCDs hit the market in 1993 and DVDs in 1995. Together, they became one of the first formats for digitally distributing encoded films on standard 120 mm (4.7 in) optical discs. The DVD as a format had two qualities that were not available in any other interactive medium at the time: enough capacity and speed to provide high-quality, full-motion video and sound and a low-cost delivery mechanism provided by consumer products' retailers.

Along with the two new technologies, digital projections systems also developed. A video projector, or a digital projector, may project onto a traditional reflective projection screen, or it may be built into a cabinet with a translucent rear-projection screen to form a single unified display device.

The DVD technology also had huge storage capacity to hold a two- to three-hour film in one or two discs, which was easier to carry and could be sent via a simple courier. DVD is an optical disc technology with a 4.7-gigabyte storage capacity on a single-sided, one-layered disk, which is enough for a 133-minute movie. DVDs can be single- or double-sided and can have two layers on each side; a double-sided, two-layered DVD will hold up to 17 gigabytes of video, audio or other information. With further developments in photography and DVD technology, films across the world have shifted to this technology, changing the entire production and distribution system of the medium.

FILM SOCIETIES ENTER DIGITAL ERA

Together, the digital technologies, VCD and DVD, created a revolution of sorts across the world of films. The viewer has an option to see the films on his laptop computer in full-screen mode today. From huge boxes of celluloid films, the delivery mode of the films has now been converted to one or two CD boxed set which could be easily transported, through post or courier, crossing all international borders, cutting across all complex tax and import duties. Online booksellers, such as Amazon, began to include DVD films on their virtual shelves. The films of the world are getting digitised and reduced to compact discs, which are available readily across the globe. However, digital technology had its own issues. Through VCD and DVD, disc contents could be easily copied, and this technological aspect paved a way for everyone to copy films, making the traditional distribution systems obsolete and copyright go haywire. Adding to the agony of the film-makers, who invest deeply into the medium, was the arrival of the internet as a medium with huge storage, as well as downloading capacities. Though there are anti-piracy laws to protect the copyrights of film-makes across the world, pirated copies of popular as well as classic films are available for throwaway prices. One was surprised to see a list of all the classics I wanted to see all my life as a film society member in 1970, 1980s and 1990s for ₹5,000 in a corner of Thiruvananthapuram in 2000. Each city in India has its share of these grey market people. In Delhi, Palika Bazar can provide film buffs with the best of classics, and in Kolkata the street vendors cater to this market. In each city, there is an informal circuit to quench the new generation's thirst for the latest and best of world cinema.

However, the official FFSI history of Film Society Movement records that the availability of films in DVD format by 2000 had become a boon for film societies. Most of the classics too were available in DVD, and FFSI officially promoted the use of DVD format and projections for screenings, as it eliminated the cumbersome process of transporting films across the country.

The FFSI may have promoted the digital formats officially, but there were film enthusiasts like C. Saratchandran in Kerala and Anil Srivastava who established CENDIT in New Delhi to introduce new technologies through their interventions much before FFSI stepped in. Saratchandran, who worked with Malayalam film-makers G. Aravindan and John Abraham and had served with the British Council in the 1980s, took upon himself to popularize video and digital formats among the alternate film circles in Kerala, much before the format became acceptable elsewhere. He was not just a film enthusiast, but a product of the little magazine wave of the 1970s and 1980s in Kerala and was also exposed to changing technologies at British Council in Saudi Arabia, where he worked as a consultant. He carried a huge DVD library of world films, when he came back to Kerala in the 1990s.

While Anil Srivastava was winding up CENDIT, which promoted video technology, in New Delhi, Sarat, as he is popularly called, went around with one of the few digital projectors in Kerala and screened DVD films, including his film on John Abraham, giving a new life to the sagging morale of the Film Society Movement hit by television and video and DVDs. "He was a one man army in popularising the digital format. He also made a two-hour film on John Abraham. He went around Kerala showing his film and other films in digital format, through the projection system brought from Saudi Arabia," recalled KN Shaji, editor of *Samkramanam*, the little magazine in Malayalam of the 1970s and 1980s. Sarat was the co-founder and active organiser of the VIBGYOR Film Festival. He was also a prominent supporter of *VIKALP*, a platform to defend freedom of expression and resist censorship. At the time of his demise, he was working on documentaries on industrial pollution due to a gelatin factory near Thrissur, and a film on the state of the Chaliyar

River. He had an untimely death on 1 April 2010, when he fell out of a running train.

REGIONAL RESPONSE TO CRISIS

The crisis period did not end well for many regions, especially the eastern and northern regions. In Kolkata, films societies did not find the transition to digital technology easy. In fact, the city's film societies began to jointly organise film screenings to overcome the crisis when memberships dropped and funds were not easy to come. Though the joint screenings affected the individuality of the film societies, it helped the city continue its pioneering role among the film societies. When the FFSI celebrated its golden jubilee in 2009, the eastern region had only 70 survivors, and only 25 of them had been operating for more than 25 years. The number further dipped to 65 in 2015.

The worst affected was the northern region. Pioneers like DFS stopped screenings in 2006, following the detection of a financial fraud. After Indira Gandhi's death in 1984, government patronage slowly weaned away. The flood of video and TV channels took away members of most film societies. Unlike other regions, the shift to digital format did not bring in new enthusiasm among the potential members. In 2009, there were only 10 film societies in the region, and only four were found to be active and the rest were trying to keep afloat. However, for the serious filmgoers in New Delhi, screenings at the India International Centre, India Habitat Centre, the cultural centres of the diplomatic missions of Germany, Italy, Spain, France and Hungary, catered to the rich traditions of film appreciation in the city. The Delhi Malayalee Film Society has its own audience, and the Malayalam film-makers look to the society and its main organiser U. Radkrishnan for the screenings of quality films. Many other regional groupings like Bangiya Samaj and Kannada Society also occasionally organise screenings of regional films. The various screenings of Directorate Film Festival and the now-redundant Osian Film Festival continued with the city's annual film screening traditions. The number of film societies in the northern region stands at 11 as of 2015.

However, in a strange coincidence, the western and southern regions have seen a growth in the film societies after the crisis. This can be attributed to the emergence of the second-level leadership and the smooth adoption of digital technologies in West and South India. The western region had a growth of almost 20 film societies in the decade after the crisis period and the introduction of digital technologies. From a mere 13 societies, the number went up to 32, and there were 8,300 film society members across the region by 2009. In 2015, the continuing growth saw the number swelling to 45.

In the southern region barring Kerala, the number of film societies went up by 13, from 40 to 53 in 2015. Kerala may be the only state that has its own FFSI region, after a court battle in 1985 with the parent body. The region that was formed officially in 2000 had 70 film societies attached to it, and by 2015 it had grown to 118 units.

The crisis and the recovery period also saw the FFSI headquarters moving out of Kolkata's Bharat Bhavan. It first moved to Mumbai from Kolkata in 2006, with the election of Sudhir Nandgaonkar as the secretary of FFSI. Nandgaonkar procured a permanent office for the FFSI and its regional outfits in Mumbai from the state government and restarted its monthly newsletter. Later, when HN Narahari Rao became the FFSI president, Bangalore became its headquarters. The FFSI changed its rules to ensure that the secretary and treasurer of the organisation are from the same region/city, and that its national office works from that city/region. This change was effected to ensure effective coordination between regions and the regional leadership to get a chance to be elected for national posts. In 2015, with Premendra Mazumder becoming the FFSI secretary, the national office shifted back to Kolkata's Bharat Bhavan, where its office was from 1959 to 2006.

The crisis that plagued the Film Society Movement from the mid-1980s and 1990s due to the entry of new media and technologies ended in 2000. Ironically, the same technological revolution in projection and format of films came as a saviour of the Film Societies Movement, leading to its growth in the western and southern regions. Incidentally, both these regions are also leading the information and technology revolution in India.

NOTES*

1. http://www.iimc.nic.in/
2. https://www.facebook.com/johnabrahamdirector/photos/pb.198076013566188.-2207520000.1456938066./856293871077729/?type=3&theater
3. http://cherianwrites.blogspot.in/2016/03/amrit-gangars-letter-to-editor-times-of.html
4. http://cherianwrites.blogspot.in/2016/02/interviewwith-sudhir-nandgoanker.html
5. http://cherianwrites.blogspot.in/2016/03/cfs-cine-central-interviews.html
6. http://cherianwrites.blogspot.in/2016/02/soruce-of-films-and-film-programs-of.html
7. Interview with Kulathoor Bhaskaran Nair, MD Chitralekha Film Cooperative. http://www.prd.kerala.gov.in/towardsmorevisual.htm

8. Gautaman Bhaskaran. *Adoor: A Life in Cinema* (New Delhi: Penguin–Viking, 2010), p. 70–71.
9. https://en.wikipedia.org/wiki/Laurie_Baker
10. Gautaman Bhaskaran. *Adoor: A Life in Cinema*, p. 73.
11. http://www.cds.edu/
12. https://en.wikipedia.org/wiki/Weekend_(1967_film)
13. http://www.ddindia.gov.in/AboutDD/pages/Default.aspx
14. David Page and William Crawley. *Satellites Over South Asia: Broadcasting, Culture and the Public Interest* (New Delhi: Sage, 2001), p. 21.
15. https://en.wikipedia.org/wiki/Kumar_Shahani
16. http://cbfcindia.gov.in/html/uniquepage.aspx?unique_page_id=20...
17. https://www.kpmg.com/IN/en/IssuesAndInsights/ArticlesPublications/Documents/FICCI-KPMG_2015.pdf
18. Ibid.
19. HN Narahari Rao, ed., *The Film Society Movement in India* (Mumbai: Asian Film Foundation, 2009), p. 119.
20. http://cherianwrites.blogspot.in/2016/03/the-das-gupta-article-on-fsm-89.html
21. Compilation from FFSI documents.
22. HN Narahari Rao, ed., *The Film Society Movement in India*, p. 112.

* All websites accessed on 16 June 2016.

CHAPTER 7

The Star Film Societies and the Survivors

The Film Society Movement of India has seen many a bright spark among its member units, during the last five-and-half decades, contributing immensely to the development of film appreciation and culture. They are spread across the country, from East to West and from Chandigarh to Thiruvananthapuram. Profiling some of them who survive even today and are contributing to the movement gives a snapshot of the ups and downs of the movement itself in each region. Most of these film societies are still hoping for a rerun of the movement, and some have passed the baton on to the new generation. Some do not see a bright future, but vow to carry on the fight for the survival of the movement. Some of the new leaderships have gone for a makeover and created new societies undertaking new experiments in their region, giving a contemporary look to the movement itself. However, the older ones are serving in most regions by associating with a regional film festival supported by the state governments of the region.

THE CALCUTTA FILM SOCIETY

The history of Indian film societies cannot be written without featuring the CFS. Though it is not the first film society of India, it was the first to make a difference to the Indian film world, with just two individual contributions. The first was Satyajit Ray, the film-maker, and the second was Chidananda Das Gupta, the film writer. Both Ray and Das Gupta stand colossal in their fields, and there is no one yet to dwarf them with equal or more contributions. India is yet to witness a film like *Pather Panchali*, which excited the world, as well as the Indians, changing the path Indian films was taking, till then. 26 August 1955, the day *Pather Panchali* was released, will remain etched in golden letters in the history of Indian films.

Das Gupta described the CFS, the Film Society Movement, as follows[1]:

> In October 1947, Satyajit Ray and a group of likeminded enthusiasts, anxious to open a window on world cinema, so tightly shut during British rule, started the Calcutta Film Society. In no time, it tuned into a movement, which was spread all over the country, providing a new impetus to film viewing, film criticism and eventually to film making. Among the film makers directly or indirectly thrown up by the movement, were, apart from Satyajit Ray himself, Ritwik Ghatak, Mrinal Sen, Shyam Benegal, Adoor Gopalakrishnan and many others.

The CFS was the first film society to import a film, *Battleship Potemkin*, in 1948, and had to dodge the police to screen it in its initial screenings. The film went on to become the first film among many film societies in India, and the box carrying the print of the Russian

Image 7.1 Jean Renior at a CFS function in 1949.
Courtesy: CFS Collection.

classic criss-crossed the country. Apart from Jean Renoir, Roberto Rossellini, John Huston, Frank Capra, Vesvold Pudovkin and Nikolai Cherkassov, all film-makers were guests at CFS in those early days before *Pather Panchali*.

Though there was a period of lull following the IFFI of 1952, the release of Ray's first film and Marie Seton's frequent visits to Calcutta revived CFS in 1956, that too with a journal, *Indian Film Review*. President, Pradipta Shanker Sen, a retired journalist who had seen the revival recalled those days nostalgically.

> The CFS restarted in 1956 with the active participation of Marie Seton, who began to frequent the city to meet Satyajit Ray, who was making waves with his first film. There was already an excitement of the success of *Pather Panchali* in Calcutta. The CFS was revived with Chidananda Das Gupta as Secretary and film maker Purnendu Patri was also there. The annual fee those days was ₹30.[2]

Image 7.2 Satyajit Ray (second from the left in second row) among the audience at the revival gathering of CFS in 1956.
Courtesy: CFS collection.

The revival witnessed about 300 members joining the CFS and, in six years, the membership increased to 3,000. The huge number remained on its rolls, till other film societies like Cine Club, Cine

Central and Cine Institute came up, according to Sen. In the 1960s and 1970s, Nirmal Kumar Siddhanto, VC, Calcutta University, Apurva Kumar Chanda, Director, Public Education (DPE) of West Bengal were all important figures of CFS along with BN Sircar of New Theatres, DP Pramanick of Eastern India Motion Pictures Association were all associated with CFS. *Prachi* Cinema, an all-Bengali cinema house in the city, allowed free shows, waiving off the nearly ₹15,000 as rent. At a retrospective of Sergei Eisenstein's films at the Academy of Fine Arts, "the crowd was so much that CFS founder Ray was seen sitting on the stairs and watching the films. That was in early 1960s," Sen recounted the golden days of CFS. *The Statesman*, the city's premier daily newspaper, carried reviews of the films shown at CFS, informing the city's cultural elite about the arrivals of the new world of films. These films were procured from diplomatic missions of most countries and other sources. The annual fee went up to ₹100 from ₹30 and life membership from ₹3,000 to ₹25,000. The CFS now struggles to keep its flag up, with around 300 members, a weekly digital projection in its office and some joint screenings in theatres. Nandan's 16-mm and 35-mm screening facilities are also utilised by the society. The CFS religiously observes the release of *Pather Panchali*, with a function in the last week of August each year, where the city's who's who from the film world assemble to ruminate on the golden years of CFS and Film Society Movement of the city along. The CFS also conducts the annual lecture in memory of Chidananda Das Gupta, its other illustrious founder.

CINE CENTRAL, CALCUTTA

There are a few film societies across the country that came after the formation of FFSI, when Indian urbanites considered being a part of the movement as a status symbol in the 1960s. Cine Central of Kolkata was one such society established in 1965 and continues its activities through milestone annual events. A Children's Film Festival in collaboration with UNICEF from 2006 and the Calcutta International Film Festival in 1986 have now been taken over by the state government. The Cine Central website states that the first show of the society was held at Tiger Cinema on 31 October 1965 with the screening of *The Road to Life*, and very soon the society became an established name in the Indian film cultural arena.

The society regularly organised country, theme and director-specific film sessions and festivals. They also screened retrospectives of both young and veteran film directors. Some of them were personally present at the show, including Satyajit Ray, Mrinal Sen (India), Lester James Peries (Sri Lanka), Jiri Menzil (Czech), Paul Cox (Australia), Sumitra Peries (Sri Lanka), Sandor Sara (Hungary), Humberto Solas (Cuba), Gur Bentwich and Zsuzsa Boszormenyi (Hungary), Amanda Fox (Australia), Mrs and Mr Rock Demers (Canada), Jonathan Paz, M Bregman, Doron Eran and Ms Idit Sechori (Israel), Juan Fischer (Columbia), Isamat Ergashev (Uzbekistan), Ms Yakiki Takayama (Japan), Roland Plaus (Germany), Rafi Bukaee (Israel), Vinko Bresen (Croatia), Eddy Terstall (the Netherlands), Adak Drabinski (Poland), Meted Pevec (Slovenia), Kathryn Millard (Australia), Francoise Rossier, Erich Schmid and Narian Spandouk (Switzerland), Mrs and Mr Glorgos Skouran (Greece), Tarique Masud, Catherine Masud and Tauquir Ahmed (Bangladesh).

Cine Central has been organising successive International Children's Film Festival and Fair at Kolkata Maidan, opposite Birla Planetarium, with generous support and cooperation from the state government, UNICEF and various corporate houses. Since 2006, they have made the Children's Film Festival an annual event. The annual International Children's Film Festival has become an important programme of the society's activity. The society also ensures that underprivileged children are exposed to the festival by arranging shows in the city's slums, suburbs and in the districts.

Cine Central Calcutta also introduced "Calcutta International Film Festival" in 1986, the first-ever Independent International film festival in India. The festival began as a small local event and has now become one of the major Film Festivals of the country. In 1998, this festival underwent a major structural change and was renamed the "International Forum of New Cinema." It continues to be held every year from 11 to 18 November, under the broad framework of Kolkata Film Festival organised by the government of West Bengal.

Cine Central has also been striving to have a small art theatre to hold regular shows for its members, discerning public and children. Kolkata does not have a single hall where regular screenings of children films are held. The proposed art theatre can surely fulfil this vacuum and expected to become a rallying point for a vibrant new film culture.[3]

CINE CLUB OF CALCUTTA

The Cine Club of Calcutta, established in 1961, also had an impressive beginning, with over 1,200 members enlisting in a year. The Cine Club used to offer its films to other societies, after their screenings. Ram Haldar, its founder, was a bookstore owner who was also a member of the CFS. Haldar was the first to introduce books such as *Film Forum* and *Film Sense* by Eisenstein, *Film Technique* by Pudovkin, *Reflections of Cinema* by Rene Clair, *The Art of Film* by Lindgren and *Sight and Sound* to Calcutta. Needless to say, Satyajit Ray and Chidananda Das Gupta and the film buffs in the city feasted on Haldar's collection. He was associated with CFS until 1961, when he parted to form the Cine Club of Calcutta. Cine Club rode the high point of the Film Society Movement and Haldar steered its growth until 1968. The Club also published two journals, *Kino* in English and *Chitrakalpa* in Bengali, to which the stalwarts of cinema and Film Society Movement in Kolkata contributed regularly. In 1974, they added *Cine News* to the publications. The club became a member of the British Federation of Film Societies and instituted the Film Appreciation Award in 1974–75 for encouraging the production of quality films in the eastern region. In 1977, the club hosted a three-day film appreciation workshop, where 40 students participated. It also instituted the annual Ritwik Memorial Lecture in 1979, delivered by eminent film personalities.

THE DELHI FILM SOCIETY

DFS was the most privileged of the film societies across India. The membership and the leadership were the who's who of Delhi in the 1960s and 1970s. Diplomatic missions vied with each other to patronise the DFS by giving their films and bringing in film-makers from their countries to meet film buffs at DFS.

I asked my former resident editor, at *Financial Express*, Dr YC Halan, who was a member of DFS from the 1960s, to give me an insight into the working of the DFS in its golden days.

Dr Halan described his early days at the DFS as follows[4]:

> I am a member of DFS since the mid-sixties. I will continue to be its member as long as it is alive as I am a life-member. I was told that the best films, particularly non-commercial, from foreign countries were not shown in India. Also films from non-English speaking countries were never shown in India (outside the film society

circuits). Those were the days when foreign films were not freely allowed. Such films were brought in by the embassies and were routed through film societies. Film Society Movement was at its peak as persons like Ms Usha Bhagat, Social Secretary to the Prime Minister Indira Gandhi and serious film buffs were interested in watching such films. Since these people were the most influential persons in the city, the best films from the best directors were brought in by embassies and shown to society members.

Dr Halan went on to become a member of the executive committee, treasurer, secretary and president during the 1970s and 1980s. Dr Halan recounted his DFS experience as follows:

It was the period during which Gautam Kaul joined DFS, when he was transferred to Delhi. John Joshua was the Secretary and Gopal the President. There was intense politics between the two groups, Vinod Mehra and John Joshua. Vinod was the protégée of Ms Mulay and was able to dislodge John and held control of it. The DFS was at its peak during the eighties and the frequency of films shown was almost five to seven in a month. Slowly, a message went around that uncensored films were shown and this attracted a large riff-raff to the film society. This was the beginning of the decline of DFS. Later in the nineties the Film Society Movement became dormant because of two reasons: the advent of TV and liberal import of films. The censoring policy also became liberal.

"The membership of DFS was a status symbol in 1970s and 1980s," pointed out another life member of DFS and film-maker and writer, Deepak Roy.[5]

The DFS was obviously a privileged society to have the crème of decision makers from all sections of society, and was also a recipient of all government patronage as far as its screenings and special occasions were concerned. Hence, the admission was not automatic, but after an interview.

Dr Halan pointed out as follows:

The uniqueness of DFS was its elitist membership. Persons serious in films, particularly the appreciation part were members. Many of them became film-makers like Pankaj Bhutalia, Gopi Gajwani and Bikram Singh. Many were politically and culturally powerful like Mulay, Bhagat and Kaul. These people ensured that only serious members joined DFS. This helped to build up quality membership. It deteriorated fast as these persons left DFS.

There is an unconfirmed story that Rajiv Gandhi, then an Indian Airlines pilot, who later succeeded his mother Indira Gandhi as prime minister, was not admitted to DFS. "I do not remember why the membership was rejected. I only saw his name in the register of applicants. At that time the membership was after an interview. He may not have come for the interview," said Dr Halan, when asked about the incident. Despite the best patronage, Dr Halan finds the DFS's impact to be marginal.

> It did make an impact, but in a limited way. The fact that many of the members produced films, Gopi Gajwani was associated with DFS and other two names Punkaj Butalia and Bikram Singh directed and produced art and documentary films, adds to its impact.

The crowd at DFS became increasingly mixed in the 1980s, as those looking out for "uncensored" films began to dominate it.

There was an incident involving a French film-maker who addressed DFS members after the screening of his film. One of the members said he found the film "sadistic," much to the surprise and shock of the film-maker. "The member put his feelings about the film so rudely that the film-maker had to be admitted to the hospital after the screening," recalled Partha Chatterjee,[6] a film scholar who was present at the screening. Deepak Roy recalls the occasion where DFS had to stop the screening of Italian film-maker Pasolini's *The Gospel According to St Mathews*, as the film had no sub-titles. "It was a mixed crowd," recalled NK Sharma of Sahamat.[7]

The abrupt end of DFS came in 2006, when Gautam Kaul,[8] its last president, found that the treasurer had withdrawn a fixed deposit without authorisation. The incident, which became a police case, led to the end of screenings at DFS. Kaul, the FFSI president (2014–16), has been trying to revive DFS, which had such a glorious history. Though there are societies like Tasveer, as many as five cultural centres of the diplomatic missions and film clubs of India, International Centre and India Habitat Centre, and the regional film clubs, such as Delhi Malayalee Film Society,[9] have divided the serious film viewers in the city, a fact increasingly realised by Kaul.

FILM FORUM, BOMBAY

Film Forum Bombay will be known as the film-makers' film society, going by the film-makers it has contributed to Indian cinema. The forum was formed in 1964, by the trade unions of the then Bombay film industry. The country's first film society, The Amateur Film Society of India, merged with Film Forum. The forum itself was the creation of the film-maker KA Abbas, who was the first to bring in social and political themes to Indian films in a big way. Other illustrious names from the Film Forum stable included Basu Chatterjee, Govind Nihalani, Bikram Singh (documentary film-maker) and Khalid Mohammed.

Mrinal Sen's landmark Hindi film *Bhuvan Shome*, which kicked off the New Cinema movement in Hindi, was produced by Arun Kaul from the Film Forum. Both Mrinal Sen and Arun Kaul had also come out with a manifesto for New Cinema those days.

Image 7.3 Arun Kaul and Mrinal Sen.
Note: They produced the first major Hindi film of the new wave genre:
Buvan Shome, which was financed by FFC.
Courtesy: FFSI/ASIAN FILM FOUNDATION.

Film-maker critic Khalid Mohammed[10] entered the film field through *Close Up*, the magazine of Film Forum brought out by Basu Chattterjee and KA Abbas. "I joined the magazine to write and learn," said Khalid, who went on to become the film critic of the *Times of India*, Mumbai, and later editor of *Filmfare*, recounting his days with Film Forum. He also remembers seeing young Mani Kaul and Kumar Shahani at Film Forum. "Films of Godard, Ozu, *Battleship Potemkin*, Rashomon of Kurosawa were all big draws," added Khalid, who feasted on the experimental films which were plenty at Film Forum. He attributed the idealist leadership of people like Abbas, Basu Chatterjee and later Gopal Doothia, to be the force behind the success of the Film Forum, which had over 2,000 members by 1969. "Basu Chatterjee maintained a library of film books. The leadership inducted potential film buffs and provided them constant education through films and discussions on films," Khaild, who turned film-maker through *Fiza*, recalled. "If the young generation is inducted, the Film Society Movement can exist," he pointed out and went on to say that the society itself had changed, "There is no pure love, things have become commercial." The period of selfless, idealist leaders are over and Film Society Movement has to acknowledge that and go about it.[11]

Film Forum undoubtedly carried the flag of Indian Film Society Movement with its galaxy of film-makers and film critics in it. Apart from the film-makers, critics like VP Sathe and Jag Mohan were also associated with the forum. It also had affiliations and collaborations with the British Film Institute, Cine academies of the USSR, France, Poland, Czechoslovakia, Japan and Sri Lanka (then Ceylon). The Forum organised a retrospective of Indian Cinema in Paris in collaboration with *Cinémathèque Française* in March 1967. The best film magazine of the FFSI was also brought out by Film Forum. The magazine called *Close Up* had an editorial board consisting of Dr Gopal Dutt, Basu Chatterjee, Arun Kaul, KA Abbas, Bikram Singh, VP Sathe, Jagmohan, Ram Mahewswari, Mrinal Sen with Arun Kaul and Vikas Desai, to name a few. The Film Forum was among the few film societies that also had a vast library of books on films. The Forum was the first to introduce an award in the name of DG Phalke for the film-maker of the year from any of the Indian languages.

Image 7.4 KA Abbas, VP Sathe and Raj Kapoor.
Note: Though from different genre of films, Abbas and Raj Kapoor were collaborators, as far as story and screenplay was concerned, a combination which was appreciated by critics like Sathe. The margi (classic) influencing desi (mass appeal) was flagged off by this combination.
Courtesy: FFSI/ASIAN FILM FOUNDATION, MUMBAI.

PRABHAT CHITRA MANDAL, MUMBAI

While Film Forum has become a star of the past, it is PCM, which is carrying the flag of Film Society Movement in Mumbai today. According to Sudhir Nandgaonkar, a Marathi film critic and one of the founders of PCM, the society was established in 1968 by a group of five film critics. Vasant Sathe, an English writer on cinema was the president and Sudhir Nandgaonkar as its general secretary. All the critics were professionals involved in writing various Marathi newspapers. The name "Prabhat" was given to cherish the memory of Prabhat Film Co led by V Shantaram in the early 1930s and 1940s.

Nandgaonkar described the early days of PCM as follows[12]:

Prabhat started initially with 30 members but within three months, its membership reached to 200. The membership fee was ₹36 per annum. Slowly, we gained ground and the members' confidence due to our programming and selection of foreign films. We celebrated our first anniversary with the festival of Prabhat Films and V. Shantaram inaugurated it. Our programming was so strong that we were choosing new films to celebrate anniversary day. The films got released after our show. Since the founders were journalists; we got good support from newspapers in Mumbai and we celebrated our 10th anniversary with a package of top 10 films from the *Sight & Sound* magazine. Then I&B Minister L K Advani inaugurated the festival with a seminar on censorship. Many stalwarts from film industry such as Raj Kapoor, Shyam Benegal was its President, B R Chopra and others participated in the seminar which was a grand success.

The 1960s were the days of the Film Forum, but PCM found its own channels to sustain itself, with a Marathi flavour adding to its activities. "During the 70s Mumbai had 18 film societies, the Film Forum was the strongest with 1,500 members. However, after the departure of Basu Chatterjee and Arun Kaul, it started dwindling.

PCM's founder-leader Sudhirji, who served as FFSI secretary, when film-maker Shyam Benegal was its President, described the ups and downs of his film society as follows:

"We started our full-fledged office to serve our members better. This resulted in getting more members. Of course, in strong programming and organising of film festivals Prabhat stood first.

It had surpassed the other film societies in 1992 by organizing 27 films of Satyajit Ray to commemorate his Oscar Award. We got financial support from Govt. of Maharashtra for the Ray Film Festival. By then, the Film Forum had closed down. We were screening our films at Mini Chitra where the capacity was 80 seats. So for two shows we could have 250 members, we could not enroll members beyond that. There was waiting list for membership. However, after the advent of colour TV in 1984, witnessed the audience for cinema dwindled and the membership of film society also went down. Prabhat had only 150 members. Slowly, the craze for TV died down, with the advent of global economy and more channels. On this juncture we organised the Ray festival and enrolled 700 members. The venue was Y.B. Chavan Centre Auditorium with 625 seating capacities. PCM initially had a membership of 250 members and during the crisis period (1984–90) it went down to 150 members, then after an impressive growth of 700 in 1992, the membership has now stabilised to around 500.

Sudhirji and PCM are now fuelling the growth of film societies in the western region in the last few years with language-specific festivals and appreciation courses.

PCM has three screenings a month, all in DVD and digital projection. Every six months, the society conducts a festival and a one-day appreciation course, apart from the monthly study group and book releases on cinema. Prabhat publishes a monthly magazine called *Vastav Roopwani* for the past 20 years. The magazine has subscribers from all over Maharashtra besides society's own members. Prabhat is credited with restoring Phalke's *Raja Harishchandra*, the movie that was screened all over India. They restored and donated the film to the National Film Archive and celebrated the father of Indian cinema's birth centenary with the state government. Prabhat was also faced with a ban on using a commercial theatre for its screenings by an overzealous police commissioner and it took two years of a public interest litigation (PIL) in the Bombay High Court to overrule the ban. In the two years, they shifted the screenings to North Bombay.

Prabhat also started The Third Eye Asian Film Festival in 2002 in Mumbai, though it is now organised by a sister organisation, the Asian Film Foundation. The festival helps Prabhat increase its membership year after year. Prabhat and its leadership have been instrumental in spreading the movement to many towns in Maharashtra and they also organise film appreciation courses in Marathi. The results are there for everyone to see, as Marathi cinema is making waves at the National Awards. Just like the films from Bengal, Karnataka and Kerala, there appears to be a craving by the people for better films in Marathi too.

SUCHITRA FILM SOCIETY, BANGALORE

Image 7.5 *Suchitra* Academy, Bangalore.
Courtesy: Author.

If there is any film society in India that has fulfilled the dreams of the pioneers and is flourishing, it is the *Suchitra* Film Society of Bangalore. *Suchitra* has its own cultural complex in Bangalore with films as its focus area. Not just that, the complex is not managed by the founders of the film society, but a second generation of leadership. "I resigned from *Suchitra* in 2003, so that the new generation can manage the affairs," HN Narahari Rao,[13] *Suchitra*'s founder and former FFSI president, and a retired engineer from Bharat Electronic Ltd, a public sector unit at Bangalore, pointed out.

Mr Rao recalled as follows:

> The foundation stone for the *Suchitra* Cinema and Cultural Trust cultural complex, promoted by the Film Society was laid by Satyajit Ray, in 1980. The society was established in 1971, with the patronage of veteran film maker, MV Krishnaswamy and with the active involvement of engineers from Bharat Electronics Ltd, Indian Telephone Industries Ltd, and Hindustan Aeronautics Ltd and bank employee unions of Bangalore. There were 11 film societies those days and all of them had a waiting list for membership.

With the active support of public sector professionals from the city and the excitement created by the films of Pattabirama Reddy, Girish Karnad and BV Karanth, *Suchitra* had to close its membership by the end of the 1970s as they already had over 1,000 members. By 1979, journalist Subbha Rao, who had an enormous clout with the state government, became its president. He got the Bangalore Development Authority (BDA) and the then Chief Minister Ramakrishna Hegde to allot land for a cultural complex in South Bangalore. By 1980, the foundation stone was laid, by 1983, the trust managed state government funding, and by August 1986 the *Suchitra* cultural complex was inaugurated. "The initial purpose of the complex was for film screenings. Slowly, the centre got into other areas of culture, starting a children's wing, *Kalakendra*, a film school, and a centre for drama. The State government and voluntary donations keep the centre going," Rao said. "We may be among the few film societies who offer short term courses on film-making, apart from appreciation courses," Prakash Belawadi, who is managing the complex, pointed out. The screening theatre has 16-mm, 35-mm and LCD projection systems with a seating capacity of 150. Despite the impressive facilities, film-makers such as Girish Kasaravalli do not get a proper release of their films at *Suchitra*, as they are still in the old mould of showing a screening for their members. Film-makers feel that it has become yet another cultural complex, not an outlet to promote regional films by giving them an outlet for release.

The film society has at least five screenings every month. With 600 life members and 200 annual members, it has the patronage of film enthusiasts of the IT city. During the Bangalore International Film Festival, the society is actively associated with the Chalachitra Academy of Karnataka. A host of temporary members get added to the society in this period, as they have free entry at the Bangalore festival. Promoters see *Suchitra* as a cultural hub and assembly point of intellectuals, and also as a film school. The trust has already singed memorandum of understanding with the Guttenberg University of Sweden for a film school. *Suchitra* is also a consultant to Karnataka's Chalachitra Academy for spreading film clubs across the state and receives an annual grant for that purpose.

The first film screened by the society was the Shantaram movie, *Dr Kotnis Ki Amarkahani*. The society became the star among film societies in the city, with huge success of Ingmar Bergman Festival in 1972 and the FFC Festival 1973. The 1977 festival "Nostalgia," where 80 films screened in six theatres, caught the attention of the entire Film Society Movement of the country. *Appreciation*, a monthly bulletin, has been published for the past 31 years. From 2006 onwards, *Suchitra* has collaborated with the state government in organising the Bangalore International Film Festival and had also hosted an all-India Film Societies conference.[14]

CHITRALEKHA FILM SOCIETY, THIRUVANANTHAPURAM

In July 2015, the Kerala unit of FFSI organised a meeting of the film society activists and film buffs at the Hassan Marikar Hall at Thiruvananthapuram. The assembly, called "Experiences and Memories," was inaugurated by the initiator of the Film Society Movement in Kerala, Adoor Gopalakrishnan, the film-maker. The event was celebrating 50 years of formation of the first film society of Kerala, *Chitralekha*, founded by Adoor and his friends.

MF Thomas, a film writer, who was the last general secretary of *Chitralekha*, recollected as follows:

"It was in 1965 July 3rd week *Chitralekha* Film Society was inaugurated by the then Kerala Governor Bhagavan Sahay. Apart from Adoor, G Ramachandran (Gandhigram), KP Kumaran (later filmmaker), theatre actors, Karamana Janardhanan Nair, Gopi and Adoor's Gandhigram colleague Kulathoor Bhaskaran Nair formed the initial team of the society.

Chitralekha's arrival in the cultural scene of Kerala capital was welcomed by the media, as the society was described as an avenue to see the best of world films.[15]

Image 7.6 *Chitralekha* membership card of the author, 1980.
Note: Such cards were a priced possession of the urban elite of 1960s and 1970s across India.
Courtesy: Author.

Thomas recollected as follows:

The society had an initial membership of around 70. Adoor himself used to operate the 16 mm projector. There was one occasion where a Pasolini film had only four members. However, the Cuban film package of Thomas Alea had a good audience. When *Passion of Joan of Arc* was shown without sub-titles Adoor read the French translation. Prior to his first film Adoor was involved in such screenings, readings, brochure making after a preview. A souvenir on films, a glossary of film terms were also published by *Chitralekha*.

Gautam Bhaskaran recorded in his biography of Adoor as follows[16]:

The society (*Chitralekha*) published thought provoking literature on cinema. The first publication was planned and executed even when Gopalakrishnan was at Pune, and articles spoke not about star lives, or their love affairs, or sexual escapades, but film technique, technological innovations, performances, direction, scripts and so on. The journal was the first of its kind in Malayalam and included writings by eminent personalities, such as Ray, Ghatak, Abbas, cinematographer Mankada Ravi Varma, actor Balraj Sahni, Das Gupta, veteran journalist BK Karanjia, writer Marie Seton and Professor Satish Bahadur. A photo feature on world classics and a glossary of technical terms added to its uniqueness.

MF Thomas, who retired as an editor in the *Kerala Bhasha Institute*, recounted the initial days as follows:

There was much commotion when the Chinese film *Road to Victory* was to be screened in 1972. It was screened at the Tagore Centenary theatre with police presence, as it was a one of the first occasions where a Chinese film was screened after the 1962 war. The package of uncensored FFSI circuit films also became a big hit in *Chitralekha* too. Jiri Manzil's Czech film, *Closely Observed Trains*, was one such hit, so was *A Blonde's Love* by Milos Forman. There was also a package of films from Film Finance Corporation, the screening of which was also popular among the members. *Chitralekha* had an academic following as far as films were concerned. Dr KN Raj, who was back in town to establish Centre for Development studies, Keltron Chairman KPP Nambiar and his wife Saroj Nambiar, Novelist Padmarajan and most influencers of Kerala art and culture vied to be members of the society. Anyone, who wanted to nurture a national and international outlook in arts and culture wanted to be part of the *Chitralekha*.

Adoor's erstwhile colleague Kulathoor Bhaskaran Nair contended as follows[17]:

Actually, the *Chitralekha* Film Society was a wing of the *Chitralekha* Film Cooperative, registered in 1965, soon after Gopalakrishnan passed out of Pune. It was established with the help of a large number of friends and well-wishers. Many contributed to this, the Kerala government too, with shared participation. So we had a paid up share capital, meager though it was.

Image 7.7 Kulathoor Bhaskaran Nair, the Managing Director of
Chitralekha Film Cooperative.
Courtesy: Author.

Gautaman Bhaskaran wrote about the formation of *Chitralekha* as follows[18]:

> This was the first time a cooperative of this kind had been set up in the country to produce, distribute and exhibit pictures. The film society was a part of the exhibition and education process: to spread a healthy culture by screening different kind of celluloid fare and publishing serious literature on it.

The society had also laid the foundation for the spread of the Film Society Movement with just one act of organising screenings of 15 world classics to coincide with the fifth All-India Writers Conference at Aluva, near Kochi, in 1966. The 15-film package was also shown in all the nine district headquarters and in Nagercoil, which was a part of Kerala then, thereby exciting the cultural enthusiasts of the state to a new world of films. The films like Roman Polanski's *Knife in Water*, *La Vérité* of George Clouzot of France, *Devi* of Satyajit Ray and *Meghe Dhaka Tara* of Ritwik Ghatak paved the way for the spread of Film Society Movement in Kerala. A decade after the formation of *Chitralekha*, Kerala had 42 film societies spread across its districts.[19] A host of National Awards for Adoor's first film *Swayamvaram*, in 1973, further excited the Film Society Movement, spreading it to most small towns.

By the time I arrived in the city in 1976, a membership of *Chitralekha* had become a "status symbol" in Kerala's capital and *Chalachithra* promoted by the officers of ISRO was the stepping stone for students like me to get into a film society. *Chitralekha* was also mentoring new film societies across the state, with its advisories for formation as well as supplying films along with the relevant literature. The society could influence the universities in Kerala to conduct the hugely successful film appreciation courses, making the movement a glamorous one among the higher education circles.

By 1972, *Chitralekha* had become a huge establishment with its film studio coming up in the outskirts of the capital city. The Laurie Baker-designed studio complex, built with a generous loan of ₹1.5 million from the cooperative department of the government of Kerala under one of the most effective communists, Chief Minister C Achutha Menon, had become the pride of cultural field of Kerala. The Film Complex remains one of the unique experiments, though short lived, even today. The first two feature films of Adoor and 25 documentaries were produced by the film cooperative. Adoor became busy with making his films, and film society activity was left to a new team, most of them were working closely working with Adoor and the film cooperative's managing director Kulathoor Bhaskaran Nair. "The main advantage of *Chitralekha* was that it was formed and manned by film professionals. And throughout its active life 1965 to 1980, never even once we served from our initial motive, that is to administer and propagate a film culture in its pure form," recalled Adoor.[20]

By the late 1970s and early 1980s, the growing difference between Nair and Adoor led to the collapse of *Chitralekha*. However, Nair had already done the groundwork for the formation of the Kerala unit of FFSI. Under the leadership of the society, Nair organised state film societies under the banner of Association of Film Societies in Keralam. The association fought a legal battle with Central FFSI at the Calcutta High Court for allowing a separate region for the Kerala association, forcing the FFSI to an out-of-court settlement, and in 1985, a local unit of FFSI was formed. The local unit of FFSI also hosted the silver jubilee of FFSI in India, during the period.

The working of the film society and film cooperative came to a halt by early 1980s, though it remains on paper even today. *Chitralekha's* contribution to the film culture and Film Society Movement for Kerala is unique and historic. In 2015, Kerala has the largest number of film societies in India with 113 units functioning across the length and breadth of the state, and they celebrate Adoor as their *Karnavar* (head of the family).

Image 7.8 Function to mark 50 years of Film Societies in Kerala organised by FFSI Keralam in 2015.
Courtesy: Sasi Kumar.

CHALACHITHRA FILM SOCIETY

The *Chalachithra* Film Society, Thiruvananthapuram, always has a special place in my heart, as it were they who introduced me to a unique world of global good films. Though, I was not present for the inauguration of the society on 11 June 1976 by the then chief minister of Kerala, late C Achutha Menon, I was admitted as a member before the end of the year. *Chalachithra* was established by four ardent film lovers, N Krishna Murthy, George Mathew, SB Jayaram, KNG Kaimal and MND Nair, all working in the prestigious Vikram Sarabhai Space Centre, the Thiruvananthapuram unit of the Bangalore based ISRO.[21]

Chitralekha was perceived as an exclusive club and was patronised by literary and cultural figures, by the organisers of the Chalachitra. (Adoor counters any elitist tag on *Chitralekha* and says it is in Malayalee blood to form clubs and associations. *Chalachithra* started with a membership fee of ₹25 per year or ₹7 for three months,

Image 7.9 A Chalachitra's Aravindan Puraskaram Presentation.
Courtesy: Mr George Mathew.

and some open memberships (for festivals) became popular with government officials, University crowd and bank employees and film buffs like me. The initial membership drive in August 1976 with the inaugural programme of a week-long festival, of Indian "New Wave" films of Mani Kaul, Satyajit Ray, Aravindan, Avtar Kaul, Mrinal Sen and Basu Chatterjee, pushed the membership to 1,400 by 1977. "*Chitralekha* was the pioneer film society in Trivandrum and in Kerala and had a membership of around 700 plus till 1977. But they turned to production of films. From 1978 *Chitralekha* was almost defunct, which paved the smooth way to the growth of *Chalachithra*," George Mathew, who still runs the show, recalled.[22] Being a pioneer, Mathew remained precise with figures when it came to membership. He described the current state of affairs of his society as follows:

> *Chalachithra* reached the optimum membership of 1,450 in the second year itself, in 1977 and it remained for a decade. The membership began dwindling from the second half of 80s. It reached the least level of 260, in the first half of 90s and there was some improvement after the introduction of Trivandrum International Film Festival (TIFF) in 1996. The society has currently around 90 life members ($\times$ 3 = 270), 30 double members ($\times$ 2 = 60) and around 160 single memberships, totalling to around 500 single memberships. Since handling 35-mm films has become too expensive of

late, the society is on smaller formats like CD/DVD etc. DVD format is the order of the day even for quality films from different embassies which enabled the TIFF to be still attractive.

Though the membership rolls increased and dwindled over decades, the actual number of film buffs in the capital city remained steady around 300, Mathew summed up his years with the Film Society Movement.

The issues faced by *Chalachithra* are as almost the same as of any other societies across India. Mathew lists scarcity of auditorium and films. High expenditure on screenings combined with very thin attendance at screenings remains the bane of this society too. He pointed out:

> We are now living in a totally different environment where cinema has become so handy, where no one needs to help others. The internet does the job so beautifully for the film buffs, with available downloads of films. Film Society is now an old concept.

As such, he does see *Chalachithra* in existence till 2022. "We have to learn to go with the times, giving up false nostalgic attitudes and clinging on to old habits. Cinema survives with its own strength and not because of the support of the Film Society Movement," Mathew warned. However, he was clear about the contribution of the movement in Kerala, "Kerala Film Societies have produced some great names like Aravindan, Padmarajan, Adoor etc. and they are the all-time greats." Though minimal, he admits to the supporting role of the state government with financial and other means. *Chalachithra* remains alive in the capital city with its annual Aravindan Puraskaram awards instituted in the name of film-maker G Aravindan and TIFF.

ASWINI FILM SOCIETY, KOZHIKODE

The *Aswini* Film Society is the sister society of *Chitralekha* in the northern Malabar region of Kerala. Established in 1969, with the same by-laws as *Chitralekha*, and by the brother of Mankada Ravi Verma, Adoor's cinematographer; *Aswini* was patronised by literary figures, including writer/film-maker MT Vasudevan Nair, former editor of the prestigious *Mathrubhoomi* weekly and film-maker Aravindan and his first producer Pattathuvila Karunakaran.

Chelavoor Venu, the society's leader from 1969, remains an enigma even today with his love for films and print media, as he always edited one specialised journal after another. Venu represents the true face of the leadership of the Kerala Film Society Movement, as he is the publisher and editor of magazines apart from being a part-time political and cultural activist. *Aswini* started with ₹50 as the annual fees and with the contribution from 300 members became instrumental in the completion of John Abraham's first major movie *A Donkey in a Brahmin Village*, by ensuring that Abraham's last-minute financial troubles are taken care of. The film society was also the abode of writer and film-maker Raveendran (Chintha Ravi). *Aswini* has survived ups and downs, and with the help of a digital projector contributed by the friends of the society working in the Gulf countries is back on track with its monthly screenings. The Kozhikode-based society also played a leading role in the spread of the Film Society Movement of Malabar region of Kerala, by sharing, organising the films from embassies and NFAI with societies in nearby towns.

In the 1970s, Venu, a student and political activist, was also roped in by the Calicut University Students Union to curate a Film Appreciation course in the early 1970s, where literary figures and film-makers like Adoor and John Abraham were exciting students with their films and discussions. "We organized a hugely successful film appreciation course at Peechi dam guest house in early seventies," recalled the then Calicut University Union chairman, the late U Rajagopal, who retired as a senior editor from the *Mathrubhoomi* daily. Irrespective of political affiliations, the Students Union encouraged such film appreciation camps. Along with literary camps, film appreciation camps became the order of the day in the 1970s and 1980s in Kerala.

The *Aswini* Film Society organised a 14-day film festival in 1980, with films from NFDC. By then, the society had 800 regular members. "A local bank had given the advance amount for paying NFDC and even sold tickets for the film festival making a profit of ₹35,000," recalled Venu.

Today, the society has just over 100 members who assemble in the auditorium of a local hotel to see the films projected from a digital projector. However, Venu and *Aswini* continue to be a must visit for film-makers in the Malabar region to reach out to the right audience.[23]

THE MADRAS FILM SOCIETY, CHENNAI

In South India, the flag of Film Society Movement was hoisted by Ammu Swaminadhan. In 1957, on 30 October, the MFS was born in the "lap of the American Consulate." Ammu Swaminadhan, mother of advocate general Sri Govind Swaminadhan was the founder-president of the society. Being the capital of South India's film industry, the MFS had the full patronage of the various consulates of diplomatic missions. The MFS was also among the only film society with women presidents, among the male-dominated leadership of the Film Society Movement. Swaminadhan was also the vice president of FFSI from 1959, and she steered the growth of the movement in South India.

The first president's tenure was followed by Shantilal Mehta, one of the senior-most life members. Thereafter, Justice P.R. Gokulakrishnan, Visalakshi Nedunchezhian, G Venkateswaran (GV) of Sujatha Films served the organisation as president. Abirami Ramanathan, who was the vice president for 15 years, is the present president of the society (2012). KS Govindaraj, who is one of the founder members of the society continued as the executive vice president.

According to AG Raghupathy, general secretary, The MFS, which began with an annual subscription of ₹12, and now charges ₹700 per annum. Raghupathy claimed that many film personalities were benefited by their screening of international films. He lists K Balachander, Kamala Hassan, Singeetham Srinivasa Rao, Muktha Srinivasan, SP Muthuraman, Balu Mahendra, Suhasini and Nazar as regular guests at the screenings of the MFS. The MFS celebrated its golden jubilee from October 2006 to October 2007, where it screened more than 250 films obtained from all the embassies and consulates in India. In the celebration, MFS also held various film festivals themed "a festival, a country, and a month." The MFS has been one of the founder members of the FFSI from 1959 and is a member of the South Indian Film Chamber of Commerce, Chennai.[24]

INTERNATIONAL CINE APPRECIATION FOUNDATION, CHENNAI

The International Cine Appreciation Foundation (ICAF), Chennai, was established in 1977. Just like MFS, it had close association with the Consulate of Canada, and it existed as a film wing of the Indo-Canada Association. The conversion to an independent body enabled it to be affiliated to FFSI.

However, unlike MFS, the ICAF had more of an academic orientation and held a number of crash courses on film appreciation and
quiz programmes on cinema. ICAF also showed Tamil films as
examples for the film appreciation courses. Some of the films taken up
for studies included the Tamil New Wave film directors, Bharati
Raja's *Mudal Mariyatha,* and *Mouna Ragam,* an early film of Mani
Ratnam. RC Shakthi's *Sirai,* KS Sethumadhavan's *Marupakkam,* Balu
Mahendra's *Veedu* and the Telugu film *Kanlu* were also discussed in
the presence of the directors. The society's newsletter *ICAFO Speaks*
publishes articles on film appreciation, directors and carries a glossary
of words and phrases relating to cinema. The ICAF launched the
Chennai International Film Festival in 2003, and it is an annual feature
at Chennai with the support of the state government.[25]

There are active film societies in Assam, Jamshedpur, Jaipur,
Imphal and Pune too. Celluloid chapter of Jamshedpur, established in
1985, is the leader in the region with its active role in organising film
screenings, workshop, seminars, publications and festivals. The
Imphal Film Society was established in 1965. It is credited with establishment of the Manipur film industry. The society died out a couple
of decades ago, but the film industry survived. Ariban Siyam Sarma,
the many a national award-winning film-maker is a product of this
film society. The Guwahati Film Club, which celebrated its golden
jubilee in 2015, is the force behind new films of Assam. The Shillong
Film Club, which began in 1964, was wound up. The Jodhpur Film
Society in Rajasthan is a pioneer under Professor Mohan Meheshwari.
The lone film society in Jammu and Kashmir, Trikuta Film Society,
started in 1977 but closed abruptly in 1981 after its founder moved out
of the state.

The choice of film societies in this chapter was to examine what
has happened to the pioneering and most successful ones. While
searching for one of the oldest film societies at Faizabad, I found a new
society functioning there, but without an FFSI affiliation. The word is
out even in small towns that film society/clubs are important for
anyone who nurtures an ambition for a film career, and they organise
clubs, with or without an affiliation to FFSI. Such ambitions of youngsters have led to many a successful rags-to-riches and success stories
in Bollywood and other regional films. In the pursuit for a film career,
many have understood that film societies/clubs are training grounds,
first steps that will help them realise their dreams. And an increasing
number of regional yearly film festivals across Indian big cities give a

pull to the film societies, as those getting hooked on to contemporary international films find the film society circuit as a forum to quench their appetite for such quality films from across the world.

NOTES*

1. Chidananda Das Gupta. *Seeing Is Believing: Selected Writings on Cinema* (Delhi: Viking, 2008).
2. http://cherianwrites.blogspot.in/2016/03/cfs-cine-central-interviews.html
3. Ibid.
4. http://cherianwrites.blogspot.in/2016/02/interview-with-yc-halan-past-president.html
5. https://www.facebook.com/deepak.roy.148553
6. http://www.amazon.com/Hindi-Cinema-An-Insiders-View/dp/0195695844
7. NK Sharma is a former colleague of Safdar Hashmi of Jana Natya Manch and a theatre director. http://www.thehindu.com/features/friday-review/theatre/keeping-it-real/article4365920.ece
8. http://delhigovt.nic.in/dept/public/gkaul.htm
9. http://cherianwrites.blogspot.in/2016/03/delhi-malayalee-film-society-profile.html
10. https://en.wikipedia.org/wiki/Khalid_Mohamed
11. http://cherianwrites.blogspot.in/2016/03/notes-from-khalid-mohammed-interview.html
12. http://cherianwrites.blogspot.in/2016/02/interviewwith-sudhir-nandgoanker.html
13. http://www.fipresci.org/people/h-n-narahari-rao
14. http://cherianwrites.blogspot.in/2016/03/profile-of-bangalore-questions-1.html
15. http://cherianwrites.blogspot.in/2016/03/profile-of-chitralekha-with-mf-thomas.html
16. Gautaman Bhaskaran. *Adoor: A Life in Cinema* (New Delhi: Penguin-Viking, 2010), p. 68.
17. Interview with Kulathoor Bhaskaran Nair
18. Gautaman Bhaskaran. *Adoor: A Life in Cinema*, p. 69.
19. HN Narahari Rao, ed., *The Film Society Movement in India* (Mumbai: Asian Film Foundation, 2009), pp. 93–94.
20. Gautaman Bhaskaran. *Adoor: A Life in Cinema*.
21. http://www.isro.gov.in/
22. Notes: http://cherianwrites.blogspot.in/2016/03/profile-of-chalachitra-tvm.html
23. Notes: http://cherianwrites.blogspot.in/2016/03/notes-about-aswini-film-society.html
24. http://cherianwrites.blogspot.in/2016/02/interview-with-govindaraj.html
25. HN Narahari Rao, ed., *The Film Society Movement in India* (Mumbai: Asian Film Foundation, 2009), p. 207.

---

* All websites accessed on 16 June 2016.

CHAPTER 8

The Policy Shift and Waning Political Patronage

The last film enquiry committee of the Central government in 1980, when Indira Gandhi returned as prime minister after a gap of three years, headed by the veteran cultural icon from Karnataka, Dr Shivarama Karanth, stressed the need for a "National Film Policy" and suggested a Chalachitra Akademi. The Akademi, just as the Sahitya, Sangeet Natak and Lalith Kala Akademies, was to independently take care of the issues relating to the film field by the professionals themselves.

Justifying the new Akademi, the committee pointed out that:

> Indian cinema has to be helped to evolve its own aesthetic values from our own cultural roots. This can only be done if the cinema is given the full status of a cultural activity.... We therefore recommend that a separate Akademi to be called Chalachitra Akademi should be set up exclusively with the object of promoting cinema as an art form, on the same lines as the other Akademies....[1]

The committee wanted the government to amend the 1935 Cinematograph Act, where the censorship of films remained with the Centre and exhibition was a concurrent subject. However, since the exhibition involved various taxes to the state government, the recommendation never crossed the hurdle of getting the state government's consent.

Earlier too, the government had withdrawn a bill from the Rajya Sabha in 1956, to take full control of the production side of the film industry as recommended by the 1951 Film Enquiry Committee headed by SK Patil. The committee had recommended that legislative action should be taken to declare the control of production of films by the Union "expedient in public interest and thereby entrust the full responsibility for the production side of the industry to the Central Government." Patil had gone into the details of the nascent film industry of India in 1951 and projected a growth trajectory for the industry and strongly advocated a central intervention as they felt that the issues of the industry are "of a nature that can be comprehended only when viewed as a whole."[2]

The SK Patil committee's recommendation to establish a film and TV training institute (FTII), Film Archive (NFAI) and Film Finance body (FFC-NFDC) had indeed changed the course of the Indian film industry. Looking back, the Patil committee recommendations also laid the foundations for the development of the Indian film industry to reach the foremost position on the world film map by 2015.

However, Prime Minister Indira Gandhi's assassination in 1984 left a big void for the film industry, especially for the New Cinema and the Film Society Movement. No other prime minister gave such an importance to films ever again: neither her son Rajiv Gandhi, nor the six others who succeeded her in the years to come, from 1984 to 2015. Without patronage from the government, New Cinema and the Film Society Movement in India are now struggling to survive, though the movement is on its own steam in many regions.

"No Prime Minister, other than Ms Gandhi, including her son had any interest in films," Gautam Kaul, the FFSI president (2015) and Gandhi's cousin, declared.[3] He, as FFSI president, is struggling to get the ₹0.6 million annual sum allotted by the Planning Commission in 2009, which was granted to FFSI as a non-governmental organisation (NGO) under the I&B ministry. A retired Indian Police Service officer, Kaul is not optimistic about getting the ₹1.2 million, which is still stuck in the files for the past two years (in 2015), as there is hardly any interest in the Central government to support FFSI.

A right-to-information plea on government funding to FFSI revealed that the ministry of I&B had released grant-in-aid to FFSI under the 10th plan scheme of "Non-Government Organisation engaged in the anti-piracy works/Festivals, and under the 11th plan scheme: "Export Promotion through Film Festivals in India & abroad." Under this scheme, the I&B ministry from the financial year 2003–04 to 2006–07 granted ₹0.4 million and in 2007–2008 ₹0.3 million and thereafter doubled it to ₹0.6 million from 2008–09.[4]

THE POLICY PARALYSES

Even as the FFSI is struggling to get the annual grant, for the financial years 2012–13 and 2013–14, the report of the I&B ministry listed the following points to show their achievements in the film sector for the financial year 2014–15:

> During April 1, 2014 to October 31, 2014 this Division has produced 35 documentary films. Films Division has released 7786 prints of 39 approved films in Cinema Houses throughout the country. Films Division has entered 47 films in 16 National/International Film Festivals. News Magazines on 14th India Russia Summit-Moscow 2013, PM's visit to China 2013 and G-20 Summit Russia-2013 were

Image 8.1 Chief Guest Amitabh Bachchan and Union Minister for Finance, Corporate Affairs and Information & Broadcasting Arun Jaitley present the centenary award to Rajnikanth at the 45th International Film Festival of India (IFFI-2014), in Goa in November, 2014.
Courtesy: Press Information Bureau, GOI.

completed. Eight films completed for Non-Theatrical release as outside production and 15 films as in house production. Nine Films were completed for theatrical release as in house production.[5]

Apart from the last point, the ministry made it clear that its role is that of the propaganda wing of the Central government and to run institutions like Prasar Bharati and censor the films. The highlights in an annual report always show the priority and the achievements of the government in that sector. The annual report begins with the picture of the minister at the opening ceremony in the 45th IFFI at Goa with Bollywood film stars like Amitabh Bachchan and Rajinikanth. However, film bodies such as NFDC and Directorate of Film Festivals were not in the list of achievements.

The section of the annual report given by the ministry on film development in 2015 read as follows:

> The National Film Development Corporation Ltd. was incorporated in the year 1975, with the primary objective of planning, promoting and organizing an integrated and efficient development of the Indian film industry in accordance with the national economic policy and objectives laid down by the Central Government from time to time. By merging the Film Finance Corporation (FFC) and Indian Motion Picture Export Corporation (IMPEC) with NFDC it was reincorporated in the year 1980. Since inception, NFDC has funded/produced over 300 films in more than 21 regional languages, many of which have earned wide acclaim and won national/international awards. As a film development agency, NFDC is responsible for facilitating growth in areas/segments of the film industry that not only has a cultural bearing but also in areas which cannot be taken by private enterprises due to commercial exigencies thereby facilitating a balanced growth of the industry. However, even while its role in the Indian film industry is largely developmental, as a public sector enterprise, NFDC also has a corporate mandate and is responsible for generating a healthy balance sheet. To its credit NFDC was presented the Turnaround Award 2013 on November 1, 2013 by BRPSE (Board for Reconstruction of Public Sector Enterprises) along with three other Central Public Sector Enterprises (CPSEs), as all have posted profits for three consecutive financial years—2010–11, 2011–12 and 2012–13. NFDC further enhanced its forte in production and distribution under the brand, "Cinemas of India," production of advertisement, short and corporate films for various government agencies, film exhibition, restoration, Film Bazaar, training in digital non-linear editing, cinematography, sub-titling etc.[6]

However, the main thrust of the ministry in the film sector appears to be the National Museum of Indian Cinema (NMIC). The annual report listed the objectives of NMIC as follows:

- To encapsulate the socio-cultural history of India as revealed through the evolution of its cinema.
- To develop as a research centre focusing on the effect cinema has on society.
- To exhibit the work of the noted film-makers: directors, producers, institutions and others for the benefit of film enthusiasts and other visitors.
- To arrange seminars, workshops for film-makers and film students.
- To generate and sustain interest in films and film movements amongst current and future generations.[7]

National Film Heritage Mission (NFHM): The NFHM, a ₹5.9741 billion project, was approved by the ministry of I&B, government of India in November 2014 through the ministry of finance for restoring and preserving the film heritage of India. This is a part of the 12th Five-Year Plan, which will spill over to its 13th Five-Year Plan as per the year-wise allocation of plan outlay. This new plan scheme has taken care of digitisation/restoration of films available with NFAI, as well as other media units under the film wing of the ministry of I&B. The implementation of the plan scheme has been handed over to the NFAI, Pune, as described in the annual report of the NMIC project.

The FFSI, indeed, still gets a mention in the report as a collaborator for organising a film festival in Delhi with the European Union. As an NGO listed under the ministry, FFSI submits an annual report to the ministry for the grants-in-aid, there was no mention of FFSI or its activities in the annual report of the ministry, revealing the "importance" that the government attaches to film societies. As an NGO, FFSI also supplies its army of film scholars and discerning selectors for various Indian film festivals, state governments' annual awards and other film-related committees. The FFSI has been giving intellectual support to the government, and various other existing film promotional avenues, in identifying and promoting the quality of films in India, which can make the country proud at international film festivals, a contribution that has been increasingly overlooked by the ministry of I&B over the years.

Gautam Kaul, the FFSI President while discussing the contribution of FFSI on such occasions, pointed out as follows[8]:

> For the 2015 International Film festivals the Directorate of Film Festivals sent 15 names and gave the option of nominating five names to the Ministry. However, they have put the entire list on hold and asked for the profile of all 15, clearly indicating that the Ministry is not going by the wisdom of the Directorate in this matter.

Needless to say, such lists are normally is filled with FFSI activists.

FTII, NFDC, NFAI, IDENTITY CRISIS

In 2015, the Government of India appointed a not-so-popular actor from Hindi television serials and films serials as the chairman of the FTII. The FTII students went on a strike protesting against the appointment, as the actor had no stature, and his only qualification was he belonged to the same ideological school as the political party ruling at the Centre. Commenting on the appoint of the actor as the chairman, Adoor Gopalakrishnan, an alumnus of the institute, told *Hindustan Times*:

> A premier institute such as this one has to be given its due respect. According to FTII Society rules, its members must be eminent people from the field of cinema, art, literature and theatre. This year that was not the case, barring a few eminent people who have resigned.[9]

The question is: How seriously have such institutions of national importance been treated by the government over a period of time? Already, the post of the director of the institute has gone to serving civil servants, unlike in earlier years where eminent professionals like Girish Karnad and NVK Murthy were the preferred choices for such a post. From imparting world-class training in film-making and television programming, the institute's leadership is trying to administer curricula set up by experts. The institute, which produced almost all pioneers of New Cinema who have filled the National Awards' lists and even won an Oscar, is now reduced to yet another film training institute.

Image 8.2 Film and Television of Institute of India (FTII), Pune.
Courtesy: Photo by Hilal Savad.

In 2011, the committee headed by PK Nair, which went into the issues of the institute, had recommended wide-ranging reforms, including strengthening the infrastructure to cater to the increasing demands of the 11 courses it ran. In 2000, a committee had favoured handing over the institute to the film industry and in 2010 HR consultancy firm Hewitt wanted introduction of short-term courses at competitive rates to make FTII self-reliant.

"Government should issue grants without interfering in administration. FTII should be permitted to raise funds from outside sources. We had suggested a raised fee of ₹1 lakh per student across all courses. FTII could offer scholarships to those who cannot afford the fee," PK Nair had said then.[10]

Apart from administrative issues, the FTII appeared to be also suffering from an ideological positioning. Over the years, the FTII had produced Left liberal film-makers, and now the obviously Right wing, Hindutva-leaning government will try and change ideological moorings of the institute. "No one can Saffornise the technical aspects of film making like lighting, camera, and sound. But the ideology can matter when it comes to the narrative," commented noted film-maker Shyam Benegal on the change of guard and ideological leanings of the new FTII chairman.[11]

The FTII, which produced and supported better films and contributed to a new film culture through its extended support to the Film Society Movement, has been in turmoil for some time. This can even affect the annual residency of film appreciation at the institute, considering the way the situation has been developing. The government is clearly interested in administering the institute, rather than nurturing the talent and new culture there.

The NFDC, which is the successor of the FFC, the institution that produced most of the New Indian Cinema, is also in doldrums. It still produces and co-produces films under its extant guidelines for film production, but it encourages debut film-makers by undertaking 100 per cent production of their first feature film and co-production of good quality films in partnership with private players, both from India and abroad. Unlike earlier years, it is no longer a production house sustaining new experiments in cinema.

The annual report of the I&B ministry explained the new policy:

> The Production Department's mandate is to support and drive NFDC's mission to create artistic movies with a view to foster excellence in cinema and promote Indian culture through the cinemas of India. In keeping with this directive, the Production Department is continuously seeking to create an environment conducive to the making of cinema that reflects India's most imaginative, diverse and vibrant film culture. The Production Department endeavors to support, through production and collaboration, a community of versatile and emerging filmmakers who embody diversity, innovation and uniqueness.

From April to December 2014, the corporation financed two films and co-produced another three. Two of the co-productions were honoured at the film festivals.

A look at the list of films honoured at the yearly National Film Festival conducted by the government also shows the declining number of the NFDC-financed films in the list. In 1983–84, there were nine films, including the Oscar award-winning film *Gandhi* in the award categories, as against just one film in 2011–12. Clearly, the NFDC is no longer the storehouse of quality, award-winning films.[12]

The NFAI has a 50-year-old legacy of archiving films and a collection of 18,878 films, reported as per the 2015 March annual report of the I&B ministry. In 2015–16, the ministry has allocated ₹70 million as the annual budget for the archive, which is the largest of the sort in the last decade. The reason is the ongoing digitisation programme of old films and also the project on the NMIC. The director of the NFAI had been in the acting capacity for years and the local senior Indian information officer from the I&B ministry has been given the additional charge. This has put the archive on an autopilot mode. My first visit to the archive in 2012 revealed that it was leaderless and I felt that the organisation was drifting. However, my second visit in 2014 showed marked improvement, may be the director with additional charge was a person with some interest in the subject he/she was handling. Increasingly, the film-related institutions are being handled by administrators from the I&B ministry and professionals in the field are not encouraged to take the reign in these organisations.

All the institutions that the 1951 SK Patil committee flagged off appeared to be at crossroads. From nurturing and promoting a film culture that will put India on the world film map, these institutions are being used to administer various aspects of films. The Film Society Movement, which was the public arm of these institutions, is getting limited to pockets of influence and does not seem to have a role in influencing the film policy or cultures any more.

POLICY INITIATIVES BY STATE GOVERNMENTS

Even as the Central government's interest in films and Films Society Movement was declining from the 1980s, the state governments have shown keen interest in their regional films and film culture. Many find the Film Society Movement to be a storehouse of experience in handling the policy on films.

Notable among the states, which have been coordinating with the Film Society Movement, are West Bengal, Karnataka, Kerala and Tamil Nadu. Kolkata, where the Film Society Movement shaped into an all-India activity, led the way in the new phenomenon too. Nandan, the cultural complex in the middle of the town, was the pet project of Buddhadeb Bhattacharya, who was the then information minister. He even designed the logo of Nandan and had a room there to meet his cultural activist friends, as long as he was in power. The foundation stone of Nandan was laid by Buddhadeb Bhattacharya in 1980, and it was inaugurated by Satyajit Ray in 1985. The complex has been hosting various film screenings, and the Kolkata Film Festival over the years. Even after the Left Front was voted out of power in 2011, the centre continues to be a cultural house with films as the centre of the activity. In February 2013, the Nandan Managing Committee was headed by the Bengali film director, and Satyajit Ray's son, Sandip Ray, the members included film-maker Aparna Sen, daughter of the Film Society Movement pioneer Chidananda Das Gupta.

Around the time when Adoor Gopalakrishnan was winning National Awards, Kerala woke up to an emerging new cinematic culture. In 1975, at the height of the Film Society Movement, the state government established the Kerala State Film Development Corporation Ltd (KSFDC), the first of the sort in any state. Then, Chief Minister C Achutha Menon from the CPI was a film society admirer and even sanctioned a 35-mm projector at the Tagore Centenary Hall in the state capital, where most of the 35-mm films were screened by *Chitralekha* and later *Chalachithra*. KSFDC's mandate was to shift the Madras-centric Malayalam film-making into Kerala by giving incentives like production studio and facilities and also a subsidy.

In the last 40 years, the KSFDC has achieved its goal of shifting Malayalam film-making from Madras to Kerala. The Chitranjali Studio Complex of KSFDC, inaugurated in 1980, was truly a pioneer in introducing the latest film technology in South India, and it became the hub of award-winning film-makers like that of Shaji N Karun and KR Mohanan, two FTII graduates, who worked at KSFDC in senior positions. The corporation also owns an exhibition network with 11 fabulous theatres spread all over Kerala. Some of the theatres regularly host screenings of the offbeat films. The Thiruvananthapuram theatre complexes of KSFDC host the IFFK.[13]

Following the recommendation of the 1980 Central Film Enquiry committee, Kerala was also the first to establish its own Chalachitra Academy (Motion Picture Academy of the Kerala State) in 1998. The academy is entrusted with the conduct of the popular IFFK, the annual year-end film festival that attracts around 10,000 delegates in various categories. The FFSI Keralam is involved in the conduct of IFFK, as a partner to the academy.[14]

The office of the FFSI Keralam chapter now has 113 film society units. The Left Front government did sanction ₹5 million to the FFSI Kerala unit to encourage film society activities in 2010.

It took another 11 years for the neighbouring state of Karnataka to have its own Chalachitra Academy in 2009. The academy promotes film culture and conducts the Bangalore International Film Festival as a yearly feature from 2008, apart from conducting film appreciation courses in various parts of the state. The academy has also promoted the establishment of the film societies in the state.[15]

Tamil Nadu, which is famous for its obsession with films, also has its own International Film Festival. From 2003 onwards, the yearly event has been organised by a professional body called International Cine Appreciation Foundation (ICAF), which works for the promotion of meaningful cinema in Chennai. The ICAF has more than 500 members, mostly comprising of the film professionals and technicians. The Tamil Nadu government now patronises the Chennai International Film Festival, organised by the ICAF since 2008. Apart from the festivals, ICAF also has regular monthly screenings.[16]

Though the Centre abdicated its initial plan to mentor film appreciation as seen by the Film Society Movement and its pioneers, many state governments appeared to take the movement forward.

WANING POLITICAL PATRONAGE
The first major public consultation of films undertaken by Prime Minister Nehru's government in 1955 was to assign the responsibility of the Film Seminar to Sangeet Natak Akademi. The then Akademi chairman Dr PV Rajamannar identified its functions as "to set up high standards for this new art form without impairing its commercial value." Over the years, the academy did not find itself indulged in films leading the 1980 Film Enquiry committee recommending a Chalachitra Akademi, exclusively with the object of promoting cinema as an art form, on the same lines as the other academies, that is, Sangeet Nataka Akademi, Sahitya Akademi and Lalit Kala Akademi.

The functions of Chalachitra Akademi were listed in detail by the committee with a clear paragraph on the film society too:

> [The academy was] to act as a centre for the propagation of film culture and film consciousness in the country by providing financial help and guidance for setting up film societies film clubs and making film classics and artistic films available to these societies through the Film Lending Service.[17]

Explaining the role of the Film Society Movement in the proposed academy, the 1980 report wanted the film societies to be encouraged so that people in general can be initiated to "the art of cinema." The report went to state:

It is obvious that the Film Society Movement has a very important role to play in "initiating" audience in the appreciation of good cinema. It is in this context that we have suggested that the Academy should be assigned the task of helping the growth of Film Society Movement.[18]

Indira Gandhi's last tenure as prime minister was plagued by terrorism, a phenomenon that India was never used to. No one in the film circuit trusted any other prime minister other than Gandhi, the original supporter of New Cinema/Film Society Movement on the formation of a Chalachitra Academy. Her son Rajiv Gandhi, who succeeded her as the prime minister, had too many legacy issues to handle and films were not his priority either. A central Chalachitra Academy remained buried in the files of the Government of India.

The only recommendation of the committee in 1980, which the Central government has accepted recently, after the Indian film industry celebrated its 100 years, was the setting up of a National Film Museum.[19] However, at least two states went ahead and formed their own Chalachitra academies and many have their own art theatres in the state and district capitals. Nandan at Kolkata, *Suchitra* centre at Bangalore and 11 theatres of Kerala's KSFDC remain as remnants of an unfinished plan across the country.

The lack of political patronage for the Indian New Cinema and film society does not need further elaboration. According to Chidananda Das Gupta, from Prime Minister Nehru's regime to his grandson Prime Minister Rajiv Gandhi's period, Film Society Movement and its leaders played an important role in the film policies of the government. It was Rajiv Gandhi as prime minister who honoured the film society evangelist Marie Seton with the nation's third highest civilian honour, the Padma Bhushan.

Chidananda Das Gupta observed as follows[20]:

Film Society activists were inducted into many Government committees and had a great deal of influence over India's third International Film Festival in 1965 (the second having taken place in 1961 after nine years of the first in 1952). The fourth festival came up in 1969 and thereafter, under Ms Gandhi's Prime Ministership, a Directorate of Film Festivals was established under the Ministry of Information and Broadcasting in 1974 to hold an annual International film festival, as well as the annual National Film Festival at which President's awards were distributed. The 1960s thus laid the foundation for a government – supported serious cinema (or the "art" film) which continued to develop through the 1970s.

The crisis of the 1980s and 1990s also saw a policy paralysis of the government-supported "art" films. In his last book, Das Gupta, whose life was dedicated to this genre of films and the Film Society Movement, documented the decline of interest in the Central government.

> In the 1980s, started the decline in the support systems for the alternative cinema. The governmental will to maintain the infra-structure in prime condition wavered. It relapsed into the common illusion of culture as a decoration to be worn on one's sleeve rather than an essential ingredient of national development, expandable whenever there was any pressure on resources. The International Film Festival of India, National Film Development Corporation, the President's awards, the National Film Archive of India increasingly found their reason d'être coming into question. If they have not been abolished it has partly been due to inertia and partly the fear of alienating powerful sections of intelligentsia. They have therefore been allowed to continue listlessly, without positive faith in their necessity. This lackadaisical attitude has been further undermined by religious orthodoxies with their xenophobic compulsion.[21]

GOVERNMENT AS A CHEER LEADER FOR BOX OFFICE FILMS

In a way, Das Gupta could foresee the appointment of an actor known for his political contacts and mythological roles, as the chairman of FTII by a future regime; NFDC going through restructuring as a sick public sector unit; NFAI being administered, and the Directorate of Film Festival being without an artistic director. The Central govern-ment, which once toyed with the idea of taking effective control of film production to raise the level of the film culture and formation of a Chalachitra Akademi, has not only left such plans, but also appeared to have submitted itself to a box office-oriented film culture. Those in the government appear to be happy clicking pictures with popular cine stars at film festivals and leading delegations to interna-tional film festivals to see global stars, going by their visible interventions.

If some films of international standards are still being made, it can only be due to the legacy, which films like *Pather Panchali* has built. The National Film Awards and choice of films for international festivals from India are increasingly moving towards the so-called popular films made for mass consumption with an eye on the box office, leaving all pretensions of government as a connoisseur of art.

NOTES*

1. Ministry of I&B. *Report of the Working Group on National Film Policy* (New Delhi: Ministry of I&B, GOI, May 1980), p. 10, paras 3.8 and 3.10.
2. SK Patil Committee report, 1951, quoted in supra 1, p. 4, para 2.7.
3. Interview with Gautam Kaul.
4. RTI on grants to FFSI by the I&B ministry: http://cherianwrites.blogspot.in/2016/02/reply-from-ministry-of-i-ffsi-funding.html
5. http://mib.nic.in/
6. Ibid.
7. Ibid.
8. Interview with Gautam Kaul.
9. Adoor-HT-http://www.hindustantimes.com/education/ftii-furore-behind-the-angry-graffiti-and-empty-classrooms/story-OSHtz0v4B6CnIJKiL1XKQO.html
10. PK Nair, HT. http://www.hindustantimes.com/india/ftii-chairman-s-new-battle-students-strike-sceptical-film-fraternity/story-Y5qPb0zCtka1Tu0546ZpQJ.html
11. Shyam Benegal, HT. http://www.hindustantimes.com/india/ftii-chairman-s-new-battle-students-strike-sceptical-film-fraternity/story-Y5qPb0zCtka1Tu0546ZpQJ.html
12. http://mib.nic.in/
13. http://www.ksfdc.in
14. Chalachitra Academy, Kerala. http://www.keralafilm.com/
15. Chalachitra Academy, Karnataka. http://kcainfo.com/
16. Chennai International Film Festival. http://www.chennaifilmfest.com/
17. Ministry of I&B. *Report of the Working Group on National Film Policy*, p. 10, para 3.10.
18. Ibid., p 13, para 3.23.
19. Ibid.
20. Chidananda Das Gupta. *Seeing Is Believing: Selected Writings on Cinema* (Delhi: Viking, 2008), p. 91.
21. Ibid., p. 91.

---

* All websites accessed on 16 June 2016.

CHAPTER 9

Towards a New Film Culture: From Crass to Class!

urprisingly, cinema, though much celebrated today, was neither considered a form of art nor a legitimate past time in India till the 1950s; rather, it was looked down as a low form of entertainment. None of the prominent cultural figures, writers, painters and musicians associated with it wholeheartedly till films like *Pather Panchali* began to make headlines nationally and internationally. A close look at the history of the development of films as a medium reveals that it was the Film Society Movement, the institutions like FTII, NFDC, NFAI and New Cinema which changed this social attitude, giving films a respectable social status along with other art forms, if not make it a glamour status, which it enjoys today. This is not to take into account the occasional sparks created by films like *Darthi Ke Lal* by KA Abbas as far back in the 1940s.

CINEMA FROM AN UNCULTURED TO A CLASSIC ACT

Chronicling the New Indian Cinema, Aruna Vasudev, the eminent film writer, narrated this makeover of films in the Indian society.[1] "In the vibrant atmosphere of the 1950s, the cinema began to be viewed as a possible art form. Cinema, until this time had been treated, as worst as, a reprehensible, though unavoidable, social catastrophe, at best a barbarous pastime for the uncultured."

Adoor Gopalakrishnan, the film-maker, speaking at a convocation ceremony at Ahmedabad University observed in that initial days of films, even professional prostitutes refused to act in films as the medium had no social standing. Adoor, who spent a lifetime lifting the film to an art form with his support to film societies and his own creations, lamented as follows[2]:

> Cinema from the very beginning enjoyed a very low esteem or no esteem at all. Even professional prostitutes had refused to act in films, although the roles offered were that of the virtuous *Sati Savitri* and the like. They feared it would tarnish their image. Dada Saheb Phalke—the father of Indian cinema—had to settle for a man who looked manly every inch to enact queen *Chandramathi's* role in *Raja Harishchandra*. Fortunately, the film was silent, and the man's voice could not kill the role. It was a long time ago and the stigma attached to cinema refuses to wash away after a century.

From 1947 to 2015, the Film Society Movement, and the institutions like FTII, NFAI and NFDC established by the Central government, have given the sector once considered "uncultured," a façade of respectability and a glamorous positioning, making many writers get into the bandwagon. The world recognised the "New Wave" in Indian films with films like *Pather Panchali* and a host of film-makers who went on to win awards in various international film festivals abroad. "Retrospectives and Film Weeks of Indian films have been held at a number of international forums and today India can justly claim to have several film-makers of international status," the Shivarama Karanth committee report observed.[3] *Pather Panchali* itself was a cinematic adaptation of a popular Bangla novel by Bibhutibhushan Bandyopadhyay, opening a new vista of adaption of fictional works into films, a trend that is still popular across Indian languages.

The best example of this change of positioning is reflected in none other than Amitabh Bachchan, the Hindi film superstar. His name has often cropped up in discussions as a potential candidate to the post of president of India. Even the thought of such an honour for any film actor being considered for the top post of the country would not have been the wildest dreams of Indians until the 1970s and 1980s. The closest they could get to Parliament in the 1970s was with a Rajya Sabha a nomination for Nargis Dutt, who happened to be in the Prime Minister Nehru and Indira Gandhi's charmed circuit, since she had a huge admirer in Egyptian President Gamal Abdel Nasser courtesy the film *Mother India*. Nasser not only ensured a remake of the film is made in Egypt but even attended a Filmfare Award ceremony to catch up with his favourite star in the early 1960s. Since then, many film stars and directors have been nominated to the upper house of Parliament over the years.

The inherent contradiction of the situation of a "not-so-cultural" mass film and a cultured cinema promoted by the government manifested as a clash between commercial and art films for years. The reason for the exorbitant taxation of films in India is a legacy of the "uncultured past." Commenting on the films of those years, Vasudev pointed that the strict censorship and lack of institutional financing was a part of this social stigma on films. "It has been allowed to go its own way, but subjected to stern censorship and more damagingly, to exorbitant taxation and a series of vexatious rules and regulations," she noted, though she added that despite all these negative conditions 319 films were made in India in 1960.[4]

BK Karanjia, the editor of *Filmfare*, also noted the sad state of affairs of the Indian cinema in the 1960s and 1970s. He focused on it in every issue of the journal. In his autobiography *Counting My Blessings*, Karanjia categorised the "evils": "first was the prevalence of black money deals, which was like a cancer eating into the industry's vitals from within. The second evil was black-marketing in cinema tickets, spreading through the country like a prairie fire. And the third was the shameful practice of wholesale plagiarism from Hollywood films."[5]

Karanjia, who campaigned against such evil practices in the mainstream cinema, also had clear solutions in his mind:

> What Indian films needed then was to cultivate the values of narrative strength and clarity, living characters and real situations. The perennial theme of love, so naive in current films, had to achieve a certain maturity. Producers had to learn to come to grips with the abiding theme of poverty which, with the outstanding exception of Satyajit Ray, had never been more than a platitude in our cinema.[6]

Karanjia will be known in history as one of the few journalists who could administer his advice in real life and make a difference. In 1968, Karanjia was appointed chairman of the Film Finance Corporation, a post he continued till 1975, when the national Emergency was declared. In his seven years as the chairman of FFC, Karanjia presided over the changeover of Indian cinema from a low cultural form to a higher art called, "New Cinema of India."

The New Cinema of India, which even took Satyajit Ray by surprise, was mainly the product of the FTII-trained film-makers, apart from Ray's contemporary Mrinal Sen and Ritwik Ghatak. Under Mr Karanjia's chairmanship, the films of Mrinal Sen, Adoor Gopalakrishnan, Mani Kaul, Kumar Shahani, Avtar Kaul (*27 Down*) and MS Sathyu were financed by FFC, giving a new genre to Indian cinema, which was described as the "New Indian Cinema" to the world. Most of these film-makers were products of the Film Society Movement or the FTII. They gave new idiom and outlook to cinema as medium, which was appreciated nationally and internationally in various film festivals, thus changing older image of "a barbarous pastime for the uncultured." The New Wave films/parallel cinema, as these films are called, also gave much-needed confidence to the Film Society Movement as the harbingers of "art and culture" in Indian films. The media and the box office film industry began to describe these films as art films and also parallel cinema, attracting the attention of not just the other practitioners, but even the government of the day, as some of these films began to be honoured in international film festivals making India proud.

Commenting on these films he financed to create a "New Indian Cinema," Karanjia wrote: "Their work held out the promise of the kind of personal, perspective, provocative and socially committed cinema that we had admired in European films ever since the first International Film Festival of India."[7] The government of the day should have been contended with these statements and international honours, since most of the films were produced by the FFC and later NFDC, the public sector corporations, established specifically to raise the standards in film-making and films.

The support of the government to the Film Society Movement, which precipitated these films by creating a group of culturally oriented film appreciators, should have been another brownie point to those like Ms Indira Gandhi, who extended the political patronage to the movement.

The non-FTII film-makers of this new wave/parallel cinema admires the role that film societies played. Mrinal Sen, one of the leading figures of the Indian New Cinema, admits that he is a product of the CFS and the film society culture of the city. "Actually I learned cinema from watching films through the Film Society Movement," the veteran film-maker said and went on to call the film societies the parents of good film-makers. "Parents are very important for a child to grow. Film societies have been very important for me to grow", the senior-most Indian film-maker after Ray admitted his love for film societies. Mrinal Sen's *Bhuvan Shome*, produced by FFC, ushered in the New Cinema in Hindi.[8]

The Dr Shivarama Karanth committee on films appointed by the Central government in 1980 too placed on record the role of the Film Society Movement in raising the level of film appreciation in the country. "While the film society movement has made a distinct contribution in the propagation of film consciousness, the movement has largely confined to major urban centres," the committee noted and went on to add, "it is obvious that the film society movement had a very important role to play in 'initiating' audience in the appreciation of good cinema."[9]

Adoor Gopalakrishnan, who pioneered the Film Society Movement in his home state remarks, "I went on to start the movement in Kerala, because firstly I wanted the intelligentsia in Kerala to become aware of a cinema of high caliber that existed in the world outside." Adoor started *Chitralekha* in 1965 with his friends, after he returned from FTII. Adoor's first film, *Swayamvaram*, was produced by FFC, and had the rare privilege of paying back the entire loan back to FFC.[10] "We paid back the entire loan amount to FFC, within a year or two, as the film ran to full houses in Kerala and bagged national awards," recounted Kulathoor Bhaskaran Nair, managing director of the *Chitralekha* Film Cooperative.[11]

Kumar Shahani has had the unique privilege of being known as a film-maker whose first film, *Maya Darpan*, was celebrated in the film society circuit, but never got a commercial release.

The film was produced by FFC. Mani Kaul too comes in this category with his films *Ashad Ka Ek Din* and *Uski Roti*, both produced by FFC. Most of these films never got a theatre release and hence were a commercial flop, although were celebrated across the world for their artistic merits.

Anil Srivastava, a pioneer of the movement, who is a new technology evangelist based in the United States, summed up those days of evolution of Indian culture in films as follows[12]:

> In the Nehruvian view, culture was important for creating a new nation, and needed equal attention as economic growth. In recognition of his stature as a film-maker, Satyajit Ray was made the President of the Federation of Film Societies of India (FFSI).

Indira Gandhi served as the Vice President and Inder Gujral as the Treasurer. Later, as the minister for Information and Broadcasting, Mrs Gandhi ruled that a certification of artistic merit of a film by Satyajit Ray, in his capacity as president of FFSI, would suffice to exempt the film from examination by the Censor Board. Many great and even controversial works of cinema thus found their way to film society screenings. ...India was indeed '...the great success story of political gradualism—of a kind of "evolutionary" independence,' where cultural movements like the film society in the Nehruvian perspective were an important and integral part.

MARGI IMPREGNATING *DESI*

The success of Film Society Movement and advent of New Wave films also created a sharp debate on art films and commercial films, which almost divided the industry vertically. The debate on films, which had an artistic content, but with mass appeal, always had its detractors. The "*Margi*" and "*Desi*" division is sacrosanct for them. Film critic like TG Vaidhyanathan calls it the "confusion between the conflicting claims of art and commerce," in his book. He made a sharp division between the two streams and said:

> The champions of art are invariably cosmopolitan intellectuals (who have probably spent their formative years in the capitals of Europe) frightened at the prospect of encroaching indigenization. The champions of commerce, on the other hand, translating their box-office anxieties into the new, fashionable language of alienation, talk glibly of "Indianans" and the need for Indian Cinema to have an "identity."[13]

This sharp debate was created by the films of Kumar Shahani and Mani Kaul, which rejected the Ray model of narrative in films. They went by the Marxian and Brechtian (Bertolt Brecht) way and were literally banished by the regular theatres. "Kaul and Shahani may be regarded as the outer limit of the *margi* cinema, meant solely for the aficionado," Chidananda Das Gupta, commented.[14] The regular film circuit developed such an antipathy for them, so much so that a humorous film of Mani Kaul did not even find a distributor years later, as they got scared by his very name of Mani Kaul, goes the legends associated with them.

There are bitter critics of Kaul and Shahani in the film society circuit too. Film scholar, Partha Chatterjee, credits the two of them as having brought the entire meaningful cinema movement to a halt. "They never grew out of their class room," says Chatterjee, reminding us that they were FTII students, when film-maker Ritwik Ghatak was the vice principal there. Ritwik, though a proclaimed Marxian in his approach, never adopted the Brechtian narrative in his films and always wanted to be closer to the taste of his evolving audience, Chatterjee pointed out.[15]

Mani Kaul happened to be a nephew of a popular Hindi film star, but never ventured into his uncle's way of film-making. Kumar Shahani and Mani Kaul remain the enigma among the "New Indian Cinema" film-makers. "At my age I am forced to explain my contribution to films," a disappointed Kumar explained his predicament of not getting funds for his films.[16] Mani Kaul ended up lecturing and promoting a film festival during the last phase of his life. However, both of them remain the finest theoreticians of films among the FTII products, as few like them have shown such depth in understanding film theories and experimented with the medium.

While the Ray model of narrative had found its own path in India with its proponents finding private financers for their films, commercial films too have been moving to this narrative in search for global acceptance. "Yet while commercial cinema remains a window to the popular India's English-speaking, globalised intelligentsia, a certain ambivalence persists," observed Vinay Lal and Ashish Nandy. The scholars pointed out the contradiction in the popular cinema as follows[17]:

> It is a cinema that appears terribly flawed by the canons of the global film theory and almost entirely disjunctive which the globally dominant aesthetics and concept of good cinema. Its principal attractions – the carnivalesque atmosphere, the centrifugal story-line, the larger than life characters and stilted dialogue – also mark it out as flawed art and a curious intrusion into the world of modern art forms.

However, Chidananda Das Gupta sees this phenomenon as "signs of a rapprochement between art films and commercial cinema." Noting the films of Mani Ratnam, *Roja* (1992) and *Bombay* (1995),

Kamala Hassan's *Hey Ram* (2000), Aamir Khan's *Lagaan* (2001) and Shah Rukh Khan's *Asoka* (2001), Das Gupta observed:

> The lessons of all positive developments—the impact of technical and artistic growth centers, the success of many serious films in the regions, their winning of prestigious prizes in India and abroad, the emergence of the documentary and of television, the increasing emphasis on realism—cannot have been altogether lost in the mainstream film industry despite the hostile noises it often made about these trends.[18]

Ray himself refused to be drawn into a debate on art and commercial cinema's in one of the last questionnaire of Das Gupta and said he believed in the art of storytelling and ensuring return on investment to the producer for his films, according to Samik Bandyopadhyay, who claimed to have seen the document.[19]

Documenting a lifetime of work, Das Gupta in his last book's chapter "Precursors Unpopular Cinema" noticed the "impregnation" of art cinema into commercial cinema, heralding a closing of the gap between art cinema and commerce. The impregnation empowered the commercial cinema in terms of "concepts and techniques and qualifying it for international acceptance at World forums."[20] This was a big development for the popular films that began as a variety show mode of the Parsi theatre. In effect, the new film culture which the Film Society Movement and New Indian Cinema stood for had influenced the crass commercial cinema, giving it a better *rasiks* appeal.

The success of *Piku* (2015), a film made by a director from the film society circuit, Shoojit Sircar, is the latest example of this impregnation, making the observation of Das Gupta that "the coexistence of *margi* and *desi* within the ambit of film industry may also become more peaceful" a prophetic one. *Piku* reportedly grossed over ₹1 billion at the box office too, apart from the fact that it has been acclaimed as a film well-made with one of the best performances from popular actors Amitabh Bachchan and Deepika Padukone. "I have grown up watching these films and it has a great influence on your life and that is important to you," said Shoojit Sircar.[21] He remembers seeing *Roza Luxumberg,* an award-winning German film, and a US documentary on the Vietnam war, where the film is about letters from US soldiers serving in Vietnam in the diplomatic missions in his early days as a film buff in Delhi.

Image 9.1 Shoojit Sircar, the director of *Piku*, a product of film society circuit of Delhi.
Courtesy: His unit.

"Hungarian cultural centre was my favorite and I used to go to the British Council and USIS," recalled Shoojit.[22] *Rosa Luxemburg (German: Die Geduld der Rosa Luxemburg)* is a 1986 West German drama film directed by Margarethe von Trotta. The film received the 1986 German Film Award for Best Feature Film (Bester Spiel film), and Barbara Sukowa won the Cannes Film Festival's Best Actress Award, as well as the German Film Award for Best Actress for her performance as Rosa Luxemburg.

POSITIONING OF THE FILM SOCIETY MOVEMENT

The pioneers had positioned the Film Society Movement as an act of cultural renaissance. A medium that was considered as less than an art was elevated to a respectful cultural phenomenon by showcasing the best of the art forms and also promoting such productions in India. From the *Desi* cultural form, films got elevated to the *Margi* form as described by veteran film theoretician, Chidananda Das Gupta and pioneering film society organiser.

Gautam Kaul, president (2015) of FFSI, pointed out as follows[23]:

> The FS movement has been the nursery of directors of film festivals in India. This is a breed apart. It has people who cannot write a good essay on films and yet they work to create a whole film festival of decent standards. They like their films though have come from disparate jobs totally unrelated to their hobby. All had one common gene. They were good managers of facts and material.

His list of such managers who enriched the Indian film festival management field included the following: U Radhakrishnan of the Delhi Malayalee Film Society, for Indian Habitat International Film Festival; BB Nagpal, a journalist, for Prism International Film Festival and Children Film Festival in Hyderabad; Niranjan Desai and an IFS officer, from Osian International Film Festival; Malti Sahay, a housewife, from the Directorate of Film Festival; S Narayanan, a former Directorate of Film Festival staff from Mumbai International Film Festival; Shanker Mohan, an FTII alumnus; HN Narahari Rao, Bangalore International Film Festival, engineer and founder of *Suchitra* Film Society; E Tanga Raj, an RBI officer, Madras International Film festival through MFS; George Mathew, an officer from the ISRO, of *Chalachithra*, and one of the artistic selector to Bangalore Film Festival and officials of Cine Central, Kolkata, associated with Kolkata International Film Festival, constitute this elite club of people running film festivals in India.

There are about 21 international film festivals being conducted in various parts of the country on annual basis and four are licensed internationally. One can say, most of these film festivals are sustained by the Film Society Movement of the area and its leadership, though the state governments have come in to support them in a big way. Gautam Kaul sees film societies as a feeder channel for film students for all major film studies institutions and film critics. "It is still a feeder channel to FTII, SRFTII Kolkata, Adayar Film Institute. It is an open classroom for most of the better known film critics in India in all languages."[24]. Going by the number of delegates to the IFFK (around 10,000), one can safely say that the 100-odd film societies and various film study departments of public and private institutions are also feeder organisations to the annual film jamboree. It was at the touring phase of the IIFI at capital of Kerala where the concept of "Open Forum," with film-makers, festival organisers and delegates as a platform, was introduced by FFSI. This gave a "club-society" feeling to the organisers and the participants enriching the experiences at the film festivals. From then onwards an "Open Forum" has become a must in all the film festivals across India.

In the film city of Mumbai, at Lokandawala complex, where most young film-makers reside, a video/DVD shop offers films to create your own film festival. Indeed, a customised festival for budding and practicing film-makers. At the music and stationary shop "Rhythm House," (closed in 2016) at Kalagoda in South Mumbai, one could pick up any of the world classics, even the one from the silent film era. The FFSI president also admits the elitist bias of the Film Society Movement. Kaul observed as follows[25]:

> It has had its limitation mainly because it was not a people's movement. It remained an elitist's interest, an evening exercise for students of serious studies in other vocational subjects. In its early years, it was the only window to the cinema of the West. Even today access to classical cinema is only through FSM activities.

Mr Kaul and his team are focusing on Indian Institute of Technology (IIT) and Indian Institute of Management (IIM) campuses across India now to resurrect the waning Film Society Movement.

Sudhir Nandgoankar, the former FFSI secretary also subscribes to the view that a serious study of films can help sustain the movement in future.

Sudhirji, who is keeping the movement's flag flying in India's film capital, pointed out as follows[26]:

> It is a general feeling of the public outside the fold of the Film Society Movement that due to 24 × 7 channels screening films, DVD, downloads from internet and now on mobile, film societies have become irrelevant today. But it is not true. Take the example of literature; the books are available in bookshops and libraries even then the languages are taught at the graduate and post graduate level. This helps readers to understand the nuances of literature. The same thing is about film society. It is not irrelevant in today's

time. But a Film Society should give emphasis on study of cinema besides screening films every month. The future of movement lies in the study of cinema. So Film Society should give more emphasis on study of cinema. Those societies will adhere to it will only survive.

. However, HN Narahari Rao, the doyen from the *Suchitra* Film Society, Bangalore, the only film society with its own cultural complex, says that there is a need to redefine the concept of film society itself. Rao pointed out as follows:

Film society concept has to be redefined, there is a need accept the right to see what the members want to see. Just as in music, there must be a choice for the filmgoers to see what they want. Use of advanced digital technology can lead us to such a situation.

Rao further stated as follows[27]: From showing films, film societies have to change to curating films for the audience. They need to be in the selection process with active involvement of the youngsters. There are communications departments in all universities and they need to be involved in film studies and Film Society Movement, with localised film clubs. The booming real estate sector has also shown interest for localized film clubs. It leads to the choice of the viewers, though copyright laws can be an impediment. Ultimately the film clubs have to go local.

The present FFSI leadership also has a plan to rope in the universities, offering film studies as a part of the mass communications courses across India to start a University Film Club, an unfulfilled dream of the pioneers. An RTI query from the UGC revealed that there are over 200 campuses that offer film studies in India.[28] This is apart from the numerous film institutes that have sprung up over the years in many parts of the country. Though most of these institutes and campuses are supplying manpower to television channels across the length and breadth of the country, they have been identified as the next fertile ground for keeping the flag of the Film Society Movement flying, as film appreciation is part of the curriculum of these institutes.

Professor Mihir Bhattacharya, of Jadavpur University in Kolkata, who started the first Film Studies department offering postgraduate studies in films, admits that most of his students end up with television channels. "We have a film making and production paper with practicals and hence they find it useful to get employment in television channels," Professor Bhattacharya added. After a wait of three years, UGC approved his department's plan to start a full-fledged film studies department offering postgraduate courses in 1991 for the first time in India and the department admits around 40 students every year. The other university that offers postgraduate courses in Film Studies is the Kolkata-based West Bengal University in Kolkatta along with many others spread across India, going by the list from UGC, which oversees the academic curriculum of higher education centres in India.[29] It is not accidental that the city that has a rich tradition of Film Society Movement also pioneered film studies in universities with its Film Studies departments. Though the Film Society Movement is at its lowest in the eastern region, the routes of looking at films with a *Margi* tradition carries on in Kolkata and in the universities of the city.

Apart from focusing on campuses, there is also a suggestion to focus on states on the lines as Kerala and Maharashtra model of organisation of Film Society Movement. Sudhir Nandgaonkar pointed out as follows:

> One intervention can be further decentralisation of the Federation of Film Societies in India. At present FFSI has five regions combining three to four states in each region. An honorary worker cannot cope up with his present workload of organisation. So, instead of a Regional Council we should have a State Council, based on regional languages. Secondly, all these years' film societies were using English as medium of communication. Now it should do so in regional language. Even film appreciation course must be organised in regional languages.

He also wants increasing involvement of the state governments in activities of FFSI, just as in Karnataka and Kerala. "Government can play a major role in promoting Film Society Movement in general and film culture in particular. Kerala and Karnataka have already started this. Other states are far behind," the Film Society Movement veteran pointed out.[30] The Dr Shivarama Karanth committee of 1980 had already recommended such a step. "...Federation of Film Societies should set up organisations at State level so that it can properly liaise with the State Governments for obtaining financial help and facilities for the film societies in the State."[31]

NOT "ORGANISED, BUT WIDESPREAD"

The Mumbai Film Festival's former executive Srinivasan Narayan says that, in most metro cities, the film-viewing culture is changing and he calls it, "not organized, but widespread." He attributes the availability of DVDs and the widespread downloading of films by the youngsters for this new phenomenon. Most of them run their own blogs and social media pages, which build communities around it and exchange of views and ideas. Srinivasan, who started his career with the Directorate of Film Festivals in Delhi, was credited with the success of the Mumbai International Film Festival and has over three decades of experience in organising film festivals.[32]

In Chennai, film enthusiasts have many options to see world films. The auditorium of the South Indian Film Chamber of Commerce is open to film enthusiasts, mainly the ICAF, to screen films from across the world as weekend morning shows. ICAF along with state government conducts the Chennai International Film Festival annually. In Hyderabad, a group of film enthusiasts has an arrangement with the studio preview theatres to screen quality world films for the *rasiks*. In Thiruvananthapuram, film societies run by young professionals, such as the Banner Film Society, have weekend screenings, with eminent film-makers and film personalities choosing their favourite films. This is apart from the regular film societies; screenings at 11 KSFDC cinema halls and the annual film festivals in various parts of Kerala.

In the capital, New Delhi, the Directorate of Film Festivals, which runs the Siri Fort Theatre, uses a small auditorium to screen films that it keeps getting for various film festivals. This is in addition to the regular shows at Italian Cultural Centre, Hungarian Information Centre, Alliance Francaise, Max Mueller Bhavan and Instituto Carvantes of Spanish Embassy, which screens films from all Spanish-speaking regions, including Latin American films. The India International Centre and the India Habitat Centre, the places where the capital's decision makers from government, corporate and social sector hangout, have their own film clubs organised more or less in the good film society way. So much so the new FFSI president finds it difficult to revive the DFS, as there are enough avenues for the *rasiks* of serious films in the city.

In Kolkata, where the Film Society Movement took the shape of an all-India movement, the situation is not glossy. CFS has been revived, and it celebrates the annual release of *Pather Panchali* every year. It also conducts an annual Chidananda Das Gupta memorial lecture. Cine Central has a children's film festival in collaboration with UNICEF, state government and NGOs from 2006 and also take part in the annual Kolkata "International Forum of New Cinema." Cine Central has plans to establish an art house theatre in the city. "There are enough finances available for all kinds of films in the city," says Sandeep Ray in a conversation with the author.[33]

However, Partha Chatterjee, a Delhi-based film scholar, says he no longer sees or hears about the long queues that he used to see at Sarala Mandir school auditorium in the 1980s for film society screenings. The number of FFSI-affiliated film societies is at an all-time low in the eastern region now, with only 65 from close to a 100 in the 1970s and early 1980s. Anil Srivastava, movement's pioneer and a technologist based in the United States, pointed out as follows[34]:

> As the country talks about big investments in broadband to the village and a Digital India, we need to think of an effort at sustaining our film culture, the moving image re-telling of stories that bridge all cultural divides. I am not being facetious in my hope for a ubiquitous cinema as the next incarnation of the film society in the new India.

FFSIs MAKEOVER PLANS

In June 2015, the leaders of the FFSI assembled at Thiruvananthapuram at Malayalam film-maker KR Mohanan's residence. Mohanan was the vice president of Kerala FFSI. The occasion was a discussion on Film Society Movement as the Kerala unit was about to celebrate its golden jubilee in July 2015. The Kerala unit happens to be one of the richest and largest of the FFSI, with the patronage from the state government, as well as from the organised Left parties of the state.

The discussion on the way forward was a closed one and a second of the sort in the year. The leadership was unanimous in targeting the young people. Suggestions for University Film Clubs had total consensus from all them. "We had a similar meet at Nagpur in the first half of 2015 and each of the regional leadership was assigned to groom a young person each in their respective areas to hand over the mantle of FFSI," according to Gautam Kaul, who was among the founders of the Lucknow Film Society and is now the president of FFSI. The former IPS man turned film society activist is also devising various programmes to enlist the top educational establishments like IIT and IIMs to the Film Society fold. However, as the last president of the DFS, which had stopped screenings in 2006, his immediate priority was to restart the prestigious DFS. "I have tough competition from the cultural centers of diplomatic missions and Film Clubs of the institutions like India International Centre and India Habitat Centre," he pointed out.[35]

Film Societies affiliated to FFSI in India 1959–2014.[36]

Year	North	East	West	South	Kerala	Total
1959	3	1	1	1		6
1964						23
1967						108
1971						111
1980						216
1984						94
1998						98
2009	10	70	32	47	70	229
2014	11	65	45	54	118	292

The numbers say that the Film Society Movement in India has grown over the years. However, in the northern and eastern parts of the country, where it originated and flourished, the numbers are dwindling. However, trends indicate the FS movement is growing in the western and southern areas. The maximum number of individual film societies is in Kerala. Kerala is the only state with its own FFSI regional branch and also considerable state government support to the Film Society Movement. This obviously leads the FFSI to look at the "Kerala development model" in this aspect too. Equally interesting is the western model adopted by the western region of FFSI. It is again riding on a regional language and cultural vehicle, but not so much with the state government support.

FOCUS ON STATE UNITS, UNIVERSITIES

In Kerala, a few societies have already started subtitling world films in Malayalam, making them available to the masses. In Maharashtra, many film appreciation courses are conducted in Marathi. There appears to be a crying need for going local with medium of language and the State wise organisation of the FFSI to take the movement forward. Going by the focus of activity, so far the FFSI leadership appears to target the same educated liberals in the metro cities who were the patrons of the movement in the 1970s. However, most of them appeared to be happy with watching such films in easily available digital formats at the comfort of their homes. The opinion makers in the population appear to have changed from the government and public sector professionals to the corporates and NGOs and there is hardly any interest about film societies in these sectors, though many classics from the film society circuit have made entry into corporate training modules. Typical of such a film is an Akira Kurosawa film, *Seven Samurai*,[37] shown and discussed to show case teamwork and its effectiveness.

The hot favourite target audience of FFSI to expand in today's scenario appears to be the educational institutions. "FFSI has plans to set up campus film societies in universities and colleges to take international cinema to the student community. Instead of 35 mm film prints, FFSI will focus on providing film DVDs to these societies to ensure smoother functioning," the official website announced. The Kerala unit of FFI has moved forward in targeting the universities, with a workshop for the trainers for university film appreciation courses.

Going by the UGC's list of affiliated universities and institutions, which offer Film Studies at postgraduate, graduate levels or as an additional subject, the FFSI can easily plan a University Film Club, provided there is a committed staffer in each of institution. However, with copyright issues of available films becoming an issue many a time, it will be a herculean task for anyone trying to organise film screenings for young people for public screenings, as grey market and downloads are targeting the very same young people. The obvious question then is: How will FFSI package its programme to popularise itself in educational instructions? The old methods of screenings and discussions will not work for sure, and much of the success of this programme will depend on makeover packages that the FFSI comes up with. With little or no interest from UGC, where such a programme was grounded due to bureaucratic hurdles in the past and lack of political patronage from the present regime, it will be an uphill task for FFSI to reach these educational institutions.

The effort to build a next-generation leadership is also in doldrums, as the old guard in many places is seen harbouring vested interests. "In most places where the film societies ran successfully, there were one or two dedicated persons and when they shifted or lost their interest, the society also died," Gautam Kaul pointed out. "Wrong people went to the leadership in Delhi as the DFS membership had become a status symbol in the city," recalled Deepak Roy, film-maker and one of the life member of the society. "Many a places the old leadership refused to give way to the new," added U Radhakrishnan, former secretary of northern region of FFSI. Clearly, there is a crisis of leadership in the movement, which the FFSI leadership is grappling with.

There are exceptions like *Suchitra* of Bangalore where the second-generation leadership has taken over the cultural complex, giving hope for the future. The success of *Suchitra* in Bangalore can be attributed to smooth leadership transition. Founder President Nara Hari Rao resigned from the trusteeship of the Cultural Academy in 2003 and handed over the leadership to another set of leaders. "However my association still continues as a patron. I just go there whenever they call me. I also functioned as the Artistic Director of the Bengaluru International Film Festival for *Suchitra* for the first 6 years till 2014," said the founder of the society, Mr Rao.

Gautam Kaul, president of FFSI, had mandated the regional leadership to train and groom future leaders in their respective regions, a focus that the Dr Shivarama Karanth committee had advised. Going by the stories of success and of struggle of individual units, it is clear that FFSI needs to go for a state-wise strategy to inject new life into the Film Society Movement. "We also recommend that Federation of Film Societies should set up organisations at State level so that it can properly liaise with the State Government for obtaining financial help and facilities for the film societies for the film societies in the State," Dr Karanth report suggested.[38]

Mr Kaul is also engaged with IITs and IIMs to rope in expertise too in the training of the new leadership. He feels that being associated with the future leaders in various IITs and IIMs will give rich dividends for the movement in the long run. A film club at the administrative training academy at Mussoorie in the 1960s had its own rich dividends, with many of the civil servants exposed to the movement supporting it in various states. U Radhakrishnan was surprised to find an IAS officer in Lucknow, who after a meeting ordered all the universities to start a film society in their campuses, as he was enamoured by such societies at the Mussoorie academy. "However, after a few months his successor at the same post was not at all keen on film societies and hence the project did not take off ," Radhakrishnan recalled. The leadership of FFSI clearly understands the role of motivated regional leaders and is working to rediscover and enthuse them.

Though family membership was in vogue among film societies, with the rush of members who were the connoisseurs of uncensored films, the film societies lost women members in the 1970s and 1980s. With television serials becoming the popular flavour of evenings, it is now difficult to get women in general to film screenings. Though the diplomatic cultural centres are patronised by women in numbers, they are yet to look at the good old film societies. The history of the Film Society Movement, there were only few women leaders. Marie Seton, Vijaya Mulay, Ammu Swaminadhan and Usha Bhagat, and former Prime Minister Indira Gandhi herself immensely contributed for the movement. In the era of women empowerment, the Film Society Movement has to make it attractive to women as a group too, to make its makeover plans realistic and successful.

WHAT FILM-MAKERS SAY ABOUT FSM

The best commentators on the Film Society Movement and its future are the film-makers who made films that needed an audience, such as the *rasiks*, who have some exposure to films shown in film societies. Let me quote the big three who were also associated with the film societies from their initial days of film-making.

Mrinal Sen:

You cannot expect large number of people to see your films. Any sensible film-maker, when he makes films, his films are not that reachable to everyone. For instance fiction if you read novels. Not all novels are very popular. Popular novels are very different.... Even then I want to be popular.... But I am a popular failure most of the time... in the box office. But then that is why my arithmetic is very simple.... I make low budget films. People say film making is an expensive process. I do not agree with them.... Not all agree with them.... Films can be made low cost. I have been making low cost films. If you make low costs films and if you can get to the larger minority audience scattered across the world... the larger minority audience... who would be seeing your film...and that way I keep going.... That is in spite of the fact that I am a popular failure at the box office I keep going....[39]

Adoor Gopalakrishnan:

As for the future course of film societies, it should change its character. It should grow in to Academy of cinemas where selected outstanding films are screened regularly for the interested public and discussed. It would become possible with the institution of a chain of such cinemas in the metropolises and big towns of the country. This is an area where the government can step in and act positively. Even an enterprising distributor can do wonders to take notable cinema around the country and screen it profitably. The only way to save and foster a film culture is to introduce the young audiences in schools to the charm and beauty and worthiness of good cinema. Like good literature and good taste, they need to imbibe it early in their lives. Instead what are we feeding them on?[40]

Shyam Benegal:

The relevance of the Film Society Movement today is to encourage young people to look at Cinema as an artistic activity rather than simply as a distractive entertainment. Campus Film Societies was an initiative I took as the President of the FFSI. This does not simply mean showing films but show them as subjects for discussion and debate among the members.[41]

INDIAN FILMS AND FILM SOCIETY MOVEMENT IN TRANSITION

The film-makers who have put Indian films on the global film map stand firmly with the Film Society Movement. They want it to be the initiation of the connoisseur to "classic" (*margi*) academic part of the medium of films, knowing full well that the "classic" has always has an impact on the mass formats (*desi*) too. In 60 years, *Pather Panchali*, the classic, had a huge impact on the Indian film industry, giving it a respectable position in the Indian society, against what it was in the 1950s. Not every film is a classic, but the deep impact of the classics is increasingly felt among the new breed of film-makers, in techniques and narrative and their approach to films.

Let me narrate a story about the New Wave Cinema of the 1970s and 1980s in Europe. The then reigning superstar-director Alfred Hitchcock[42] was told about the New Wave films and he asked: "Do they tell the story in pictures?" Film Societies are the storehouses of films that tell "stories in pictures" and people who discuss and debate them to appreciate the language of films.

For anyone and everyone who wants to develop a "taste" for the language and art of cinema, they need an ambience, be it an individual act of seeing films or collective movement, like the film societies. Despite the changing socio-cultural mosaic in the digital age, film societies and screenings of classic in formats of your convenience are still a must for film buffs in their search of grooming and mastering the film language. An optimistic film society pioneer and techno-evangelist, Anil Srivastava observed as follows[43]:

> Now we seem to prefer a more mechanistic view of socio-cultural development. Technology is transforming the way moving images are created and projected. Gone are the days of the rickety projector, the noise of the moving sprockets, the celluloid. The iconic Kodak is no longer pivotal. Recording a moving image is as simple—and often better in quality—as pointing your iPhone. You can stream *Battleship Potemkin* or find *The Louisiana Story* from Netflix on your television or even your tablet. All of this is making possible a new culture of cinema where everyone can participate.

It is up to the Film Society Movement of India, which has a glorious past, to find its moorings in the changed scenario and place itself as the gateway to the world of films. With or without the "movement," a country that produces over 10,000 films a year will undertake film appreciation as the very basic of the act of film-making through the emerging digital technology platforms.

NOTES*

1. Aruna Vasudev. *The New Indian Cinema* (New Delhi: McMillan, 1980), p. 2.
2. http://indianexpress.com/article/cities/ahmedabad/varsities-in-india-have-always-kept-cinema-out-of-bounds-adoor-gopalkrishnan/
3. Ministry of I&B. *Report of the Working Group on National Film Policy* (New Delhi: Ministry of I&B, GOI, May 1980), p. 9, para 3.2.
4. Aruna Vasudev. *The New Indian Cinema.*
5. BK Karanjia. *Counting My Blessings* (New Delhi: Penguin, 2005), p. 182.
6. Ibid., p. 191.
7. Ibid., p. 192.
8. http://vkcherian.blogspot.in/2012/06/mrinal-sen-at-90-riding-wave-of.html?view=timeslide
9. Ministry of I&B. *Report of the Working Group on National Film Policy,* p. 13, paras 3.23 and 3.24.
10. http://cherianwrites.blogspot.in/2016/02/adoorgopalakrishnan-on-film-society.html
11. Interview with Kulathoor Bhaskaran Nair, MD, Chitralekha Film Cooperative. http://www.prd.kerala.gov.in/towardsmorevisual.htm
12. http://cherianwrites.blogspot.in/2016/03/on-fsm-by-anilsrivastava-pioneer-and.html

13. TG Vaidyanathan. *Hours in the Dark: Essays on Cinema* (Delhi: OUP, 1996), p. 86.
14. Chidananda Das Gupta. *Seeing Is Believing: Selected Writings on Cinema* (Delhi: Viking, 2008), p. 95.
15. Interview with Partha Chatterjee.
16. Interview with Kumar Shahani.
17. Vinay Lal and Ashish Nandy. *Fingerprinting Popular Culture: The Mythic and the Iconic in Indian Cinema* (Delhi: OUP, 2006), introduction.
18. Chidananda Das Gupta. *Seeing Is Believing*, p. 93.
19. Interview with Samik Bandyopadhyay.
20. Chidananda Das Gupta. *Seeing Is Believing*.
21. Interview with Shoojit Sircar.
22. Ibid.
23. Interview with Gautam Kaul, President, FFSI.
24. Ibid.
25. Ibid.
26. http://cherianwrites.blogspot.in/2016/02/interviewwith-sudhir-nandgoanker.html
27. Interview with HN Nara Hari Rao.
28. http://cherianwrites.blogspot.in/2016/03/universities-with-film-studies.html
29. Ibid.
30. http://cherianwrites.blogspot.in/2016/02/interviewwith-sudhir-nandgoanker.html
31. Ibid., p. 13, para 3.27.
32. Interview with Sreenivasan Narayanan.
33. Interview with Sandeep Ray.
34. http://cherianwrites.blogspot.in/2016/03/on-fsm-by-anilsrivastava-pioneer-and.html
35. Interview with Gautam Kaul.
36. Compiled from the available FFSI documents.
37. https://en.wikipedia.org/wiki/Seven_Samurai
38. Ministry of I&B. *Report of the Working Group on National Film Policy*, p. 13, para 3.27.
39. http://vkcherian.blogspot.in/2012/06/mrinal-sen-at-90-riding-wave-of.html?view=timeslide
40. http://cherianwrites.blogspot.in/2016/02/adoorgopalakrishnan-on-film-society.html
41. http://cherianwrites.blogspot.in/2016/02/interview-with-benegal.html
42. https://en.wikipedia.org/wiki/Alfred_Hitchcock
43. http://cherianwrites.blogspot.in/2016/03/on-fsm-by-anilsrivastava-pioneer-and.html

* All websites accessed on 16 June 2016.

ANNEXURE 1

Genesis of Indian Films

India was one of the few countries to be an early witness to the birth of the new medium called cinema, invented by Lumière Brothers, Auguste and Louis, in 1895. The first of the screenings by the Lumiere Brothers took place on 22 March 1895 at 44 Rue de Rennes in Paris at an industrial meeting where a film, *Workers Leaving the Lumière Factory*, was shown especially for the occasion.

Louis photographed the world around him. Some of his first films were "actuality" films, like the workers leaving the factory. The brothers began to open theatres to show their films (which became known as cinemas). In the first four months of 1896, they had opened *Cinématographe* theatres in London, Brussels, Belgium and New York.

The Celluloid Train Steams into Bombay on 7 July, the announcement for the first film show was made in 1896, at the Watson's Hotel Bombay. The city's elite, including the British officials and their *memsahebs*, had paid a rupee each and had braved inclement weather to witness Lumiere's *Marvel of the Century, Wonder of the World*. As the large grainy images flickered back to life and the locomotive made its first appearance in a Parisian parlour barely six months earlier and steamed into the Bombay hotel room, the audience broke into an enthusiastic applause. This event remained a historic one, as it kick-started an entire new medium of entertainment called cinema in India.

The development of the Indian film industry—as one of the world's largest—is as old, as varied, and as exciting as the history of the medium itself. The first of a short film in India was directed by

Hiralal Sen, starting with *The Flower of Persia* in 1898. The first Indian feature film, *Raja Harishchandra*, however, made much later in the year 1912, coincided with the appearance of the first full-length features in the United States. The first Indian talkie hit the screens in 1931, two years after the first British and French "all-talkies" were made.

Film historians Rani Day Burra and Maithili Rao wrote as follows:

> At the turn of the century—when cinema dawned—India was poised for a major social and political reform. Technological innovations, such as cars, planes and gramophone records which took classical music to the masses, were transforming a society that had remained unchanged for centuries. A new force in the formation of public opinion, the press, was making its presence felt. (*Source NFAI*)

Encouraged by the response, the exhibitors moved the cinema shows to Novelty Theatre, and introduced a broad set of prices for both patrician and plebeian. The cheapest tickets were for four *annas* (quarter of a rupee)—creating the four *anna* class audience that in decades to come would dictate the form and content of Indian commercial films and determine the rise and fall of its stars.

Though the initial stories for films were mostly from the epics of India, there was hardly any literary or cultural figure getting involved in films. The conventional literary and cultural traditions did not accept cinema as a medium of expression, though there was an effort by the modernists like Prime Minister Jawaharlal Nehru to give it acceptability. However, the leader of the freedom struggle, Gandhi, had dismissed the new medium.

During the early days, the patron of the "bioscope" was the literate, urban and ruling class, while the average Indian found the imported films (*The Queen's Funeral Procession, Assassination of President McKinley*) shown in the tents of Calcutta and Bombay as too exotic. Enterprising young Indians began to cover local events, such as the celebration of Edward VII's coronation, with cameras from London. With the rise of exhibitor magnates in India like Jamshedji Framji Madan and Abdulally Esoofally, films from all over the world were jostling for a slice of the Indian market, as recorded by the film historians.

The first Indian movie released in India was *Shree Pundalik*, a silent film in Marathi by Dadasaheb Torne on 18 May 1912, at the Coronation Cinematograph in Mumbai. Torne is also considered the "Father of Indian Cinema."

However, the first full-length motion picture in India was produced by Dadasaheb Phalke. Dadasaheb was the pioneer of the Indian film industry. He was a scholar on Indian languages and culture, who brought together elements from Sanskrit epics to produce his *Raja Harishchandra* (1913), a silent Marathi film with inter-titles in English and Hindi. The female roles in the film were played by male actors.

The story of how the first film was made is as follows: "Phalke appeared to have visited every cinema show, studying films, experimenting with his cheap camera 20 hours a day till his health failed. Pledging his life-insurance policies, Phalke sailed to England and having trained there for a week with *Cecil Hepworth*, returned with a Williamson camera, a film perforator, processing and printing machines, and raw stock. He was all set to make India's first feature film...all he needed was money. His wife Saraswati Phalke, who supported him through it all, allowed him to mortgage her ornaments." Interestingly, almost five decades later, Satyajit Ray would pledge his wife's ornaments to make *Pather Panchali*, the first film to put Indian cinema on the world map.

The first Indian chain of cinema theatres was owned by the Calcutta entrepreneur Jamshedji Framji Madan, who oversaw production of 10 films annually and distributed them throughout the Indian subcontinent.

In South India, Raghupathi Venkaiah Naidu pioneered the production of silent movies and later talkies. Starting from 1909, he was involved in many aspects of the history of Indian cinema and travelling to different regions in Asia, to promote film work. He was the first to build and own cinema hall's in Madras. The Raghupathi Venkaiah Naidu Award is an annual award incorporated into Nandi Awards to recognise people for their contributions to the Telugu film industry.

During the early 20th century, cinema as a medium gained popularity across India.

In 1927, the British government, in order to promote the market in India for British films over American ones, formed the Indian Cinematograph Enquiry Committee (ICEC). The ICEC consisted of three British and three Indians, led by T Rangachariar, a Madras lawyer. The committee introduced the censorship and ensured that only British and US films entered Indian market.

But these governmental policies did not stop Indian film-makers to experiment with new developments in technology of cinema.

Ardeshir Irani released *Alam Ara*, which was the first Indian talking film, on March 14 1931. HM Reddy produced and directed *Bhakta Prahlada* (Telugu) and released it on 15 September 1931, and *Kalidas* (Tamil) was released on 31 October 1931. *Kalidas* was produced by Ardeshir Irani and directed by HM Reddy. These two films were Southern India's first talkie films to have a theatrical release. As sound technology advanced, the 1930s saw the rise of music in Indian cinema, *Indra Sabha* and *Devi Devyani* marked the beginning of song-and-dance routine in Indian films. Studios emerged across major cities such as Chennai, Kolkata and Mumbai, as film-making became an established craft by 1935, exemplified by the success of *Devdas*, which had managed to enthrall audiences nationwide. Bombay Talkies came up in 1934 and Prabhat Studios in Pune had begun production of films to cater to the Marathi language audience. Film-maker RSD Choudhury produced *Wrath* (1930), which was banned by the British Raj in India as it depicted actors as Indian leaders, an expression censored during the days of the Indian Independence Movement. *Sant Tukaram*, a 1936 film based on the life of Tukaram (1608–50), a Varkari saint and spiritual poet, was screened at the 1937 edition of Venice Film Festival, the first Indian film to be screened at an International Film Festival. The film was subsequently adjudged as one of the three best films of the year in the world.

The Indian *masala* film—a slang used for commercial films with song, dance, drama and romance—came up following the Second World War. South Indian cinema gained prominence throughout India with the release of SS Vasan's *Chandralekha*. During the 1940s, cinema in Southern India accounted for nearly half of Indian cinema halls and cinema came to be viewed as an instrument of cultural revival. The partition of India following its Independence divided the nation's assets and as a result, a number of studios went to the newly formed Pakistan. The strife of Partition became an enduring subject for film-making during the decades that followed.

IPTA, an art movement with a Leftist inclination, began to take shape through the 1940s and the 1950s. A number of realistic IPTA plays, such as Bijon Bhattacharya's *Nabanna* in 1944 (based on Bengal famine of 1943), prepared the ground for the solidification of realism in Indian cinema, exemplified by Khwaja Ahmad Abbas's *Dharti Ke Lal* (Children of the Earth) in 1946. The IPTA movement continued to emphasise on reality and went on to produce *Mother India* and *Pyaasa*, amongst India's most recognisable cinematic productions.

ANNEXURE 2

Memorandum of Association: FFSI

The Memorandum of Association of FFSI was as follows:

1. The name of the Society shall be the Federation of Film Societies of India, hereinafter referred to as the 'The Federation'.

2. The registered office of the Society shall be situated in the State of West Bengal in the city of Calcutta.

3. The objects for which the Federation is established shall be:

    (a) To promote the study of film as an art and social force.

    (b) To encourage the production of films of artistic value.

    (c) To promote public appreciation of films of artistic value.

    (d) To promote and coordinate the activities of film societies towards the achievement of the above aims, particularly in the matter of organization of showing film classics and outstanding current films from all over the world.

    (e) To promote research on the cinema.

    (f) To cooperate with national and international organizations having similar objects.

4. The above objects will be realised through the following activities:

    (i) To enroll individual film societies as its members.

    (ii) To promote the formation of film societies and the development of the Film Society Movement all over the country.

(iii) To raise funds and or loans from member societies and from other sources and receive and pay grants, bequests, donations, subscriptions, etc.

(iv) To establish and maintain museums, collections, libraries, auditoria etc., and to translate, compile, collect, publish, purchase o sell any literature bearing upon any subject relating to films.

(v) To organize and participate in film festivals, lectures, seminars, conferences etc., in India and abroad.

(vi) To establish and maintain liaison with national and international organizations having similar aims and objects.

(vii) To own, buy or sell or purchase, hire or mortgage all property.

Source: FFSI.

ANNEXURE 3

Presidents of FFSI
(1959–2016)

1. Satyajit Ray
2. Mrinal Sen
3. Anil Chatterjee
4. Chandran Nair
5. Vijaya Mulay
6. Moinul Hasan
7. Shyam Benegal
8. Kiran Shantaram
9. HN Narahari Rao
10. Kiran Shantaram
11. Gautam Kaul

Source: FFSI.

Index

About the Author

VK Cherian grew up as a film society member and activist with the celebrated film-maker Adoor Gopalakrishnan's *Chitralekha* Film Society from 1976 to 1980 at Thiruvananthapuram. He organised film study and theatre groups at Mar Ivanios College and University Centre, Trivandrum, and also at his hometown in Kayamkulam in Kerala. Mr Cherian writes occasionally about films in English and Malayalam. A regular visitor to the various international film festivals for over 35 years, he is an ardent film enthusiast who has been engaged with the film fraternity as a writer and promoter of good cinema. Maker of several video documentaries, he has authored and edited three books, as well as promoted the Indo-Afrikhadi Foundation. An alumina of the Indian Institute of Mass Communication, New Delhi, Cherian is a journalist-turned-communications professional residing in New Delhi for the last 35 years.

His published books include *The Scam and the Rajas of the Money Market* (1993), *Satyagraha—Indian and South African artist's tribute to the spirit of 9-11-1906—Collection of Essays and Catalogue* (2006) and *Crisis of Corporate Communism—Politics of Murder in Kerala* (2013). He also wrote numerous articles in English and Malayalam in mainline media and journals across India and abroad. Produced many television series as independent content editor for Doordarshan, Asianet and Jain TV. Made video documentaries, *Khadi, The Metaphor of Hope* (2003) and *Afri-khadi—a thread that binds* (2005).

Widely travelled, he plans to cover all continents. Interested in politics, social trends and technologies, he is passionate about art and films and networking with right-thinking people across the world.